CREDIT UNIONS IN IRELAND

Anthony P. Quinn

Oak Tree Press

Dublin

Oak Tree Press
Merrion Building,
Lower Merrion Street, Dublin 2

© 1994, 1999 Anthony P. Quinn

A catalogue record for this book
is available from the British Library.

First Published 1994 (ISBN 1-872853-21-8)
Second Edition 1999 (ISBN 1-86076-122-4)

Printed in Ireland
by Colour Books Ltd, Dublin

CONTENTS

Dedication .... *xiii*

Acknowledgements .... *xv*

List of Cases .... *xvii*

Legislation .... *xix*

Disclaimer .... *xxi*

Foreword .... *xxiii*

Introduction .... *xxv*

Chapter 1: The Co-operative Background 1

    Co-operative Context 2

    Historical Outline 2

    Co-operative Principles 7

    International Co-operative Principles 7

    Credit Unions and the Co-operative Principles 10

Chapter 2: The Irish Credit Union Movement: Origins and Development 11

    The Co-operative Context in Ireland 11

    Agriculture Credit Societies 12

    Lessons from Failure 14

    Friendly Societies 14

    Social and Economic Studies 15

    UCD Course 15

    Ideas into Action: Dublin Central Co-op Society Ltd 17

    German and American Influences 18

    Credit Union Extension Service 18

Pioneers and Inspirational Leaders..19

Committee on Co-operation...22

Credit Union Legislation...23

Irish League of Credit Unions (ILCU).....................................25

Chapter 3: Basics of Credit Union Membership...................27

Forming a Credit Union...27

Joining a Credit Union..30

Common Bond Enshrined in Law..32

Rules...34

Insurance..34

Savings and Loans in Summary..35

Main Benefits of Membership...35

Chapter 4: Rules in General...37

Specific Requirements..37

Registrar's Role..40

Standard Rules: The Bible of a Credit Union.........................40

Legal Effects of Rules...43

Chapter 5: Meetings and Voting...47

Organisation Meeting...48

Annual General Meeting (AGM)...49

Special General Meeting (SGM)...53

Resolutions...55

Active Participation by Members..57

Chapter 6: Governance: Board of Directors, Supervisory and other Committees, Officers and Management...........59

Officer..60

Board of Directors..60

Officer: Principal Posts and their Functions..........................64

Supervisory Committee...67

Other Committees...71

General...73

Disqualification of Persons from Board or
Other Functions 76

Practical Issues 78

Conclusion 81

**Chapter 7: Financial Transactions: Members' Savings,
Loans and Insurance...83**

Membership 84

Shares.. 85

Deposits 87

Loans 91

Remedy for Debts from Members............................. 97

Insurance.. 97

Savings Protection: Section 46, Rule 55 99

Transfer of Member's Financial Interest upon Death 100

Additional Services to Members............................... 103

Tax... 106

**Chapter 8: Wider Operations by Credit Unions:
Contracts, Investments, Special Funds and
Borrowing Contracts 107**

Land: Acquisition, Holding and Disposal 107

Investments: Section 43, Rule 52............................ 108

Borrowing by Credit Unions.................................... 112

Insurance... 114

ATMs and Computerisation 116

**Chapter 9: Registrar of Friendly Societies: Supervision and
Control; Complaints and Disputes.......................117**

Mission Statement.. 118

Registration.. 119

Time Limits on the Registrar................................... 121

Cancellation of Registration..................................... 122

Limits to Registrar's Functions............................... 122

Prudential Role 123

Control and Supervision of Credit Unions
    by the Registrar 124

Regulatory Directions 126

Inspection 129

Statutory Report and Weaknesses Observed during
    Inspection 131

Registrar's Follow-up Action 133

Investigations 133

Investments 138

Disputes and Complaints: Settlement and Arbitration 140

Administrative Functions 141

Conclusion 142

Chapter 10: Accounts, Auditors and Watchdogs 145

Basic Requirements 146

Accounts and Records 147

Treasurer's Functions 148

Auditing and Auditors 149

Statutory Requirements 150

Exclusions 151

Appointment and Removal of Auditor 152

Auditors' Duties Distinct from those of Credit Union 153

Accounting Guidelines 154

Resignation of Auditors 155

Annual Return 156

Monitoring of Accounts 157

Responsibilities of Auditors and Credit Unions 158

Chapter 11: Administrators and Examiners 161

Examiners 161

Administrators 171

Conclusion 173

Chapter 12: Termination: Winding-up; Dissolution, Amalgamation, Transfer of Engagements and Cancellation...**175**

    Winding-up...176

    Amalgamations and Transfers of Engagements 184

    Cancellation of Registry of Society...186

    Conclusion..188

Chapter 13: Irish League of Credit Unions (ILCU)...........189

    By What Magic?..189

    Format and History of the League..190

    Specific Highlights..191

    League Rules...195

    Objects..196

    Vision and Mission Statement 197

    Annual Convention/AGM and Elections to Board.................198

    Supervisory Committee of ILCU..199

    Other Committees...199

    Ineligibility...199

    Regional Chapters 200

    ILCU Administrative Structure..201

    Computer Monitoring 202

    Central Investment Management Service (CIM)....................203

    Central Financial Services 203

    Insurance Services..204

    Wider Community Involvement...204

    Affiliations..206

    ILCU International Development Foundation Ltd. 206

    Other International Connections...206

Chapter 14: Credit Union Advisory Committee (CUAC)..**209**

    Background 209

    Early Members..210

Why an Advisory Committee?...210

The ILCU and the Advisory Committee 211

Current Statutory Provisions...212

Chapter 15: Northern Ireland...215

Background 215

Credit Unions in the North 216

Some Comparisons between Legislation in the Republic of
Ireland and Northern Ireland (NI)...................................224

Credit Unions in Britain...227

Conclusion 228

Chapter 16: Future Trends and Developments 229

Main Agents of Change 229

The Credit Union Act, 1997..230

Involvement with the Wider Community
and the Social Economy 233

EMU, the Euro and Lower Interest Rates............................234

Demographic, Social and Other Trends
in the Irish Economy...235

Balance between the Voluntary Ethos and Professional
Management..237

Strategic Planning by the Credit Union Movement under the
ILCU's Leadership 238

Appendix 1: Profiles of Credit Unions...............................241

Ballyphehane Credit Union Ltd., Cork.................................241

Donore Credit Union Ltd..244

Ballyjamesduff Credit Union Ltd...246

Tallow Area Credit Union Ltd..248

St Raphael's Garda Credit Union Ltd..................................251

Law Library Credit Union Ltd. 255

**Appendix 2: (A) Credit Union Operating Principles
(B) Statement of the Co-operative Identity**......................**257**

   Introduction 258

   Principles..261

**Appendix 3: Credit Union Invocation / Achainí an Chomhar
Chreidmheasa**...**263**

In Memoriam: Séamus P. MacEoin..**265**

Glossary of Terms **267**

Useful Addresses **283**

Select Bibliography **285**

   1. Credit Unions..285

   2. Co-operative Background and History...............................289

   3. Co-operative Reports, Laws and Principles........................291

   4. Specialist Periodicals..293

   5. Annual Reports 293

   6. Co-op and Credit Union Reports from Abroad 294

   7. Miscellaneous including General Legal Texts....................294

   8. Parliamentary Debates on Credit
      Union Legislation, 1996–1997...296

Index **297**

DEDICATION

In Memoriam

Séamus MacEoin

Co-operative pioneer and co-founder of the
Irish Credit Union Movement
who passed to his eternal reward on 14 October 1993.
Ar dheis Dé go raibh a anam.

ACKNOWLEDGEMENTS

I record my thanks to the many people who encouraged my efforts
and gave me advice, information and support during my research
and writing. A general thanks to my colleagues over the years in
the credit union and wider co-operative movements, the civil
service, the legal profession and the Irish Writers' Union.

To Ann and our family, especially Anthony M. Quinn for his
computer and journalistic skills and Paul for suggesting the
profiles of credit unions, my daughters Blaithín and Jeannette,
my brother John and my hill-walking friends.

To the many activists in credit unions and the wider co-
operative movement, particularly Seamus MacEoin, RIP, to whom
this book is dedicated and to Eilis MacEoin and family; Pat
Bolger, Lifford; Michael Kennedy, Dalkey Credit Union Ltd; Jim
Ivers, former director general of the Law Society; Frank Lynch,
president ILCU; Mary Griffin and Sean Redmond, board
members; John O'Regan, treasurer and Tony Smyth, general
secretary and the staff of the Irish League of Credit Unions,
especially Pat Fay, Jim O'Dwyer, Brian Douglas, and Grace
Perrott (former head of marketing and promotion); John Brady,
SJ, Society for Co-operative Studies and Dermot McKenna, SJ,
Co-operative Development Society; Paddy Candon, New Ross
Credit Union Limited and the Co-operative Way group; Michael
O'Brien, St Raphael's Garda Credit Union Ltd., Geraldine
Mitchell for original material on the late Muriel Gahan and on
Nora Herlihy, RIP; and also the credit unions which provided
material for profiles.

To Noel Martin Sisk, Registrar of Friendly Societies, Dublin
and the Registry staff especially William Roe, professional
accountant and Geraldine Parker; Eamon Carey, former

Registrar; Gerry Darcy, Mary Solan and Annette Whelan, Department of Enterprise, Trade and Employment; Raymond McKeag, Registrar of Credit Unions, Belfast and the Registry staff, especially Sylvia Davenport.

To Sam McAughtry, chairman Irish Writers' Union, 1998/9, who as a Senator facilitated my access to the Seanad stage of the Credit Union Bill, enacted in 1997, and Senator and former TD, Helen Keogh, who accorded similar facilities in the Dáil.

To the members and staff of the Bar Council and Law Library, Four Courts, Dublin, especially the participants in the Law Library Credit Union Study Group for their practical enthusiasm. Thanks particularly to Ercus Stewart, SC, Sinéad Ní Chúlacháin, Dan Feehan, Rosemary McLaughlin, Mary Phelan, Caroline Carney, John McCoy, Francis Gallogly, Vivian McDonnell and Teddy O'Neill. Their commitment culminated in the Law Library Credit Union Ltd., being registered. Thanks to James O'Reilly, SC and also to Pádraic Clarke and Brendan Conway for commenting on some draft chapters of the book and to Des Mulhere, librarian.

Thanks also to David Givens and the staff of Oak Tree Press, especially Janet Brown and Jenna Dowds. Placing credit unions in a wider context was facilitated by the Consumers' Association of Ireland and its magazine, *Consumer Choice*; and by Jim Bardon, director, Irish Bankers' Federation; Felix O'Regan, manager, Irish Banks Information Service; Des Byrne, Irish Mortgage and Savings Association and William Fagan, then Director of Consumer Affairs.

Although I drew from many sources and am presently an officer of the Society for Co-operative Studies in Ireland and the Law Library Credit Union and an associate of the Plunkett Foundation, Oxford, the interpretation of the material is my own and does not purport to represent the views of any individual or organisation.

LIST OF CASES

Eley v. Positive Government Security Life Assurance Co.
(1876) I Ex D 88... 44

Beattie v. Beattie (1938) 3 All E.R. 214 44

Frizelle v. New Ross Credit Union Ltd no ref
High Court Flood J 30.7.97 70

Re City Equitable Insurance Co Ltd [1925] 1 Ch 407 (CA) 77

Irvine and Fullerton Building Society v. Cuthertson [1905] 45
SLR 17 (Murdoch (1993) p. 489 85

The Prison Officers Credit Union v Registrar of Friendly Societies
[1987] ILRM 367 ICLSA R 62................................. 122-3

McMahon v. Ireland, the Attorney General and the Registrar of
Friendly Societies [1987] ILRM 198 122-3

In re Haughey [1977] IR 217 136

re Kingston Mills (No 2) [1896] 2 Ch 279 c 288/9 145

Irish Commercial Society Ltd (unreported judgments by Barron J
High Court 17.5.86 & Finlay CJ)
Supreme Court 16.6.86 .... 137, 273

Irish Woollen Company Ltd v Tyson [1900] Fitzgibbon LJ 26 The
Accountant Law Report 13 158

re Thomas Gerrard & Son Ltd [1967] All E.R. 525 Chancery
Division 158

re PMPA Insurance Co [1986] ILRM 524
and [1988] ILRM 109 173

LEGISLATION

REPUBLIC OF IRELAND

Acts

Arbitration Act, 1954 (No. 26 of 1954), as amended by the Arbitration Act, 1980 (No. 7) and the Arbitration (International Commercial) Act, 1998 .... No. 14 of 1998

Bills of Sale (Ireland) Acts, 1879 and 1883

Building Societies Act, 1989 .... No. 17 of 1989

Central Bank Acts, 1942 to 1997

Companies Acts, 1963 to 1990

Consumer Credit Act, 1995 .... No. 24 of 1995

Credit Union Act, 1966 .... No. 19 of 1966

Credit Union Act, 1997 .... No. 15 of 1997

Friendly Societies Acts, 1896–1977

Industrial and Provident Societies Acts, 1893–1978.

Industrial and Provident Societies (Amendment) Act, 1978. .... No. 23 of 1978

Powers of Attorney Act, 1996 .... No. 12 of 1996

Solicitors (Amendment) Act, 1994 .... No. 27 of 1994

Statutory Instruments Act, 1947 .... No. 44 of 1947

Statutory Instruments

Companies Act, 1990 (Auditors) Regulations, 1992, S.I. No. 252

Credit Union Act, 1997 (Commencement) Order, 1997, S.I. No. 403 of 1997: provided that the Act with specified exceptions (mainly regarding the provision of new services and some details about auditors' reports) would come into effect on 1st October, 1997.

Credit Union Act, 1997 (Fees) Regulations, 1998, S.I. No. 155 and 274

NORTHERN IRELAND

Credit Unions (Northern Ireland) Order 1985 (SI 1985/1205, NI 12), consolidating with amendments and repealing provisions of the Industrial and Provident Societies (Northern Ireland) Act 1969.

Credit Union Deregulation (Northern Ireland) Order, 1997. SI 1997 No. 2984 (NI 22).

DISCLAIMER

No responsibility for loss occasioned to any person acting or refraining to act as a result of material in this publication can be accepted by the author or publisher. While every care has been taken in preparing this publication, there may be errors or omissions for which the author and publisher cannot accept legal responsibility. Professional advice should be sought on legal, financial, accountancy and insurance matters where considered necessary.

FOREWORD

If I were asked what is the most important work I have done in my lifetime, the answer would be very clear to me. I am very proud of my work, begun as a young man aged twenty-three, in the foundation of the Irish credit union movement.

I was heavily involved in the foundation of Derry Credit Union in 1960, the first credit union in the North. In an effort to encourage and help with the establishment of other credit unions, I travelled throughout Ireland, spending many evenings discussing details of credit union philosophy and organisation with community groups.

The credit union movement is the most successful co-operative in the history of Ireland. Its positive work for individual human beings, families and communities is invaluable. Credit unions directly help working and unemployed people financially at individual, community and local business level. Credit unions are a powerful community resource. They retain millions of pounds that would otherwise have been lost from the community to commercial financial institutions.

I hope that before long some of our universities will begin detailed research into the effects of the credit union movement on the social and economic history of our country. It will be a powerful story.

I wish this book every success and trust it will be of practical use to credit union activists and those with an interest in the development of the movement in Ireland.

John Hume, MP, MEP
April 1999

INTRODUCTION

The remarkable success of the Irish credit union has often been stated but the degree of success of this co-operative venture cannot be fully appreciated until details are considered. The story can be illustrated by a few statistics: in 1959, there were three credit unions with 200 members and £415 in shareholding representing members' savings; by 1998, there were almost 600 Irish credit unions with total savings of about £3.4 billion (c €4.3 billion). As total outstanding loans reach almost £2.3 billion (c €3 billion), the gap between loans and savings continues an upward trend.

Even allowing for individuals who are members of more than one credit union, total membership throughout Ireland at over 2.2 million represents more than a third of the population. A higher proportion, almost one-half of Irish families, benefit from credit union membership with greater concentration in some areas.

There is a wide spread across all social classes, with concentrations in the skilled working class C2 category and among white-collar office and service employees. The upper middle class, especially professionals and managers, represent an increasing proportion of credit union members. That trend, however, does not necessarily prove a dilution of co-operative principles as no specific group has a monopoly of that ethos. Barristers as well as public servants and skilled workers can co-operate. Despite the co-operative tradition in the dairy and agricultural sectors, a declining proportion of farmers are members of credit unions.

Most credit unions are affiliated to the all-Ireland body, the Irish League of Credit Unions (ILCU). The figures shown above include about 70 credit unions in Northern Ireland and a few in the Republic of Ireland which are not affiliated to the ILCU.

PURPOSE

This book's purpose is to trace the background to that remarkable community achievement, to pay tribute to the visionary pioneers and other leaders, and to explain concisely the legal framework and procedures, financial operations and practical workings of credit unions. The material in the first edition of this book, published in 1994, has been substantially revised in this edition, especially to take account of the Credit Union Act 1997 (referred to as the 1997 Act, except where the context otherwise requires the full title of the Act). There were significant changes in the legal framework and scope of credit union operations consequent upon that stand-alone Act, a major landmark in the history of the Irish co-operative movement.

I hope that the general reader, as well as credit union officers and members, and also legal, financial and accountancy professionals, will benefit from this book.

CREDIT UNIONS IN CONTEXT

The main thrust of this book deals with the history, background, legal framework, functioning and future of Irish credit unions. Simply defined, a credit union is a mutual society organised for the benefit of its members and basically providing them with a savings and loan service, with extras such as loan protection and life-savings added on. "Credit" derives from the Latin verb, *credere* — to trust, to believe — and the Latin noun, *creditum* — a thing entrusted to another person, such as a loan. Trust is a vital part of credit union operations. Savings rather than credit have an increased role as money is now attracted by relatively high credit union dividends.

Before providing a detailed treatment, it is necessary to place credit unions in the wider context of the financial services sector. Having regard to their substantial membership and assets, and the scale of operations, credit unions should not be regarded as charities nor as amateur players on the money field. Despite an increasingly middle-class base, however, credit unions still play an important social role by providing savings facilities and access to credit in poorer communities and through household budgeting systems. About 40 per cent of members who save in credit unions are low-income earners. A substantial proportion of loans are made to members in the C, D and E socio-economic categories as distinct from the A and B higher income groups who have greater access to the mainstream financial institutions such as banks and building societies. There is an overlap between users of such services and credit union membership.

Credit union activists were pioneers in combating illegal moneylending, breaking chronic cycles of personal debt and establishing programmes which have now official support through the Money, Advice and Budgeting Service (MABS) under the aegis of the Department of Social, Community and Family Affairs. MABS offers a free, confidential and independent service and advice on debt management.

Credit unions are user-friendly because of their basic nature as mutual organisations and the inherent co-operative philosophy. Interest rates cannot exceed the statutory limit of 1 per cent per month on outstanding loan balances, a rather high threshold in the declining interest rate regime of the European Monetary Union. There no hidden charges in credit unions although the total costs of borrowing may be inflated by the requirement on members to maintain a savings' ratio. Commercial financial sectors are increasingly consumer-conscious and must provide more information on charges and fees because of statutory requirements. The Irish Banks' Information Service (IBIS) and the Irish Mortgage and Savings Association play an active role.

Credit union members are not consumers in the precise meaning of that term but, as a credit union becomes larger and more impersonal, members tend to relate to it as consumers, a trend that could dilute the mutual ethos. In general, credit unions are expected to provide an efficient and competitive service.

Comparisons with Banks

A credit union differs substantially from a mainstream commercial bank but each has its own slot in the wider financial services sector. Credit unions are owned and organised by member shareholders on a mutual co-operative basis while banks are owned by shareholders and managed on a commercial basis to maximise profits. A member shareholder has only one vote at meetings of a credit union, irrespective of the extent of the individual's shareholding. Although there are many individual shareholders in Irish banks, large institutional investors can exercise a dominant influence through their voting power.

Each credit union is a separate legal entity and does not usually have branches but may have sub-offices. Banks operate a substantial branch network, over 950 nationwide. Credit unions have traditionally depended on members' savings to provide sources of credit but banks operate in the wider financial market. Flowing from that difference, bank interest rates (on loans and deposits) are heavily influenced by market trends, both domestic and international. Trends such as competition from banks, European Monetary Union and the Euro and also, in the 1997 Act, facilitation of borrowing by credit unions on a wider basis, make credit unions more sensitive to commercial interest rates. Generally, however, credit union interest rates tend to follow long-term trends, rather than fluctuate in accordance with short-term trends.

As interest rates and loan conditions vary, individuals should check current details with their own credit unions, banks, building societies and finance houses. The insurance built-in to credit union loans and savings is vital. Details of financial transactions in and with credit unions are given in Chapter 7 of this book.

Banks employ many more people, over 23,000, including part-time staff, compared with over 1,500 employees in credit unions. Because of the latter's dependence on over 16,000 volunteers, precise figures for employment are difficult to obtain. According to IBIS, total bank group assets in the Republic of Ireland for 1998 were approaching £60 billion (around €75 billion), which seems very high compared with about £3 billion (c €3.8 billion) for credit unions in the Republic. Credit union assets, however, are owned by the individual members who are also the shareholders and users. Banks' assets are owned by shareholders, but only some of them may be also consumers and users of the banks' services.

Total membership of credit unions in the Republic, over 1.8 million, compares favourably with commercial banking statistics of about 2.2 million current account holders and 4.4 million deposit/saving accounts which are likely to become less popular as interest rates decline. There is some overlap between account holders in different categories and extensive use of plastic money through credit cards and innovations such as laser cards. Credit union members also hold accounts in banks and other financial institutions and in some cases may also be members of more than one credit union.

The Central Bank is the official supervisory authority for banks and building societies although the Consumer Credit Act, 1995 gave the Director of Consumer Affairs an increased role in the financial services sector.

Credit unions are exempt from the Central Bank Acts, 1942 to 1997, the Building Societies Act, 1989, and the Consumer Credit Act, 1995. The Registrar of Friendly Societies and the Registrar of Credit Unions in Northern Ireland are the official regulatory authorities for credit unions. There is pressure for one overall regulatory authority for all financial institutions, broadly defined to include credit unions. It has been suggested, for example in a report (1998) by the Oireachtas Joint Committee on Finance and the Public Service, and supported by government policy, that one independent financial services authority be established to regulate the various sectors, including banks, building societies and credit unions.

Co-operation and Competition

Credit unions and banks have co-existed peacefully. Good relations were exemplified by the advertisements placed by local branches of banks in anniversary brochures of credit unions. As valued customers, credit unions (and their members) use banking services, for example, for cheques and money transmissions. The ILCU has developed the IQ Cash network by which members may access their funds through technical facilities — such as ATMs — in the main associated banks as well as credit unions. Despite such co-operation, competition between banks and credit unions is likely to intensify as credit unions expand their services. The banking sector has criticised and challenged in the European Union context what is perceived as the favourable State treatment for credit unions. Criticism was specifically directed at taxation policy and credit unions' exemption from corporation tax and from consumer credit and banking legislation on the basis of their mutual status.

Comparisons with Building Societies

Building societies were similar in origin and ethos to credit unions as both types of societies sprang from the same Victorian stable of self-help organisations, owned by their members for mutual benefit. In recent years, some building societies have changed from mutual status to become public limited companies (plcs), as facilitated by the Building Societies Act, 1989 which in some respects influenced the Credit Union Act, 1997 in its regulatory aspects. Credit unions compete with building societies which are also increasing their range of financial services. It is a tribute to the success of credit union systems that one building society launched a credit union-style service. For example, building society consumers who save for five months may borrow twice the sum accumulated, up to a maximum of £10,000.

Building societies traditionally dominated the mortgage market but in recent decades banks have played a larger role. That dominance of housing finance may be challenged by credit unions to some extent, for example in respect of home extensions or purchase of local authority dwellings, because higher loan limits and longer term loans are allowed under the 1997 Act.

Other Financial Options

The insurance industry provides a wide range of financial services, including savings and investment schemes, some of which are loosely based on credit union concepts of saving.

In some limited ways, the Post Office Savings Bank is comparable with credit unions because of the nationwide network of public offices and the emphasis on the small saver. An Post provides a wide range of banking-type services, including deposit accounts with easy access for withdrawals, and also tax-efficient systems such as savings certificates, bonds and national instalment savings. Like credit unions, An Post operates payroll deductions schemes from salaries and wages. Interest rates on post office savings follow general commercial trends but are not, in the short term, as sensitive to interest rate fluctuations in the wholesale money market. An Post also acts as agent for other financial services such as foreign exchange.

Finance houses provide substantial monies for the purchase of cars and household durable goods. Leasing is another option for purchase of items such as cars and computers.

Moneylenders have traditionally provided credit in poor and deprived communities but interest rates are inevitably high because of household collection systems and inherent risks of default. The credit union movement has been in the forefront of the fight against the adverse effects of moneylending, especially the unlicensed illegal type. New procedures under the Consumer Credit Act, 1995, including effective powers for the Director of Consumer Affairs, have provided greater official control over licensed moneylending. It remains, however, a much more expensive form of credit than that provided by credit unions.

In general, individuals should seek information from the relevant credit union or financial institution and from independent bodies such as the Consumers' Association of Ireland and the Office of Consumer Affairs. Choices depend on the various and distinctive needs of individuals, including access to savings, expected risks and reward, credit ratings and the length of commitment to savings and loans.

NEW LEGISLATION

Most of the changes in respect of supervision and new services heralded under the heading "New Horizons" in the first edition of this book in 1994 have been included in the Credit Union Act, 1997. That stand-alone Act replaced in respect of credit unions, the Industrial and Provident Societies Act, 1893 — 1978, including the short Credit Union Act, 1966 which was repealed.

The new legislation marked the start of a new era for the Irish credit union movement, especially in respect of additional services, longer and larger loans, balanced by a stricter supervisory regime by the Registrar of Friendly Societies (the Registrar). The enactment was a major achievement for ILCU and a tribute to the determination and lobbying power of the Irish credit union movement at individual, local, regional and national level. The position in Northern Ireland, with separate rules and legislation, dealt with in Chapter 15, was changed by statutory regulation to allow greater flexibility but a new comprehensive Act is necessary.

Parliamentary Process

The Registrar and the Department of Enterprise and Employment contributed significantly to the new Irish legislation which was steered efficiently through the parliamentary process by the then Minister of State, Pat Rabbitte, TD. Opposition members, especially Ned O'Keeffe, TD, and Maureen Quill, then a TD, were active during the debates.

This book deals with the main aspects of the 1997 Act in relevant chapters according to the subject matter. My comments on the various sections reflect my own experience: As a practising Barrister and former civil servant concerned with the proper regulation of credit unions, as an activist in the co-operative movement including the Society for Co-operative Studies Ltd, and in the Law Library Credit Union Study Group. That resulted in the Law Library Credit Union Limited being registered as the first one under the 1997 Act on International Credit Union Day, 15 October 1998.

Also included throughout the book are my comments on specific provisions following my attendance at the Dáil and Seanad during the parliamentary process. To some extent, that was a frustrating experience in this era of open government and freedom of information. Unlike, for example, the citizens' open access to the Swedish parliament, as a general rule with some exceptions visitors to Leinster House may attend only as guests of TDs or senators. (Helen Keogh and Sam McAughtry facilitated me.)

With due regard to parliamentary procedures and press gallery arrangements, it is particularly frustrating that an individual seeking to follow the democratic processing of legislation during debates in the Dáil or Senate chambers is strictly forbidden to take notes in the public gallery. Legal authors and commentators should be facilitated, for example by temporary access to the privileges of the Oireachtas Press Gallery. The position is improving as parliamentary debates become available on the internet at the Oireachtas website, www.irlgov.ie/oireachtas. Extensions to buildings at Leinster House should facilitate greater public access.

In the Dáil Select Committee on Enterprise and Economic Strategy, the atmosphere was constructive and informal. The committee chairman, Michael Bell, TD, having conducted the proceedings fairly and efficiently, thanked the visitors, including credit union activists for their interest and attendance.

It was disappointing during the parliamentary process that there was no effective debate on many important aspects of the new credit union legislation, for example the innovation of examiners and administrators for credit unions. The main concerns of the credit union movement — financial limits on savings and loans, and some supervisory aspects — were taken on board by the Minister and dealt with through amendments to the original Bill. By the end of the second stage a record number of over 60 TDs had spoken. After that slow start when time was wasted in repetition of some points and the inevitable local references by TDs, the legislative process moved very fast, apparently by consensus to meet the deadline of the ILCU's annual convention.

There was insufficient discussion on some aspects of the legislation. Many TDs and senators with financial and legal expertise could have, and arguably should have, contributed constructively to other areas of the legislation apart from the obvious ones about financial limits. While political party considerations and time constraints probably inhibited some TDs and senators from contributing to the debate, constructive and objective analysis could reasonably have been expected, especially from independent members. Provisions which were not examined in detail during the parliamentary process may cause problems later when the legislation is being applied.

In commenting on the various provisions of the 1997 Act, I consulted the official published reports of the Oireachtas debates which are available to the public. By providing the background and context, such reports are a guide to understanding legislation. Such reports, however, are limited by the extent and quality of the debates and confined by the standard rules on statutory interpretation, including the literal rule, the golden rule, the mischief rule and relevant legal maxims. In summary, the Credit Union Act, 1997, as a statute directed to the public at large, should be understood by giving a word or expression its ordinary or colloquial meaning. Some terms have special meanings as explained in the glossary and in section 2 of the Act on interpretation. Courts may have to interpret specific statutory provisions especially in respect of technical and regulatory provisions. Eschewing the awkward but fashionable politically correct terms such as " him/her, he/she, chairperson," the 1997 Act uses the traditional forms of him, he, and chairman. From statutory interpretation and common practice in credit unions, it is clear that both genders are included in those terms and no reflection is intended on significant contribution of many women since the pioneers, Nora Herlihy and Muriel Gahan.

The explanatory guide published by the Department of Enterprise, Trade and Employment, the ILCU's guidelines and standard rules, and also the Irish Current Law Statutes Annotated (ICLSA) R 62, August 1998 (Bird, 1998), referred to throughout this book, also help in understanding the practical aspects of the 1997 Act. The glossary of common terms simply explained with cross-references to relevant chapters, included in the book, should also be useful to readers.

ANTHONY P QUINN

International Credit Union Day
15 Deireadh Fómhair, 1998

Chapter 1

CO-OPERATIVE BACKGROUND

"Co-operation as a constructive expression of man's age-old
instinct for mutual aid holds out hope."

W.P. Watkins, British and international leader;
Co-operative Principles, Today and Tomorrow, 1986.

Credit unions are mutual organisations, owned by the members,
who have democratic control through the principle of one-member-
one-vote. That system contrasts with the usual format of banks
and other commercial companies which are normally dominated
by large shareholders and management.

The practical purposes of credit unions, as financial co-
operatives, are to encourage thrift among members and to provide
loans at fair and reasonable rates of interest for members. Those
objectives are achieved by using voluntary effort to administer
and organise credit unions and by paying a relatively modest rate
of interest on savings, that is, monies subscribed by members as
shares and deposits. The thrust is voluntary with no State
involvement except for supervision and control in the public
interest. The increased levels of savings and loans and also the
thrust towards expanded services, however, led to stricter State
supervision under the Credit Union Act 1997. The trend is also
towards more professional management. Further details on the
practical workings of credit unions and the laws governing them
will be provided throughout this book.

CO-OPERATIVE CONTEXT

First, it is necessary to place credit unions in their appropriate context as part of the wider co-operative (co-op) movement. A co-op differs from mainstream forms of business in a number of ways reflecting co-op ethos and principles. While co-op structures take different forms at various times, in diverse places and businesses, some general badges or indicators are common to most. The thrust of these indicators means that co-ops aim in business dealings to serve the members and to benefit society at large.

Co-ops must obviously be managed on business lines. That is especially true of the credit union movement. With its substantial financial assets, it has a distinct and separate identity apart from the wider financial services sector. Sometimes, parts of the co-op movement may have to dilute or adapt the strict principles to compete and survive in business. For example, Irish agricultural co-ops formed public limited companies (plcs) to raise extra capital on the stock exchange. Some building societies have moved away from mutuality principles on which they were historically based.

HISTORICAL OUTLINE

Co-operation, a basic human process, is evident informally in families and communities. The Irish *meitheal* is often quoted as an example of co-operation in which neighbours helped one another with the harvest. The origins of modern formal co-operation can be traced to the self-help movement of the eighteenth and nineteenth centuries, which took various forms in different countries, as described below.

Germany

Schultze-Delitzsch Societies

Herman Schultze-Delitzsch a lawyer from Prussian Saxony, organised co-ops to provide insurance in sickness and death. His greatest success, however, was organising people's banks on a mutual basis among craftsmen and small-scale merchants. By 1859, there was a federation of one hundred and eighty co-ops with nearly twenty thousand members. By 1882, there were over three thousand societies.

The German Schultze-Delitzsch societies are interesting and relevant for the modern credit union movement because of those societies' features especially:

- The principle of mutual help which excluded Government hand-outs. The financial base of each co-op must be its own capital raised by small monthly or weekly contributions from members;

- Limited interest was paid on capital deposited by members;

- Short-term loans only were granted;

- Economic self-sufficiency was promoted;

- The main criteria for borrowing was individual character rather than collateral;

- Open membership to all suitable applicants.

German Raiffeisen Societies

A Rhinelander named Frederic Raiffeisen founded savings societies among rural communities during the mid-nineteenth century. That credit movement grew to a formidable extent and by 1883 there were over four hundred societies. In contrast to the Schultze-Delitzsch societies, which served urban craftsmen, the Raiffeisen societies were organised on Christian principles to serve farmers. Some features of the Raiffeisen societies or land banks are relevant to modern credit unions:

- The character of the individual member is the most important condition for admittance to the society;

- Members would be accepted only from a particular group and within a particular area such as a parish. The common bond requirement in credit unions is based on a similar concept;

- Officers perform duties on a voluntary basis;

- The period of loans limited — from two to ten years;

- Societies to operate on a non-profit basis with earnings added to reserve funds but such funds took priority over distribution of profits;

- No profits distributed until reserve funds were established.

Italy

The modern co-operative credit movement was also influenced by two Italians of the nineteenth century, Luigi Luzzatti and Leon Wollenborg. Luzzatti, a professor of political economy at Padua, organised a co-op bank in Milan in 1866. By 1909, there were over seven hundred societies in Italy. Dr Leon Wollenborg's credit unions were small, required entrance fees and made small renewable loans to members.

Some of Luzzatti's innovations, suitably adapted, feature in modern credit unions:

1) Limited liability to protect individual members;

2) Restriction on each individual member's share capital;

3) An annual renewal of members of the board of directors by the retiral of one third each year.

North America

Alphonse Desjardins was born in Quebec Province, Canada, in 1854. As a newspaper journalist, he became interested in the problem of usury and abuse by moneylenders who charged high interest rates. At the turn of the 20th century, in his native town of Levis, Desjardins organised the first credit union in North America, called *La Caisse Populaire de Levis*, a type of people's bank. Some relevant features of early American co-ops which influenced modern credit unions were:

- The borrower's character was the main security for any loan;

- Loans were granted only for productive or emergency purposes;

- Members had limited liability, as in the Italian Luzzatti societies

- The co-ops, although engaged in monetary transactions, were not to be considered as part of regular financial institutions

- The co-ops expressed a high social ideal in the field of economics.

Caisses populaires developed in French-speaking Canada as credit and savings co-ops organised on a community and local basis, the prototype of Irish credit unions based on the common bond of living or working in a neighbourhood. *Caisses d'économie* were organised on the basis of members' occupation, employment (like the Irish industrial credit unions) or ethnic group. The English-speaking credit unions were organised as "centrals" and the Credit Union of Canada.

Dr J.H. Tompkins and Monsignor Moses Coady of St Francis Xavier University, Antigonish, Novia Scotia founded the Antigonish movement just before World War Two. Local study clubs resulted in co-op stores and credit unions among the farming and fishing communities of Nova Scotia. Monsignor Coady had a world-wide influence through his writings, especially *Masters of Their Own Destiny*, published by Harper Collins. A few credit unions in Northern Ireland still follow the Antigonish model.

In 1938, Pope Pius XI gave express approval to the Antigonish movement as a practical expression of the Papal encyclicals, *Rerum Novarum* and *Quadragesimo Anno* for reconstructing and perfecting the social order by improved living conditions.

A commentary on those Papal encyclicals, *Forty Years After: Pius XI and the Social Order* (Miller, 1948) explains the relationship between Catholic social teaching and the co-operative and credit union movements, especially in North America. In that context, a co-op was defined as a group of ordinary people who unite to do business for themselves, save expense, break the hold of monopolies and ultimately improve living conditions within communities.

In the USA, credit union pioneers during the early twentieth century included Pierre Jay and Edward A. Filene. Filene believed that credit unions should teach workers the habits of thrift, leading to control of their own destiny.

Although the general movement is non-sectarian, the Roman Catholic Church influenced the formation of the early American credit unions as an expression of Catholic social teaching. Prior to 1900, there was a co-op banking system in the St Louis archdiocese but the first credit union was formed in 1909 in St Mary's parish, Manchester, New Hampshire. Diocesan agencies encouraged the spread of the movement into many parishes nationwide under both State and Federal charters.

The American efforts led to the Credit Union National Association (CUNA) and the development of the modern worldwide movement.

The Influences of the Wider Co-op Movement

It is necessary at this stage, however, to revert to the nineteenth century and to trace the influences of the wider co-op movement. General principles developed to mirror the features in the emergent credit union movement in Germany, Italy and North America.

The early British co-operators were inspired by idealism. For example, in Scotland, New Lanark was founded by Robert Owen in the early nineteenth century. Rejecting capitalism, Owen set up model conditions for his spinning mill. To use modern terminology, it was a people-centred business. In contrast to the dark satanic mills of the Industrial Revolution, self-governing communities at New Lanark were called Villages of Co-operation. Owen combined moral earnestness with visionary insights. He elaborated a theory of co-operation instead of competition.

William Thompson, a social and political theorist from Roscarberry, Co. Cork, influenced Owen who helped to devise a world free from poverty, greed and ignorance. An Owenite community was founded at New Harmony, Indiana, USA.

At New Lanark Visitor Centre, between Glasgow and Edinburgh, modern tourists are taken on a "Quest for Universal Harmony" based on the ideals of Robert Owen who is generally regarded as the father of modern co-operation.

CO-OPERATIVE PRINCIPLES

Facets of the self-help movement of the Victorian era included friendly societies for insurance purposes and also co-op stores. One such store, formed at Rochdale, Lancashire, England in 1844, adopted rules to facilitate people working for mutual purposes, sharing the benefit of joint efforts on an equitable basis.

The rules of the Rochdale Equitable Pioneer Society emphasised democratic control and equal voting rights for all members and also elected management committees. Discrimination on religious or political grounds was prohibited. Surplus funds were set aside for education. A century and a half later, the thrust of those rules is universally relevant to the co-operative movement. The Rochdale Rules led to the formulation of the modern Co-operative Principles, adopted in 1966 by the International Co-operative Alliance as marks or badges of genuine co-ops including credit unions.

INTERNATIONAL CO-OPERATIVE PRINCIPLES

1. Open And Voluntary Membership

Membership of a co-op should be voluntary and available without artificial restriction or any social, racial or religious discrimination, to all persons who can use its services and are willing to accept responsibilities of membership.

2. Democratic Control

Co-ops are democratic organisations. Their affairs should be administered by persons, elected or appointed in a manner agreed by members and accountable to them. Members of primary societies should enjoy equal voting rights (one-member-one-vote irrespective of extent of shareholding) and participation in decisions affecting their societies. In societies other than primary societies (for example, a co-op consisting of many primary co-ops of individual members), administration should be on a democratic basis in a suitable form.

3. Limited Return on Share Capital

Share capital should receive only a strictly limited rate of interest, if any. The principle is sometimes explained on the basis of capital being subordinate to people in a co-operative enterprise, as distinguished from mainstream business where the emphasis is on the level of return on capital invested.

4. Disposal of Surplus

Surplus monies or savings, if any, arising out of a society's operations, belong to the members. Any such surplus should be distributed in such manner as would avoid one member gaining at another's expense. The distribution of any surplus may be done by members' decision to provide for the following:

- Development of the business of co-op

- Common service to benefit all members

- Distribution among members in proportion to their transactions with the society.

5. Education

All co-op societies should provide for education of their members, officers and employees and of the general public, in the principles and technique of co-operation, both economic and democratic.

6. Co-operatives Co-operate

All co-op organisations, to best serve the interests of their members and the communities, should actively co-operate in every practical way with other co-ops at local, national and international levels.

The Co-op Principles are basic but may be adapted to suit evolving needs and specific types of co-ops. For example, principle No.1 as applied to credit unions means membership is open to all suitable members who meet certain requirements and specifically the common bond of occupation or residence or employment within a specific locality. The International Co-operative Alliance as a statement of co-operative identity adopted a revised version of the co-operative principles at Manchester in 1995 which are listed in Appendix 2, with the *Credit Union Operating Principles*.

The credit union movement is especially committed to the fifth principle above by training its members and the wider community in the merits of mutual saving and borrowing facilities and also in wider co-op principles. Such involvement is facilitated by the Credit Union Act 1997, as reflected in the revised standard rules adopted by the ILCU in 1998. For example in section 6(2) of the Act, included in ILCU standard rule 5(1) — the objects for which a credit union may be formed and section 44, rule 53, — empowering a credit union to establish a special fund for social and cultural purposes including community development.

There are limits to what can be achieved in practice and there is scope for more education. Some critics claim that the credit union movement neglects educational initiatives to raise awareness of co-operation. Other practical applications of the Co-op Principles to credit unions are considered throughout the book.

It is necessary to distinguish between principles, on one hand, and rules and practice on the other. For example, the principle of one-member-one-vote is impracticable in federations of co-ops but is vital for the practice of democracy in primary co-ops, such as credit unions, consisting of individuals. Some co-op activists favour a flexible approach to the principles and stress the achievement of objects.

CREDIT UNIONS AND THE CO-OPERATIVE PRINCIPLES

The credit union movement throughout the world is inspired by co-op principles. The specific application of those principles, however, depends on circumstances which may vary between countries depending on the local legislative framework which may enshrine the co-op principles in various degrees of detail.

The Irish League of Credit Unions (ILCU) at its 1984 Annual General Meeting, adopted a Statement of Credit Union Operating Principles which reflect the international co-op principles.

The statement issued by ILCU in 1992, however, expanded the original principles to suit the specific needs of credit unions. For example, new headings include "Service to Members", to improve the economic and social well-being of members, whose needs shall be a permanent and paramount consideration, rather than towards the maximising of surpluses. Education and social responsibility are stressed. The operating principles are now included as Appendix 1 to the standard rules for credit unions affiliated to the ILCU and Rule 6 requires compliance with the framework of the principles.

In the rules of the ILCU, the objects clause includes: To encourage its members to operate in accordance with the *Credit Union Operating Principles*, which are listed in Appendix 2 to this book. So, the principles, originating in Victorian Rochdale and modernised in Manchester in 1995, have been adapted to suit credit unions in modern Ireland in the new millennium.

Chapter 2

THE IRISH CREDIT UNION MOVEMENT

"History affords no support for the belief that co-operative
credit societies could be successfully established."

Economic Development, Department of Finance,
Dublin, 1957

THE CO-OPERATIVE CONTEXT IN IRELAND

The roots of the modern Irish credit union movement were in the
wider context of co-operation as outlined in Chapter 1. There were
also specific Irish aspects. Robert Owen, the pioneer of the British
co-op movement, visited Dublin in 1823. At a successful meeting
in Dublin's Rotunda, Owen was warmly welcomed by an
influential audience which listened to his ideas on co-operation
and a new moral world. The Hibernian Philanthropic Society,
formed to propagate Owenite ideas, strongly influenced a County
Clare landlord, John Scott Vandeleur. He started Ireland's first
formal co-op at Ralahine, Co. Clare and recruited as manager a
disciple of Owen named Edward Thomas Craig. In 1833, that
mutual experiment in communal agriculture and manufacturing
failed due to the human weakness of Vandeleur who indulged in
gambling.

The tensions between British co-ops and Irish producer,
orientated co-operators in the 1890s was traced in an article:
"Irish Co-operatives, from Creameries at the Crossroads to
Multinationals" (King and Kennedy, 1994). There were competing
visions between a co-op commonwealth based on consumers and
one based on producers. The path to consumer co-ops was

virtually closed in Ireland although farmers did purchase seeds, tools and fertilisers communally through agricultural societies. The Cork co-operative society which tried during World War One to reduce the price of bread and other basic foods failed because workers and their families did not support it.

AGRICULTURE CREDIT SOCIETIES

The growth of the Irish co-operative movement, mainly in the agricultural sector, during the later Victorian period and the early twentieth century has been well documented and described. *The Irish Co-operative Movement, its History and Development* (Bolger, 1977) and *Horace Plunkett, Co-operation and Politics, An Irish Biography* (West, 1986), provide a comprehensive picture of the movement.

The main leaders were Sir Horace Plunkett, George Russell (Æ), and Fr Tom Finlay, SJ. Plunkett's aims of "Better farming, better business and better living" were effected under the aegis of the Irish Agricultural Co-operative Society (IAOS). Now called the Irish Co-operative Organisation Society (ICOS) to reflect the wider co-op movement, it celebrated its centenary in 1994. Co-op ideals in the agricultural sector have been diluted by involvement in mainstream companies and stock exchange funding.

At the turn of the century, Plunkett's ideals were translated into practical initiatives. The Plunkett Foundation, Oxford, established in 1919 to promote co-op education, celebrated its 75th anniversary in 1994. Other initiatives under Horace Plunkett included establishing agricultural credit societies, called village or agricultural banks, were registered with the Registrar of Friendly Societies as specially authorised societies. These should not be confused with the National Land Bank which the incipient Irish parliament, Dáil Éireann, established in 1919. The specific co-op initiative, spearheaded by Fr Tom Finlay SJ, was based on the German Raiffeissen societies' system as outlined in Chapter 1 of this book and in "Irish Credit Unions, a Success Story" (Quinn, 1995).

As examined by Ivers in his MBA thesis, "The Further Development of Credit Unions in Ireland" (UCD, 1970) and by King and Kennedy (*ibid.*), the first credit society was set-up in Doneraile, Co. Cork, in 1894. The main features were:

- Membership was confined to the local village or parish;

- Loans were made for productive purposes only and society members scrutinised loan applications;

- As in the Raiffeisen system, membership entailed unlimited liability. (This was because of registration under the Friendly Societies Acts, rather than the Industrial and Provident Societies or Companies legislation);

- If the society experienced financial problems, each member would be held liable for the society's debts. This deterred careless lending;

- The emphasis was on trust and honesty, as in modern credit unions;

- Unlike credit unions, however, agricultural credit societies were disproportionately based in the poorer areas, especially the Western seaboard;

- Voluntary communal effort kept interest rates much lower than those charged by ruthless local shopkeepers, the so-called gombeen men, who exploited small farmers.

Weaknesses in the agricultural credit societies included insufficient deposits to match loans, a reluctance to disclose personal business to neighbours on the committees, a dependency on State support and inadequate control procedures. These agricultural credit societies, however, did fill a basic communal need in combating indebtedness among small farmers.

The success of the Doneraile credit society encouraged IAOS to expand that system. By 1914, there were 233 credit societies alongside 350 dairy or creamery co-ops and over 200 agricultural societies which supplied farm inputs.

LESSONS FROM FAILURE

Increased prosperity of Irish farmers during World War One ironically helped the decline of the credit societies by decreasing the demand for their services. Due to financial constraints, government support was withdrawn and commercial banks became more active. Only about 50 credit societies remained by the early 1930s. The economic recession did not stimulate their revival and they went into terminal decline.

The agricultural credit societies failed to live up to the high expectations of their founders. Although the societies did not survive into modern Ireland, they provided a base for credit union ideas and salutary lessons in pitfalls to be avoided. In some ways, however, the lack of success associated with the agricultural banks reinforced prejudices against co-op credit. In 1938, the Irish Banking Commission concluded that there was little prospect that any useful development of co-op rural credit could be achieved by government initiative or through the Agricultural Credit Corporation. The negative quotation about co-op credit societies cited at the start of this chapter from an official Irish government document was presumably influenced by the agricultural bank experience.

FRIENDLY SOCIETIES

Mutual loan and insurance societies were an expression of the self-help ethos of Victorian Britain. In Ireland, according to contemporary reports, there was a reluctance to utilise small savings banks and friendly societies. The habit of depositing savings was lacking but farmers hoarded cash. Friendly societies were organised to some extent among the emergent urban working classes especially the better-off skilled tradesmen in the East and North East. Irish friendly societies developed in different forms and some societies called tontines divided their funds among members at Christmas.

Societies like the Irish National Foresters and the AOH provided mutual insurance on a wide scale before the modern Welfare State.

In a link with the past, the very successful St Mary's Credit Union, Navan, Co. Meath, was founded in the front room of the old Foresters Hall, Navan. In general, however, the friendly society movement lacked deep roots in Ireland and had only a minimal influence on the modern Irish credit union movement.

SOCIAL AND ECONOMIC STUDIES

In the period after the World War Two, or the Emergency as it was called in Ireland, some informed individuals stimulated the study of the problems of emigration and unemployment within a wider social and philosophic context. In 1946, courses of adult education lectures were organised in University College, Cork — now National University of Ireland, Cork — by its president, Professor Alfred O'Rahilly. His role in stimulating the co-operative spirit and educating people to achieve more control over their money supply was acknowledged in Gaughan's, (1992) *Alfred O'Rahilly, III: Controversialist, Part 1: Social Reformer*.

Nora Herlihy in her pioneering days in spreading the credit union message quoted from Dr O'Rahilly's writings on social and economic policy. In correspondence with Nora Herlihy he expressed hope about the practical effects of the proposed credit unions on rural communities. In *A Labour History of Ireland* (1992), Dr Emmet O'Connor related the UCC initiative to the social teaching of the Catholic Church and trade union fear of communist and other secular influences.

UCD COURSE

An evening Diploma course in Social & Economic Science at University College, Dublin (UCD) in the late nineteen forties was directed by Fr Edward Coyne, SJ, President of IAOS. He was a protégé of Fr Thomas Finlay, SJ, co-operative pioneer and co-founder of the Irish Agricultural Organisation Society (IAOS, later ICOS). Dr Alfred O'Rahilly's influence on the Dublin course was acknowledged in *Nora Herlihy: Irish Credit Union Pioneer*, (Culloty, 1990). The UCD initiative was supported by the Congress of Irish Unions, part of a divided Irish trade union movement and distinct from the Irish Trade Union Congress. The UCD course, organised by the extra mural studies board, was aimed at people who would not usually have had access to third level qualifications.

In the UCD course, ethics and sociology lecturer, Dr Cornelius Lucey of Maynooth, and later Bishop of Cork, related the Rochdale Co-operative Rules and Principles (explained in Chapter 1) to Christian social teaching on human dignity and the subsidiarity of the State. The concept of the State supplementing but not supplanting private effort for the public good reinforced co-operative ideas. That thrust reflected the prevailing Catholic ethos of the period as expressed in social welfare initiatives by Dr John Charles McQuaid, Archbishop of Dublin during the period after World War Two.

The Papal encyclicals, *Rerum Novarum* and *Quadragesimo Anno* on reconstructing and perfecting the social order by improved living conditions, referred to in Chapter 1 in the North American context, were also relevant in Ireland. The philosophy of the encyclicals that authority should be devolved to local and occupational groups was central to credit union philosophy. Both the UCC and UCD extra-mural courses were available in some localities outside the cities. Therefore seeds were sown widely. Maurice Gaffney, later an eminent Senior Counsel at the Irish Bar and Bencher of King's Inns, lectured on trade union studies at the UCD diploma course. He remembered that period of the late nineteen-forties, early nineteen-fifties, as a great time for stimulation of ideas among enthusiastic participants eager for practical and theoretical information. He recalled the resurgence of national spirit at that time. A student on the UCD course, the late Séamus MacEoin, credits Maurice Gaffney with sowing the seeds of co-operative ideas during his lectures.

IDEAS INTO ACTION:
DUBLIN CENTRAL CO-OP SOCIETY LTD

Having completed the UCD diploma, an experience which profoundly affected him, civil servant Séamus MacEoin, helped to form an economics study panel to debate topical social issues. Each panel member took turns in presenting a paper for discussion. Séamus MacEoin spoke about the co-op movement at a open meeting on 9 December 1953 at 35, Lower Gardiner Street, Dublin, where the printers' trade union was based. The paper stimulated interest in credit co-ops among an audience which included Nora Herlihy, a school teacher based in Dublin, who became a prominent leader of the Irish credit union movement.

Following the economics panel meeting, addressed by Séamus MacEoin, an initiative was taken to tackle unemployment and emigration through worker co-op development and low-cost credit. 1954 was the centenary of the birth of Irish co-op pioneer, Sir Horace Plunkett, and also of Alphonse Desjardins, who initiated the *Caisse Populaire*, the prototype of modern credit unions. So it was propitious that the Dublin Central Co-op Society (DCCS) held its first meeting on 6 March 1954 in Moran's Hotel, Talbot Street, Dublin. Séamus MacEoin recalled the venue as being suitable for a public access, yet near the printers' union office in Lower Gardiner Street, where the National Co-op Council was based. The modern Moran's hotel on the Naas Road, Dublin is by coincidence used as a venue in more recent years for seminars on co-operative education held by the Co-operative Education and Promotion Group, organised by Paddy Candon and other enthusiasts with support from the ILCU.

The DCCS, whose registered office was at 85, Lower Abbey Street, formed an investment bank, but its legal basis was not clear and further research was necessary. Séamus MacEoin remembered that information was received from Denis Byrne, a civil service colleague in the Land Commission and a member of the National Co-op Council and the DCCS. The information from Byrne led Nora Herlihy to obtain data on credit unions from the

Credit Union National Association (CUNA), Madison, Wisconsin, USA.

GERMAN AND AMERICAN INFLUENCES

As explained in Chapter 1, the modern credit co-op concept owes its origin to various influences. They included the Raiffeisen societies formed in Southern Germany in the nineteenth century when small farmers associated to provide purchasing power for the mutual advantage of all participants. Following initiatives by the French Canadian Desjardins, Monsignor Coady of Nova Scotia, and Americans, including Edward Filene, the movement spread in Europe and India.

The credit union movement drew on the German Raiffeisen principles reflecting wider co-op concepts:

- The members would own, control and administer credit unions;

- Only members could save or borrow from the union/society;

- Members' character would be vital as security for loans;

- Loans were made for provident or productive purposes at affordable rates of interest.

CREDIT UNION EXTENSION SERVICE

Despite the decline of the earlier agricultural credit societies and the negative conventional wisdom quoted at the start of this chapter, the concept of co-op credit was developed in the late 1950s by a small group of Irish enthusiasts who drew on experiences in other countries, especially North America. The leaders — Nora Herlihy, Séamus MacEoin and Seán Forde who are all now deceased — started a ginger group called the Credit Union Extension Service. Community groups including Muintir na Tíre, National Farmers Association (now IFA), and also the Irish Countrywomen's Association (ICA) were represented. The National Co-operative Council, (NCC), under its president Brendan Ó Cearbhaill, a printers' trade union leader, was also active. The Credit Union Extension Service was originally a sub-committee of that council.

According to Geraldine Mitchell (1997) in her biography of the late Muriel Gahan, an ICA and country market activist, she also joined extension service meetings held at the Country Shop, a focus point for communal initiatives. On behalf of Country Workers Ltd, which was closely connected with the ICA, Muriel Gahan put the first money ever into an Irish credit union. Although the sum was small, £5, a "fiver" in the parlance of the time, the money was regarded by the pioneer Seán Forde as "manna from heaven" and helped to buy over a thousand postage stamps to spread the credit union message.

The extension service initiative aimed to create a reliable system of low cost credit based on the Raiffeisen principles.

PIONEERS AND INSPIRATIONAL LEADERS

By 1958, the first Irish Credit Unions were at Donore Avenue, Dublin 8 and Dún Laoghaire, which was confined to members of Dún Laoghaire Grocery Co-op, managed by Eamonn Quinn. He was father of Senator Fergal Quinn, a successful supermarket operator and uncle of Ruairí Quinn, leader of the Irish Labour Party and former government minister.

Eamonn Quinn and his brothers operated Red Island Holiday Camp, at Skerries, North County Dublin, where Folk High Schools (daonscoileanna) were organised on the Danish model during the late 1950s and early 1960s. John O'Halloran, the camp manager, was also active in the National Co-operative Council.

Themes discussed at the residential Folk Schools included co-operation and community development. Séamus MacEoin explained the background in his contribution to *The Golden Triangle, the Æ Commemorative Lectures*, (ed. Quinn 1989).

In May 1957, a Folk School organised at Red Island by the National Co-operative Council under its chairman, Brendan Ó Cearbhaill, was opened by Éamonn de Valera, An Taoiseach — Prime Minister. Noelle Davies, TCD lecturer, inspired the concept. The Director was Con Murphy, an admirer of the Folk

High Schools founded by Grundvig in Denmark to promote community development, and providing the basis for the successful Danish and Scandinavian co-operative movements.

Séamus MacEoin recalled that a special guest at the High School was the veteran William P. Watkins, director of the International Co-op Alliance from 1951 to 1963. Although aware of human frailty in the co-op movement, Watkins stressed in his writings and lectures the importance of education as a means to achieving perfection. Education became a vital key to spreading the credit union ethos.

As an educational aid, an American credit union film, *King's X*, received from the Columban priests at Dalgan Park, Navan, Co. Meath was shown at the Folk School in May 1957. The name *King's X* derived from an allusion to the marking, under Royal authority, of debtors' doors, during the days of debtors' prisons. The innovative audiovisual aid was helpful in spreading the fledgling credit union message.

The film was supplemented with an address from Nora Herlihy, a Cork-born teacher who was based in Dublin. The sincerity and determination of Nora Herlihy (1910–1988) has been documented in a biography (Culloty, 1990). Nora Herlihy had been strongly influenced by the writings of Monsignor Moses Coady, of Antigonish, Nova Scotia, who had formulated a co-operative philosophy. She made a deep study of the Coady philosophy, including practical details such as people's right to assert control of their monetary and consumer rights. That was in the era when many Irish people depended on expensive credit under schemes such as provident cheques, hire purchase, moneylending and informal savings funds, sometimes called "diddly" clubs in Dublin slang.

In the specific area of co-operative credit, Nora Herlihy was convinced of the need for education and fresh thinking to help tackle national problems. Her enthusiasm was tempered by caution. She had also studied the weaknesses of the Irish agricultural credit societies and was conscious of the need for a proper legal code to provide adequate controls. Within the

National Co-op Council, Nora Herlihy focused on credit unions. Muriel Gahan, activist of the ICA and country markets, also attended the Folk School at Red Island in 1957 where she met enthusiasts who had already started to spread the credit union message. Her role was peripheral but influential.

The pioneers of the Irish co-operative movement such as Sir Horace Plunkett, Æ and Fr Tom Finlay and also the German Raiffeisen provided inspiration for the fledgling Irish credit union movement. It also drew on other sources especially the Credit Union National Association (CUNA), Wisconsin, USA, where the World Council of Credit Unions (WOCCU) is now based. As outlined in Chapter 1 the *Caisse Populaire* of Quebec, the Antigonish model and the German credit banks provided prototypes for modern credit unions. There was also an influence from the Southern Hemisphere through Mrs Helen Fowler from the Australian parish credit unions.

As well as those involved in UCD and other extramural courses, Irish clergy who contributed to setting the spark which inspired the Irish credit union movement included: An t-Athair D. Ó Floinn, SP, spiritual director of the Legion of Mary in Dublin; Dr W. Philbin, later Bishop of Down and Connor; Fr E Fitzgerald, Cork; Dr C. Lucey, Bishop of Cork; Fr O'Brien of Dalkey, Co. Dublin and parish priest at Rathdrum, Co. Wicklow, Fr Paddy Gallagher, Canon Peter McKevitt, PP, Termonfeckin, Co. Louth and also Church of Ireland Canon Cormac Lloyd, Inch, Co. Wexford. The Society of Saint Vincent de Paul was also active.

Séamus MacEoin, during his final illness in 1993 at St. Michael's Hospital, Dun Laoghaire reflected on the pioneering days of the Irish credit union movement. He compared those days to a space rocket's different stages — each giving way in turn to a further stage as the momentum gathered pace.

The first stage, the UCD extra-mural diploma course, 1948–1950, gave way to the Economics Study Panel and its seminal meeting addressed on co-ops by Séamus MacEoin in 1954. The Dublin Central Co-op Society started in 1954. That led to the Folk Schools and the Credit Union Extension Service (originally a sub-committee of the National Co-operative Council) and ultimately to the Credit Union League of Ireland (1960) which evolved into the Irish League of Credit Unions (ILCU). Another body, the Co-operative Development Society (CDS), founded in 1954 to fund and register worker co-ops, was revived in the late 1980's by a group which included Séamus MacEoin. The CDS formulated standard or model rules, under the Industrial and Provident Societies Acts, to suit the Irish situation outside the agricultural co-ops which were under the aegis of IAOS, Plunkett House, Dublin. There was an increasing awareness of the need for legislative reform, especially for credit co-ops.

COMMITTEE ON CO-OPERATION

During the Lemass era, Ireland moved forward towards a modern economy. Following lobbying by co-op and other community groups, a Government Committee on Co-operative Societies (1957–1963), was appointed by Seán Lemass, then Minister for Industry and Commerce and later Taoiseach. The committee was chaired by the Registrar of Friendly Societies, Kevin Mangan, a barrister attached to the Attorney General's Office. The committee included credit union activist Nora Herlihy. She had been nominated on Muriel Gahan's initiative by the Irish Countrywomen's Association (ICA) which had originated as the United Irishwomen, (1910–1935), a sister society of IAOS (now ICOS) during the co-operative efforts of Sir Horace Plunkett.

Civil Servants in the relevant Department of Industry and Commerce, including committee secretary Patrick McAuliffe praised the quality and scope of Nora Herlihy's work on the committee.

The recommendations in the committee's report included proposed new legislation for credit unions. Some of them, mainly from the Community Development Movement, were registered under the Industrial and Provident Societies Act 1893 which was drafted in a different era for the wider self-help movement.

Due to the complex nature of its brief the committee on co-operatives deliberated thoroughly rather than swiftly. Meanwhile, the educational and research efforts of the fledgling credit union sector continued. Submissions to the committee included detailed documents from the Credit Union Extension Service and the Dublin Central Co-op Society Ltd. The signatories to the submissions, Nora Herlihy and Séamus MacEoin, made their informed comments relevant to economic development and quality of life in the context of co-operation as a viable philosophy.

The submissions also pressed for new laws and the committee recommended new legislation. The government accepted the need for a new legal framework for credit unions. Nora Herlihy and Kathleen Matthews (subsequently manager of Premier Navan Road Credit Union, Dublin) prepared a draft Bill. The legislative process was stimulated by representations from the League's Legislative Committee who met Jack Lynch, who had succeeded Sean Lemass as Minister for Industry and Commerce. The late Sean Flanagan, as parliamentary secretary (now called junior minister) to the Minister, Dr. Patrick Hillery, steered the Bill through its parliamentary course.

CREDIT UNION LEGISLATION

As she stood beside President de Valera as he signed into law the Credit Union Act 1966, Nora Herlihy was justly proud of the efforts of herself and the other pioneers. This was a legislative reform vital to the growth of the Irish credit union movement. The legal basis of Industrial and Provident Societies legislation was retained as a basic framework but the new Act (No. 19 of 1966) provided for the registration of co-operative societies. These co-ops were to be known as credit unions for the encouragement of thrift and the creation of credit, and to provide for the regulation of credit unions. The Act was a landmark for the wider co-operative movement because of statutory recognition of co-op concepts including the mutuality of members in the ownership and organisation of their societies.

Basic Industrial and Provident legislation, enacted to meet the special circumstances of the co-op movement, as interpreted by the Registrar had facilitated co-op principles to some extent. For example, by requiring one-member-one-vote on special resolutions for specific purposes under section 51 of the 1893 Act. That earlier legislation, however, was wide and flexible in scope. Thus it was subsequently used for commercial purposes for example registration of investment and deposit-taking enterprises which clearly were not *bona fide* mutual societies.

The Registrar of Friendly Societies (the Registrar), an independent officer under the aegis of the Department of Industry and Commerce, was designated as the regulatory authority under the Credit Union Act. The name of the relevant Department has undergone many changes over the years and has become the Department of Enterprise, Trade and Employment.

Basic Provisions

At this stage it is necessary to be alert to basic legislative provisions, some originating in the 1966 Act (now repealed) which are included in both the comprehensive Credit Union Act, 1997 (No. 15) and the standard rules, following an extensive consultation process between relevant bodies, especially the Registrar and the ILCU.

Common Bond

Membership of credit unions, is based on the basic concept of a common bond between members now provided for by section 6(1) (b) and (3) of the 1997 Act and ILCU standard rules 1 and 14. For example, members must be in the same occupation, live or work in the same locality or be members of the same association (other than for the purpose of forming or conducting a credit union, so it must be a *bona fide* body).

Legal Entities Run by Volunteers and Professionals

Each credit union is a separate legal entity, a corporate body, controlled by its members through annual meetings. Credit unions have not evolved as branches of the ILCU although that body assists and provides services for groups to ensure viable credit unions. Like registered companies, credit unions are corporate bodies, with a legal existence distinct from their members, who are protected by limited liability. Members elect a board of directors, with officers such as chairman, secretary and honorary treasurer. No remuneration is payable to such officers but treasurers may be paid, usually by honorarium, for duties performed.

The board of directors appoints a credit committee to consider loan applications. Members elect a supervisory committee to carry out statutory functions such as examining books and records of the credit union as an extra precaution. There is an increasing trend towards the employment of salaried staff as professional managers and cashiers. Officer is now defined in section 2(1) of the 1997 Act (rule 1) to include employees. As explained in Chapter 10, a qualified auditor must also be appointed in accordance with law to audit and certify the accounts.

IRISH LEAGUE OF CREDIT UNIONS (ILCU)

In Dame Street, Dublin near College Green, a plaque on a Telecom Éireann building which replaced the old Jury's Hotel, commemorated the foundation on 7 February 1960 of the Credit Union League of Ireland, now the Irish League of Credit Unions — ILCU. The credit union movement spread to Northern Ireland in the sixties under the leadership of John Hume, later to become an MP, MEP, leader of the Social Democratic and Labour Party (SDLP), Northern Ireland Assembly member and Nobel laureate. The ILCU, a non-sectarian and non-political organisation which is the representative and service body of the Irish credit union movement, maintains its all-Ireland dimension. About one-fifth of all credit unions affiliated to the ICLU are based in Northern Ireland. Chapter 13 of this book deals specifically with the ICLU and includes a table highlighting its history and development.

A branch of a British-based umbrella body, the National Federation of Savings and Co-op Credit Unions, NFCU, became active in some unionist areas of Northern Ireland. As explained in Chapter 15 on Northern Ireland, the Ulster Federation of Credit

Unions (UFCU) was formed in recent years as a representative group for over 50 credit unions.

There are about 600 credit unions throughout Ireland and most are affiliated to the ILCU. It is a non-statutory service body which provides schemes such as assisting individual members if their credit union gets into financial difficulties. ILCU retains the voluntary impetus through its board directors. Professional staff provide a back-up service for affiliated credit unions but voluntary input on the League board and various committees is fundamental to the co-operative ethos.

Among the ILCU's services, insurance is provided for loans and savings through ECCU Assurance Company Ltd. Commission on insurance payments by credit unions provides funds for the ILCU. The Irish credit union movement consists of over two million members with about £3.5 billion Irish pounds in personal savings and assets. Those impressive figures belie negative notions about the lack of success of co-operative credit, quoted at the start of this chapter, and conveyed officially in Ireland of the 1950's as conventional wisdom.

Chapter 3

BASICS OF CREDIT UNION MEMBERSHIP

"We practical folk keep a poet (Æ) in the office of our society from whom the most fruitful inspirations are derived."

Sir Horace Plunkett,
founder of modern Irish co-op movement.

Inspiration and ideas are vital but practical action is necessary to translate concepts into reality. The credit union movement is motivated by practical idealism. Therefore, careful planning is necessary especially concerning financial matters. Following the tradition set by the pioneers of the Irish credit union movement — Séamus MacEoin, Nora Herlihy and Seán Forde — study groups are essential before a new credit union is formed. The pioneers' motto remains apt: No education, no credit union.

Because of the study group system, proposed organisers and members have an opportunity to educate and train themselves in the theory and practice of co-operation and credit unions. Relevant legal formalities and requirements together with functions of boards and committees are studied so that intending members and officers are alerted to their rights and responsibilities. Thus practical effect is given to Co-operative Principle No. 5: Education, as explained in Chapter 1.

FORMING A CREDIT UNION

Before recommending a proposed credit union for registration by the Registrar, the ILCU insists on pre-formation study groups which undergo intensive training. That is considered essential to proper understanding of the ethos and operations of co-operative credit. Each member of the study group should be given the opportunity by rotation of presiding over meetings and acting as secretary. The ILCU educational programme for emergent and new credit unions operates at local level in the regional groups of credit unions, which are called chapters. Study groups, preferably consisting of about twenty people, are encouraged to contact local chapters and the credit unions affiliated to them. Experienced credit union officers are assigned to attend new study groups to encourage and monitor progress. Field officers and other ILCU officials and also board members give regular advice on insurance and assist in interpreting rules and legislation. The ILCU route is not a legal requirement but it would be much more difficult for a group to form a credit union without the League's assistance.

At the pre-registration stage, a group may commence a savings fund. For practical and legal reasons, however, loans should not be issued. Without the legal framework, it would be difficult and probably illegal to administer a loans system. Unregistered groups would not have corporate existence and limited liability, nor would they benefit from section 184 of the Credit Union Act 1997 which provides that certain enactments do not apply to credit unions: the Central Banks Acts, 1942–1997; Building Societies Act, 1989 and Consumer Credit Act, 1995 which includes restrictions on moneylending.

Caution is advised before starting a new credit union. Most centres of population are covered by the common bond of a credit union. For villages or outlying districts, the extension of the common bond of an existing credit union might be preferable to starting an entirely new operation with doubtful viability. A community basis may be more viable than an industrial basis because of the rapid changes in industrial sectors and consequent redundancies. Potential members should realise that the savings of members, in the form of shares or deposits, constitute the funds available for loan to members. Unless an adequate core of people understand and accept the system of co-operative credit, there is no point in proceeding to actually forming a credit union. It is vital that information and study group meetings are organised properly in a suitable venue to encourage effective participation. A formal venue such as the boardroom of an organisation could inhibit junior personnel from becoming involved. If the study group meets the expected standards and the ILCU is satisfied about the common bond, and the expertise, viability and potential membership, affiliation to the League is followed by formal application to the Registrar under section 7 of the 1997 Act. A minimum of 15 persons, including the secretary, but excluding family members is now required to sign the application and three copies of the proposed rules. They would generally be the standard rules of the ILCU. It is legally possible to register and form a credit union outside the League system but such a course would be difficult. The ICLU provides a support service including submitting the registration application to the Registrar and assisting fledgling credit unions to get started with practical matters such as providing office stationery and complying with statutory requirements including holding an organisation meeting after registration in accordance with the strict time scale in section 77 of the 1997 Act, rule 127.

Variations in Rules

Subject to complying with the 1997 Act and wider law, credit unions have scope to vary details in some ILCU standard rules numbered as follows:

a) Rule 2 — the credit union's name;

b) Rule 7 — the registered office;

c) Rule 14 — membership and the common bond;

d) Rule 16(1) (iii) — entrance fee, usually £1;

e) Rule 16 (iv) minimum shareholding — at least one share of £1 and not more than ten shares or such larger sum as may be prescribed in accordance with section 17 (3) of the 1997 Act;

f) Rule 52(8) — amount of cash funds for petty cash and practical operational purposes;

g) Rule 64 — number of directors — an odd number of not less than seven nor more than fifteen in accordance with section 53 (2) of the 1997 Act;

h) Rule 78 — number of members of supervisory committee — three or five in accordance with section 58 of the 1997 Act.

The signatories to the application form for registration must also sign three copies of the proposed rules which should be suitably adapted to include the variations in rules listed above.

New credit unions have been formed in recent years, for example, in Manorhamilton, Co. Leitrim, and to cater for niche membership for barristers and staff of the Law Library and for staff of University College Dublin's Belfield campus.

JOINING A CREDIT UNION

As the movement is now widespread, people who are interested in becoming members usually have the opportunity of joining existing credit unions. These are mainly organised in localities or employment places or service sectors. For example, there are credit unions in towns, suburbs, factories or within a professions like teaching or employments, for example, Telecom Éireann or Garda Síochána.

Creditworthiness is related to the mutual relationship of members within a workplace or community as well as savings records. The largest proportion of credit unions, about 87per cent, are community-based and members work or live within particular locations. Many of the largest credit unions, however, especially in terms of total assets are industrial, based on employment, for example in public services and semi-State companies such as the Garda, (St Paul's in Cork and St Raphael's in Dublin, which is profiled in Appendix 1), Telecom Éireann and ESB (St Patrick's). Signatories to the registration application together with the duly admitted members comprise the membership.

Applicants for membership must comply with section 17 of the 1997 Act and rules 15 and 16. Formalities before formal approval of new membership include: being eligible under the common bond; filling in an application form; paying a small entrance fee (£1 maximum) and purchasing a share for a small sum of money (maximum £10 or such larger sum as the Minister may prescribe). Applications must be approved by the affirmative vote of a majority of the directors or by a duly appointed and authorised membership committee (rule 16(1) (ii)).

Persons under the age of 16 may now be members under section 17(5), rule 17, but there are restrictions: such persons cannot act in specified posts as members of boards or principal committees or be office managers. Loans may be granted to members under 18 provided that an indemnity is given. Section 17(7), rule 18, provides that incorporated or unincorporated bodies may become members of a credit union if a majority of the body's members are eligible for membership of the credit union.

To ensure fair procedures, section 18, rule 19, provides that potential members who are refused membership may appeal in writing to the District Court in the area where the credit union is situated. That court may either confirm the refusal of membership or direct the credit union to admit the appellant to membership. The District Court's decision shall be final although questions of law may be referred to the High Court, with further appeal to the Supreme Court by leave of the High Court.

Individuals may be members of more than one credit union at the same time provided that common bond criteria are met.

Section 17(4) of the 1997 Act introduced the concept of a "non-qualifying member", who ceased to have the common bond. Such members may retain their membership and voting rights but would not be included in determining whether a common bond exists between members. The concept was controversial during debates on the legislation. By agreement during negotiations on the revised standard rules, the term was not used in the relevant rule 20 which is headed "Members ceasing to have the common bond." Loans to such members are restricted to 10% of total outstanding loans, or such larger percentage as the Registrar may approve: section 35(4), rule 44 (6).

COMMON BOND ENSHRINED IN LAW

The Credit Union Act 1997 (No. 15) defines common bond. Section 6(3), (rule 1) (interpretation) specifies the acceptable types of common bond which are essential to membership of a union:

a) Following a particular occupation.

b) The most frequent common bond is residing or being employed in a particular locality. That is self-explanatory and forms the basis for credit unions in neighbourhoods and parishes. To avoid confusion and overlapping, the limits or borders of each locality are defined in rules and ILCU procedures.

c) Being employed by a particular employer or having retired from employment with a particular employer. Employees of large organisations such as Telecom Éireann, ESB or Garda Síochána may work at diverse locations but they still have a common bond of employment. Many large industrial credit unions such as those mentioned above were reclassified by the registrar under category e) below, "other" to cover pensioners as members under the earlier legislation. Pensioners would now be included in Category C under the 1997 Act.

d) Being a member of a *bona fide* organisation or being otherwise associated with other members of the society for a purpose other than that of forming a society to be registered as a credit union. That definition excludes people whose only common bond would be forming or joining a credit union. That would exclude a group of people who would have nothing in common except their membership of a credit union. *Bona fide* is the Latin for good faith and conveys a meaning of being genuine and not artificial.

e) Any other common bond approved by the Registrar. On that basis, the Registrar has discretion to register as a credit union a society the rules of which require a common bond among its members of a nature not provided for in the specified categories.

Section 6(1) (b), rule 14, provides that membership is restricted to persons, each of whom has in relation to the other members, at least one of the common bonds specified above.

Family Members

A member's relatives who live in the same household as a member come within the scope of a common bond. Section 6(5), provides that if the rules so provide, a person shall be treated as having the qualification required for admission to membership stated in the rules if he is a member of the same household as, and is a member of the family of, another person who is a member of the credit union and who has a direct common bond with those other members.

The ILCU rules provide for family membership in rule 16(2). For that purpose, section 2 of the 1997 Act, rule 1, defines "member of family" to include the obvious members of the extended family such as father, mother, children (including adoptees), grandparents, grandchildren, uncles and aunts, nephews, nieces, in-laws and first cousins. Current social trends such as cohabitation or partnerships outside of marriage are not covered in the definition of "member of family".

The Irish Constitution has not defined "family" but, as noted in Bird's annotations in ICLSA R62 on the Credit Union Act 1977, definitions of "family" have been considered in some court cases as discussed in *The Irish Constitution*, Kelly J.M, 3rd edition, Hogan G and Whyte G, 1997, pp. 997 *et seq*.

Common bonds provide the mutual cement which keep credit unions working for the community. The wide definition of common bond, however, is open to criticism from people outside the credit union movement, including financial institutions. In contrast, common bonds based on localities in cities and suburbs may be artificial and unrelated to actual communities and their shopping patterns.

RULES

Organisations need guiding principles or regulations. These are called the memorandum and articles of association in the usual limited liability company. In industrial and provident societies and in credit unions, rules are required by law and approved by the Registrar under the relevant statutory provisions which are now in section 13 of, and the First Schedule to, the Credit Union Act, 1997. People proposing to form credit unions or intending to join an existing union should be aware of the rules. Members have rights and duties under the rules. To facilitate registration with the Registrar, the ILCU provides model or standard rules and these are referred to in this book after the relevant sections of the 1997 Act. Credit unions which are not affiliated to the ILCU would have their own rules based on the Act. Detailed statutory requirements for inclusion in the rules, including name, objects, registered office, and membership are dealt with in Chapter 4, Rules in General.

INSURANCE

Through the ILCU and its associated ECCU Assurance Co. Ltd credit unions provide life insurance protection for both savings and loans without any direct cost to members. Individual members should check details with their credit union as there may be variations in cover according to the relevant contract. There is also a maximum coverage which may vary between credit unions.

Insurance benefits are in proportion to savings and benefits are payable only on a member's death. Participants must be under 70 years of age and actively at work, or if not working, in good health. Members under 55 years of age would have full cover which means that additional benefits on death would equal pound for pound of savings. After age 55, there is a sliding scale so that from age 65 to 70 insurance cover would be only 25p for each pound saved.

Outstanding loan balances of eligible members are automatically insured, up to specific limits, at no direct cost to members.

They can take out loans in the confidence that their dependants will be protected against the debts on death. Insured borrowers who meet the health criterion or are actively at work, and who sign a promissory note when the loan is granted, are generally protected. If borrowers die, the loan is paid out in full. Debts die with the member. The balance of loans outstanding is paid in full by the insurance company. Some insurance contracts also provide cover for disablement up to age sixty. Other types of insurance are also provided including the Home Union scheme for household cover. There is an increasing range of insurances services available through the ILCU.

Members' savings are also protected by a Savings Protection Scheme operated by the ILCU to cover credit unions in financial difficulties subject to guidelines laid down by the ILCU board.

SAVINGS AND LOANS IN SUMMARY

Success depends on the ability to generate savings. The more members save, the greater will be the funds available for loans to members. Interest on monies loaned generate income. The virtuous cycle then leads to bigger reserves and higher dividends and subsequently to increased membership, as explained in an article on British Credit Unions by Donnelly and Haggett (1997). Members have access to loans at interest and conditions which are relatively favourable compared to those in commercial financial institutions.

MAIN BENEFITS OF MEMBERSHIP

The liability of members is limited to their shareholding in the credit union. That means that members cannot be called upon to pay more than their shareholding if the credit union experiences financial problems. Each credit union is a legal entity distinct from its members, other credit unions and ILCU. Members are protected by the legal framework of the Credit Union Act, 1997, the related standard rules, the Registrar's supervisory powers and also services of the ILCU if affiliated to it. Financial accounts may be inspected by members in the credit union offices and annual statutory returns to the Registrar are open to public inspection. Audits to required official standards ensure that proper accounts are kept. The Registrar and the ILCU maintain prudential checks to protect members' interests. Information and training are available from local groups, known as chapters and from the ICLU.

On becoming a member, individuals have access to facilities on loans, savings, and insurance as outlined above and detailed later in this book, especially in Chapter 7 on Financial Operations.

Members should be aware that membership of a credit union also involves commitments to a mutual society in which participation is expected, at least at annual meetings and preferably more often. Although professional and other full-time staff are becoming more common both at local and League levels, voluntary efforts are vital.

Following the tradition of co-op visionaries such as the poet Æ, referred to at the start of this chapter, voluntary enthusiasm and high ideals motivate credit unions. More than poets and idealists, however, are required to organise contemporary credit unions and their busy offices.

Chapter 4

RULES IN GENERAL

"If rules were results there would be little need of lawyers."

Karl Llewellyn, American Jurist, in
Twining and Miers (1982).

Rules are essential for communal life. Most people have to deal daily with rules in households, on roads, in employments, colleges, clubs and games. People in authority such as parents, police, teachers, umpires, officials and lawyers have the extra responsibility of interpreting and applying rules. Legislation on self-help mutual societies has provided that specified matters be included in the rules which form the constitution of a society. In general, registered societies are allowed some scope in how the specified topics should be dealt with.

The law governing mutual societies does not follow the company law approach which provides specimen forms of memorandum and articles of association for example in Tables A–E, Companies Act, 1963, which can be adopted *en bloc*. Standard or model rules are provided by co-op organisations to facilitate members and provide cohesion.

SPECIFIC REQUIREMENTS

Industrial and provident societies must comply with the requirements of the Industrial and Provident Societies Act, 1893 which provides in Schedule 11 for matters which must be contained in the rules, including:

- Objects

- Name

- Registered office

- Terms of admitting members

- Mode of holding meetings

- Voting

- Making, altering or rescinding rules

- Appointment and removal of management committee and of managers and other officers

- Loans

- Deposits

- Shares

- Audits of accounts and auditors

- Investment of capital, and

- Custody of the seal.

The Credit Union Act, 1966 did not contain a schedule of matters for inclusion in rules but provided in section 6(1) that rules should be in a form approved by the Registrar. The Minister could prescribe what the rules should contain. The 1997 Act, which repealed the 1966 Act and removed credit unions from Industrial and Provident Societies legislation, reverted to the traditional system of society law by specifying in section 13(1) (a) that rules contain provisions with respect to matters in the First Schedule. The general thrust of Industrial and Provident Societies precedents was followed but there were differences of detail and emphasis. The objects listed above for industrial and provident societies apply in general but some distinctive points in the First Schedule to the Credit Union Act, 1997 are outlined below:

1. **Name** must comply with section 10 which requires that the words "credit union" or the Irish language equivalent *"comhar*

creidmheasa" shall be included in the name and that business shall not be carried on under a name which includes the words "bank", "banker" or "banking" or translation, derivatives or variants of those words. Banking laws and specifically the Central Bank Acts, 1942 to 1997, do not apply to credit unions. Some co-op activists, however, aspire to starting a cooperative bank but such a project may be too ambitious in the context of the current financial services sector. A misleading name or one which is undesirable in the Registrar's opinion cannot be used.

Section 10(6) of the 1997 Act, and rule 2(1), require the registered name to be engraved legibly on the official seal and displayed prominently outside its registered office and other place of business and in all notices, advertisements and other official documents including cheques, promissory notes, bills and invoices. Credit unions cannot use any title other than their registered name but may change their name in accordance with the detailed procedures in section 11 and rule 3, including the passing of a resolution at an AGM and the prior approval of the Registrar. He must subsequently register the change of name as a rule amendment. The formalities of section 14(2) on rule amendments do not apply to a change of name.

Under section 12(3), the use of the words "credit union" or *"comhar creidmheasa"* or any derivatives of those words cannot be used by persons which are not credit unions. It is an offence to breach that prohibition. There are exceptions, however, under section 12(4) in respect of officers of credit unions using their title or descriptive expression indicating an office or function, and for the ILCU or groups of credit unions as approved by the Registrar.

2. **Objects** included in the rules shall comply with section 6 of the Act as reflected in rule 5. The specified objects must include basic credit union aims such as promoting thrift by accumulation of members' savings, creation of credit for mutual benefit at a fair and reasonable rate of interest and wider

co-op principles such as community education and well-being. The effect is to confine registration to genuine credit unions.

3. **Shares** — According to 7 of the First Schedule to the 1997 Act, the rules must determine the maximum amount of interest which a member may hold in shares, subject to section 27(4) of the 1997 Act. It provides that a member's share maximum when aggregated with the amount held on deposit may not exceed £50,000 or 1% of total assets of a credit union, subject to a maximum deposit of £20,000 by an member. Shares are dealt with in more detail in Chapter 7 on Financial Operations. Rules must also provide for the mode of withdrawing shares and payment of balances due.

REGISTRAR'S ROLE

Chapter 9 deals with the Registrar's functions in detail but attention is drawn to some aspects at this stage. Section 13(1) (b) of the 1997 Act empowers the Registrar, after consulting the Advisory Body (CUAC) and other expert bodies, to require provisions in the rules additional to those in the First Schedule.

Section 14 of the 1997 Act, rule 10, provides that the rules shall not be amended except by a resolution approved by not less than two-thirds of the members present at an AGM or present at a special general meeting, SGM, called to consider a resolution amending the rules. The Registrar also has to register amendments of rules within three months or issue a notice of reasons for refusal.

STANDARD RULES: THE BIBLE OF A CREDIT UNION

In accordance with general practice in the wider co-op movement, the ILCU provides model standard rules to help groups starting a credit union and to facilitate faster registration at lower than standard fees with the Registrar. The standard rules are revised and updated at the annual conventions and AGMs of the ILCU, and affiliated credit unions are expected to carry the amendments into their own rules either at a special general meeting or at the

AGM. These standard rules are distinct from the ILCU rules governing the operation of the League and the relationship between credit unions, as outlined in Chapter 13 on the ILCU.

There are also distinct standard rules for chapters, the local groups. Unless otherwise indicated, references to standard rules in this book are those of the ILCU for affiliated credit unions in respect of their operations to reflect related sections of the Credit Union Act, 1997. The standard rules are divided into numbered sections for the various topics including interpretation, registration, rules, membership, operations including loans and savings, board of directors and committees, management, meetings, elections, accounts and audit, disputes and complaints, amalgamations, winding up, examiners, records and affiliation with the ILCU. In this book, to avoid confusion with sections of the 1997 Act the standard rules are not referred to by numbered sections. The numbers of the relevant ILCU standard rules, however, are shown after references to sections of the Act.

Following the 1997 Act, the legislation committee of ILCU and its legal and secretariat services under Jim O'Dwyer, BL, assisted by Clare Brennan, prepared revised standard rules after discussions with the Registrar and taking account of previous standard rules. The revised rules reflect provisions of the 1997 Act as appropriate to the constitutions of credit unions but generally exclude areas specific to the Registrar's supervisory functions and matters such as offences and sanctions. Additional provisions in the rules provide for extra procedures required by the ILCU. Seminars were held throughout the country to clarify and explain the revised standard rules to representatives of local credit unions prior to the adoption by the ILCU convention, April 1998.

Until individual credit unions adopt and register the revised standard rules, some provisions of the 1997 Act cannot be availed of, for example, the longer time span for loans under section 35(2) and rule 44(4), and, therefore, existing stricter statutory provisions would apply. Rules are subject to the provisions of the 1997 Act and cannot apply until the relevant parts of the Act are commenced by Ministerial Order. For example, rule 59 on the power to provide additional services specifically includes a proviso "when commenced" because sections 48 to 52 on additional services were excluded from the main commencement order, SI 403 of 1997, Pn.4459.

For simplicity and ease of style, the standard rules follow the Act's format by using terms such as "chairman", "he" and "him" rather than the fashionable gender neutral language. In accordance with standard statutory interpretation, however, the masculine shall when necessary include the feminine and the singular shall include the plural (rule 1, interpretation). In accordance with the tradition of the co-op movement and equality principles, all posts in credit unions are open to, and are held by, either men or women without any discrimination.

As outlined in Chapter 3 of this book in the context of new credit unions, individual credit unions may vary some of the details in the standard rules in matters such as name, registered office, common bond, entrance fees, minimum shareholding, number of directors and supervisors, and funds for petty cash. Any such variations, however, must comply with the 1997 Act and general law.

It is advisable to use the standard rules which have been carefully drafted as precedents to meet legal and practical requirements. Some adaptations may be considered desirable to suit local or specific needs and diverse sizes but rule 10(2) provides that a credit union shall not unilaterally amend the standard rules of the ILCU. Rule 10(4) provides that a copy of any notice of rule amendment shall be sent to the ILCU at the same time as it is sent to members. Standard rules are without prejudice to the duties and rights of the promoters or the Registrar.

Appendices to Rules

Appendices to the ILCU standard rules include the credit union operating principles; revised forms for basic operations such as applications for membership, shares, deposits, loans, transfers, promissory notes and receipts; and a declaration of fidelity and secrecy to be executed annually by each officer and voluntary assistant.

In *The Prison Service Credit Union Ltd.* v *Registrar of Friendly Societies* (The High Court [1987] ILRM 367), the net effect of the judgment in the case was to limit the Registrar's scope in registering rules or amendments to rules. Mr Justice Barrington found that the function and jurisdiction of the Registrar was solely limited to an enquiry as to whether or not such a proposed amendment would result in any breach of the relevant Acts.

Credit unions seeking to register amendments to rules may find it worthwhile to consult the Registrar and the ILCU to prevent problems arising at the registration stage. The ILCU, like other co-operative service or promotional bodies in agricultural and housing areas, owns the copyright to standard model rules which groups or societies intending to register should not use, without permission of the relevant co-op body.

LEGAL EFFECT OF RULES

Members and the Credit Union

Rules are important, not only for their practical effect on organisation and management of a credit union, but also because of the legal impact. Rules govern legal relationships between one member and another and also between members and the credit union as a legal entity with a corporate existence distinct from the members.

Section 15 of the 1997 Act and rule 11, provide that the rules bind the credit union and its members and all persons claiming through them respectively as if each member had subscribed his name and affixed his seal to those rules and had covenanted to conform to them, subject to the provisions of the Act. Members cannot be bound by amended rules requiring them in the absence of written consent to subscribe for more shares, to pay more than the unpaid amount on shares or otherwise to increase the relevant members' liability to contribute to the share capital. Persons claiming through members, for example because of entitlements on a member's death as executor, administrator or assignee or a nominee on a nomination, would have similar rights and duties.

The net effect is that members and credit unions have duties imposed on them by the rules without proof of a contract at common law. There is a complex relationship between members and the credit union under the rules as outlined above. In a dispute, legal questions would require professional advice.

Similar provisions about the memorandum and articles of association binding members under section 25 of the Companies Act, 1963, based on section 20(1) of the UK Act, 1948, have been interpreted by the courts with a limited scope to rights and obligations. For example, to come within the scope of the sections a member must be bound in the relevant capacity or have benefited as a member.

Provisions dealing with an individual member acting in another capacity — such as an adviser to a company and, by analogy, to a credit union — would not come within the scope of contracts created by section 25, Companies Act, 1963, section 22 Industrial and Provident Societies Act 1893 or section 15 of the Credit Union Act, 1997.

A professional adviser such as solicitor would not be part of the contract created by those sections on the basis of precedents: *Eley* v *Positive Government Security Life Assurance Co (1876) I Ex. D 88*; and *Beattie* v *Beattie [1938] 3 All E.R 214*

Members and the Rules

As the rules are very important both for members' rights as individuals and in the wider sphere of practical functioning and mutuality of purpose in the credit union, familiarity with rules is vital. Members are entitled to obtain on request copies of rules and amendments. During meetings of boards, committees and at general meetings, officers and officials should be familiar with the rules and use them constructively.

Due to rule variations, it is necessary for officers and members to update themselves about changes. This book is based as far as possible on current information but all rule amendments may not necessarily be included. Some credit unions do not revise their own rules within a reasonable time to take account of all amendments advised by the ILCU. Officers and members interested in specific applicable rules should check with their own credit union about the actual rules.

Difficulties of interpretation may be clarified by the Registrar or the ILCU but specific problems would require consultation with lawyers and other professional advisors. Despite best intentions, rules do not necessarily achieve the results or objectives intended. Hence the relevance of the quotation at the start of this chapter.

Chapter 5

MEETINGS AND VOTING

"Corresponding to Abraham Lincoln's idea of government
by the people, the role of the members in a co-operative
must be active rather than passive."

W.P. Watkins, veteran British and international co-op
activist, *Co-operative Principles, Today and Tomorrow*
(1986).

Democratic control in accordance with co-operative principles can
only be achieved if members participate in meetings and related
voting and elections. Legal provisions on meetings and voting, as
reflected in the rules, are vital. The First Schedule to the Credit
Union Act, 1997 requires at no. 5 that matters to be provided for
in the rules should include: "The mode of holding meetings, and
the method of notice, including provision as to the quorum necessary for the transaction of any description of business, and the
mode of making, altering, or rescinding rules." Those provisions
are an expanded form of the requirements in Schedule 11 to the
Industrial and Provident Societies Act 1893.

The Credit Union Act, 1997, especially part V, sections 77–83,
as reflected in the ILCU's revised standard rules 127–133, includes specific provisions regarding meetings and related matters.
General legal principles, often reflected in the legislation and
rules, should be followed, including natural justice and fair procedures such as *audi alterem partem* — hear the other side,
whereby both sides must have a reasonable opportunity to make
their case and *nemo iudex in sua causa* — no one should be a
judge in their own cause. In the absence of specific provisions,
general common law procedures would apply to meetings.

ORGANISATION MEETING

When a new credit union is being formed, interested people meet in a study group where basic procedures for meetings should be followed to train participants in procedures for meetings. In accordance with section 77 of the 1997 Act and rule 127, the first formal meeting is known as the organisation meeting. It must be called in a written notice to all members, by the signatories to the application to register not later than one month after registration of the credit union. The notice shall state the date, time and place of the meeting and shall be delivered personally or by post to each member. Postal deliveries shall be at the member's address recorded in the credit union books. There are also time limits for the notice of the meeting: a maximum of twenty-one days and at least seven days before the meeting. It is vital for the founder members of new credit unions to be alert to procedures, especially the strict time scale for calling and holding the organisation meeting after formal registration.

Members present at the organisation meeting (usually the signatories to the registration application plus other study group participants accepted as credit union members at that stage) shall elect by secret ballot: in accordance with section 53 of the 1997 Act, rule 65, an odd number of members, not less than seven nor more than fifteen, to be members of the board, known as directors; and under section 58 and rule 79, three or five members to form a supervisory committee (subject to exclusion of specified persons such as directors and employees) to carry out relevant statutory duties. The functions of the board of directors and supervisory committee are dealt with in detail in Chapter 6 on Governance. Persons under sixteen years of age are excluded from voting or being members of the board or the principal committees or office managers: section 17(5)(6) and rule 17(1)(2).

Only new credit unions hold an organisation meeting. It is a once-off event, called by the signatories to register the credit union and held in accordance with the procedures in section 77 and rule 127, not later than one month after registration. The first board of directors and the supervisory committee are elected by secret ballot at the organisation meeting. The previous procedure for the organisation meeting to appoint auditors is replaced by the appointment by the directors of the first auditor before the first annual meeting, under section 113(3) and rule 149(3).

ANNUAL GENERAL MEETING (AGM)

For all credit unions, the statutory annual general meeting (AGM) is vital for efficient control and also for the democratic role of members. Special general meetings may also be called in specified circumstances. Sections 78–83 of the 1997 Act and standard rules 128–133 provide detailed procedures for calling meetings and conducting business at them.

Each eligible member must be notified in writing, personally or by post at their recorded address, not later than seven days and not earlier than twenty-one days before the date of any general meeting. The Registrar, as a logical consequence of his right to attend and speak at any general meeting, and also the auditor, must be notified. If the Registrar considers that exceptional circumstances exist, there is statutory provision in section 80(4) and (5) and rule 130(4) and (5) for notice of general meetings to be given by publication in at least two appropriate newspapers (one local and one national would suffice) published in the State and circulating in the area in which the credit union's registered office is situated. The notice shall be in any other manner which the Registrar requires as being necessary for bringing the notice to the attention of persons entitled to attend the meeting.

In normal circumstances, there should be no need to use that special notification procedure which is intended for difficult and urgent situations. There is a fall-back system to deal with failure to comply with the specified procedures in section 80(6) and (7) and rule 130(6) and (7): proceedings shall not be invalidated by the accidental omission to give notice to any member or the non-receipt of notice by any member; at least two-thirds of members entitled to vote and the auditor may agree in writing, either before or during the meeting, to convene a general meeting with less than seven days' notice.

The notice must specify the date, time and place of the meeting and be accompanied by the agenda. Rule 130(2)(c)(e) and (f), in respect of credit unions affiliated to the ILCU, add to the statutory requirements the following: the notice must also include the number of vacancies to be filled at the meeting, the nominating procedure and availability of nominating forms. The notice must be sent to the ILCU and also be displayed in the credit union's public offices.

Many procedures, specifically those regarding notice, in the Act and in the rules apply to all general meetings but there are some distinctions between procedures for annual general meetings, AGMs, and those for special general meetings, SGMs, as outlined under that heading below.

The general meeting must be held in the State during specified months, October to January inclusive, according to section 78(2), rule 128(2). There are supplemental provisions for all general meetings in section 82 and rule 132, including the Registrar's right to attend and speak at any general meeting. Rule 132(2) allows authorised representatives of the ILCU to be present and to speak at any general meeting. Such rights of audience would only be exercised in special circumstances requiring urgent action.

Under section 81(4) and rule 131(5), the quorum or minimum number of members required to be present before business can be conducted, is ten per cent (10%) of members or 30 members whichever is the lesser number. It should be noted that the figure of 30 replaces that of 15 under previous legislation. A quorum cannot fall below a minimum of ten members, but the rules may provide for a lesser quorum for an adjourned general meeting. Section 81 and rule 131, provide for adjournment of a general meeting and the reconvening of an adjourned general meeting to deal with unfinished business, subject to adequate notice to relevant persons including the auditor. Adjournment may be for not more than 90 days or such longer period as the Registrar may require. The secretary must keep minutes of all general meetings.

Voting Procedures

Voting at general meetings shall be on the basis of one-member-one-vote, for each question arising, irrespective of shareholding or the number of accounts held in a specific credit union. That is vital to the ethos of mutuality and co-operation expressed in International Co-operative Principle No. 2, Democratic Control, as outlined in Chapter 1. Co-op Principle No. 2 was given statutory effect in section 82(2) of the 1997 Act, and is embodied in rules 131 and 138 and in Appendix 1(2) to the ILCU standard rules. Membership of other credit unions, however, would also confer voting rights in those credit unions. Rule 131(1) provides that in voting at elections, the presiding member shall have a second or casting vote if there is equality of voting. That is a specific and limited exception to the general principle of one-member-one-vote.

Proxy voting is a procedure normally allowed in companies and societies to permit members' authorisation of their nominees to vote on their behalf at meetings. Under section 82(3) and (4) of the 1997 Act and rule 132(4), in credit unions proxy voting is restricted at general meetings to members who are not natural persons, so that groups or bodies may authorise an individual member to vote on their behalf and the authorisation is accepted by the board of directors. That restriction may be criticised but it is logical having regard to the mutual nature of credit unions in which individual members participate on a equal basis. Proxy voting is also allowed under section 161 in considering proposals for a compromise or scheme of arrangement, dealt with in Chapter 11 on Examiners.

Business at Annual General Meetings

The order of business is listed in rule 128(4) but may vary according to the rules of specific credit unions. Formalities common to most meetings include: acceptance of proxies (if any) by the board of directors; ascertaining that quorum is present; adopting standing orders to govern procedure; and also approving and if necessary correcting the minutes of previous AGM and any inter-vening SGM.

When the formalities have been dealt with, the essential busi-ness of the meeting is considered, including receiving, discussing and adopting various reports including those of the board of direc-tors, other committees, the treasurer and the auditor. After tellers have been appointed, elections are held to elect the auditor and fill vacancies on the board and the supervisory committee. After any other business, election results are announced before the meeting is formally closed. Members present may vote by a two-thirds majority to suspend the order of business.

The above procedures, broadly similar to most meetings of companies and societies, are vital for the proper running of busi-ness. Credit unions due to their special nature also have to con-sider specialised reports of the supervisory and credit committees and of any other committees.

Elections

There must be elections to the board of directors and the supervi-sory committee even if candidates are not being opposed and if there is no competition for specific positions. At AGMs, members vote on candidates who were validly nominated for election to va-cancies on the board of directors and supervisory committee. Nominating procedures in rules 134–6 help to ensure that there is a least one candidate for each vacancy for which an election is held. Thus, greater participation by members is stimulated. The Registrar in his annual reports for 1994/6 and 1997 drew atten-tion to the need for foresight in seeking suitable replacements for long-serving board members.

Under rule 134, the nomination committee, consisting of at least three members including a director, reports to the board when necessary. Other members may also nominate candidates, with a proposer and seconder, for vacant positions, subject to rule 135 which excludes non-members, a body corporate and members under eighteen years from being nominated to vacant positions.

Further nominations to fill vacancies may be taken from the floor of the meeting, if that would be in the interests of the credit union. That exceptional procedure under rule 136 requires a two-thirds majority of members present, ascertained by a show of hands.

Three or five members are also elected to the supervisory committee. The functions of the board and various committees are dealt with in Chapter 6 on Governance. Except at the start of a new credit union, when under the 1997 Act appointment is by the board, the auditor must also be elected at the AGM. Voting at general meetings is by secret ballot and election by majority voting in accordance with rule 137. The system of voting is not specified so that proportional representation is not required but may be used. Rule 140 prohibits multiple resolutions which are defined as motions for the election or appointment of two or more persons as officers. Names of persons elected should be notified to the Registrar and the ILCU.

SPECIAL GENERAL MEETING

For special general meetings, section 80(2) (c) and rule 130(2) (d), require that the notice must include a statement that annual accounts for the most recent financial year may be obtained at the registered office not later than seven days before the meeting. The purpose is to provide members with up-to-date financial information which would be available at an AGM.

Special general meetings (SGMs) may be convened by the board of directors or the Supervisory Committee under section 79(1), reflected in rule 129. That rule also provides for involvement by the ILCU as the body representing the savings protection scheme, and by the ILCU's general secretary in calling SGMs in the exceptional circumstances specified in rule 129(2) and (3). Under section 79(3) and (4), rule 129(4) and (5), at the request of a qualifying group of members (50 members or, if it is less, 10% of membership), the board of directors shall convene a SGM. The board cannot ignore such a request. If, within one month of receiving the document from the members, the board have not convened a SGM to take place within six weeks of the date of receipt of the members' request, any ten members acting on behalf of the qualifying group which made the request may convene a SGM. The Registrar may also direct, in the interests of members and creditors or proper regulation of the business, that no SGM be held for a period not exceeding nine months.

As explained in Chapter 6 on governance, under the heading of Supervisory Committee, a SGM must be called under the provisions of section 66(1) (b) and rule 115(1) (b), by that committee when an officer has been suspended.

Many of the relevant statutory provisions of the Credit Union Act, 1997 and the standard rules apply to a SGM as if it were an AGM. That parallel between general and annual meetings is for procedural purposes. Otherwise, the two types of meetings are different.

Specific types of situations, dispersed in various parts of the 1997 Act and the related rules, require the calling of a SGM including:

Expulsion of a Member from a Credit Union

In accordance with section 19 of the 1997 Act, (based on section 24 of the 1966 Act), rule 25, a member may be expelled. A two-thirds majority of members present and voting at the meeting on the expulsion resolution is required. "Voting" means that non-voting members would not be taken into account in calculating the two-thirds majority.

It is a very serious step to expel members and deprive them of rights. The grounds for expulsion could include:

- Grave and sufficient reasons such as wilful breach of rules, or refusal to comply with rules;

- Divulging confidential information obtained as an officer;

- Deceit regarding money borrowed and its use;

- Maliciously and knowingly spreading false rumours about the management of the credit union finances; or

- Wilfully making any entry, or erasure in, or omission from any pass-book, record or return with intent to falsify.

To ensure fair procedures, the member concerned must be given at least 21 days written notice of the meeting and be afforded a reasonable opportunity of being heard at the meeting under section 19(1) and rule 25(1). There is a right of appeal to the District Court against expulsion under section 19(2) and (3) and rule 25(2) and (3).

Removal of Supervisory Committee member

Section 61 of the Act and rule 87, provide that subject to specified provisions, a credit union may, by a resolution of a majority of members present and voting at a SGM called for the purpose, remove a member of the supervisory committee from office. To ensure fair procedures, the secretary of the credit union must give the member at least 21 days' notice of the meeting and (unless the Registrar decides otherwise) the member may require that any written representations made by him be notified to credit union members and be read out at the meeting. Those procedures are without prejudice to the person whom it is proposed to expel being heard orally.

RESOLUTIONS

Ordinary resolutions are used for much of the business of an AGM such as adopting reports or ratifying proposed dividends. Such resolutions are passed by a majority of members who are present and voting.

Special Resolutions

Section 2(1) of the Act and rule 1 on interpretation define a special resolution as a resolution which:

a) is passed by a majority of not less than three-quarters of such members of a credit union for the time being entitled under the rules to vote as may have voted in person at any general meeting of which notice, specifying the intention to propose the resolution, has been duly given according to the rules; and

b) is confirmed by a majority of such members for the time being entitled under the rules to vote as may have voted in person at a subsequent general meeting of which notice has been duly given held not less than 14 days and not more than 28 days from the date of the meeting at which the resolution was first passed.

Section 83 and rule 133, specify the basis for adopting a special resolution at a general meeting, including signature by the chairman of the meeting and countersigning by the secretary. Registration with the Registrar, to whom the resolution must be sent within 21 days, is a requirement for its coming into effect, and failure to comply would be an offence with penalties on conviction.

Special resolutions are required for specific purposes, including amalgamations under section 128 and rule 159, and also, except in special circumstances, for transfers of engagements under section 129 rule 160. Chapter 12 of this book on terminations, and part IX of the 1997 Act deal with the amalgamations and transfers of engagements in more detail.

The requirement for special resolutions and a three-quarters' rather than a simple majority vote has been controversial especially for amalgamations and transfers of engagements under the Industrial and Provident Societies Act, 1893. In that Act the definition of special resolution was mainly followed in the Credit Union Act, 1997 to ensure that serious decisions affecting a credit union's future would not be taken without adequate consideration including a confirmatory meeting.

CHAPTER MEETINGS

The guide for local groups called chapters and related standard rules, published by the ILCU, include practical points about the efficient conducting of meetings. While some aspects are specific to regional chapters and their educational and training role, many points are of wider interest including:

- Plan meeting in an active and businesslike way;

- Circulate planned agenda in advance to members;

- Start and finish meetings punctually;

- Keep to fixed time scale;

- Keep to procedures and the agenda.

ACTIVE PARTICIPATION BY MEMBERS

Members' participation in all meetings at relevant levels open to them is essential to ensure that business is dealt with in a democratic way. Fair procedures are vital especially where serious decisions are being taken affecting members' rights, such as expulsion of members or removal of a director from the board. It should be borne in mind that such persons have rights to be heard and put their side of the case in accordance with the principles of natural justice.

Members attending meetings at local, regional, national or international levels should do so in a constructive way. When participating in discussions, procedures recommended by the ILCU should be followed to avoid time-wasting such as arguing over well-trodden paths or repeating points already made by other speakers.

Personality clashes, an unfortunate feature of some voluntary organisations, are destructive. An objective and professional approach is desirable. For practical participation, officers and other members should be familiar with legal requirements, rules and procedures. Active rather than passive roles are vital.

Chapter 6

GOVERNANCE: BOARD OF DIRECTORS, SUPERVISORY AND OTHER COMMITTEES, OFFICERS AND MANAGEMENT

"Efficient decision making is essential in any business enterprise. Involvement in decision making is essential in any
co-operative enterprise. The interface between those two
premises is sometimes conflict, sometimes harmony, but it
is the nub of the question when considering the internal
management structures of co-operatives."

Berry and Roberts, Co-op Management and Employment,
Industrial Common Ownership (ICOM), London, 1984

The words quoted above, written in the context of worker co-ops,
are relevant to credit unions. All co-operative enterprises must be
managed in a businesslike way. There are special considerations
due to the nature of co-ops as mutual organisations involving
voluntary effort combined with salaried employment. The trend is
for credit unions to employ professional managers. Members'
participation is part of the democratic process in line with Co-
operative Principle No. 2, outlined in chapter 1 and reflected in
the Credit Union Operating Principles, set out in Appendix 2 to
this book.

Governance means the way in which organisations are controlled, while management indicates how the ordinary business is
conducted. Governance and management functions may overlap,
especially in mutual organisations such as credit unions, and
minimum statutory requirements also apply. A greater degree of
transparency is necessary in credit unions than in the usual
commercial enterprise.

Under credit union law, rules and ethos, there is no provision for directors from outside the organisation, similar to non-executive directors in commercial companies. That lack could cause structural weaknesses as identified by Professor E. Cahill, NUI–Cork in his address to the ICOS AGM, 1998 on co-operative governance and investment.

Management

Part IV, sections 53 to 76 of the 1997 Act, reflected in ILCU standard rules 64 to 126, includes detailed provisions for management of credit unions by the board of directors, and also by the supervisory and other committees, and other related matters.

OFFICER

It should be noted that officer is defined in section 2 of the 1997 Act (rule 1) as including: chairman (or president), vice-chairman (or vice-president), treasurer, secretary, member of board of directors or of principal or supervisory committee, employee, credit officer or credit control officer. Auditors appointed under the Act are excluded.

BOARD OF DIRECTORS

Section 53, reflected in rules 64, 65 and 66, specifies the general functions of the board of directors and sets out certain provisions in relation to the directors: their numbers, the manner of election from and by the members of the credit union, eligibility for election and the length of terms of office.

The board must have an odd number of directors: at least seven (increased from five under the 1966 Act) but not more than fifteen members. The number shall be specified in the rules and the ILCU standard rule 64(2) refers. Section 53(3) and rule 65, provide that the first board shall be elected from among the members by secret ballot at the organisation meeting. Subject to section 57(4), rules 66 and 77(3), which provide for a situation where, due to resignations or suspensions, there would be no functioning board, subsequent vacancies on the board shall be filled from among the members by secret ballot at an AGM.

As an exception to the general rule that the board is elected by the members, the Registrar has power under his supervisory function, as explained in Chapter 9, to appoint a director in special circumstances, as specified in section 95, in the interest of the orderly and proper regulation of business. Such an appointee shall not be entitled to vote at board meetings and would not count for the purposes of the statutory maximum or minimum membership of the board.

Under section 53(6), a body corporate or a minor cannot become a director but employees are eligible, reflecting partnership trends in wider society.

The term of office, beginning at the conclusion of the AGM at which the director is elected, shall not exceed three years: Section 53(4) and rule 66, replacing the old rule 83 which also provided for a three-year term. Except where the rules provide otherwise, it is now specifically provided that retiring directors are eligible for re-election. To ensure continuity and democracy, regular terms should be fixed so that at each AGM the same number of directors should retire.

At the organisation meeting at which the first board of directors is elected in a single stage, new credit unions should arrange for lots to be drawn under independent supervision to decide the order in which board members should retire.

Special Provisions

Section 54, reflected in rules including 67, 68 and 74, requires *inter alia* for the board to meet as often as necessary to conduct its business, provided that:

- it endeavours to meet monthly but, as a minimum, holds not less than ten meetings annually,

- the interval between any two meetings shall be not greater than six weeks.

Following comment from the ILCU and individual credit unions, section 54 was amended at the select committee stage in the Dáil to provide flexibility on monthly meetings. The purpose of the revision was to facilitate small credit unions which might decide not to hold a meeting during holiday months. It will also facilitate credit unions in occupations where there are fairly long vacation periods and members would be absent from places of employment.

Casual vacancies may be filled by the board and persons appointed shall hold office until the next general meeting at which an election to the board is held.

Functions of Board of Directors: Control, Direction and Management

Section 53(1), reflected in rule 75, provides that the board shall be responsible for the general control, direction and management of the affairs, funds and records of a credit union. That wide-ranging provision on governance should be construed in the context of wider law and also the specific provisions of the 1997 Act and the rules. Relevant provisions of the Companies Acts, 1963-1990 would also apply as appropriate, for example in winding up situations as explained in Chapter 12 on Termination.

In general, there is a heavy onus on directors to carry out their responsibilities in accordance with members' wishes, as expressed in general meetings, and in accordance with law.

Without prejudice to the generality of section 53(1), outlined above, specific powers and functions are set out in section 55, (an expanded version of section 13(2) of the 1966 Act), and the related rule 75.

The main functions of the board are deciding on:

- Membership applications, including appointing a membership committee account should be taken of the open membership principle for qualified applicants and the implications of refusing an application, including a possible appeal to the District Court under section 18 and rule 19;

- Loan applications including appointment of a committee or credit officer;

- Interest rates charged on loans and paid on deposits;

- Surety bond, required by section 73 of the Act and rule 122, for officers who have custody of funds or property, and authorising the payment of relevant premiums by the credit union;

- Recommended rates of dividend;

- Maximum sums of shares, deposits and loans applicable to every member;

- Investment of funds;

- Employment and terms of employment of staff;

- Purchase, sale, renovation, repair and alteration of property;

- Borrowing money by the credit union;

- Signatories to cheques, drafts or similar documents drawn on credit union accounts;

- Removal from office of officers or committee members, except the Supervisory Committee for failing to perform their duties;

- Submitting accounts for audit;

- Arrangements for general and special general meetings, and board meetings;

- Sanctioning of expense payments whether by way of expense claim or invoice;

- Filling of casual vacancies on the board or relevant committees;

- Establishment of appropriate internal structures, including committees and officers, to assist in the proper discharge of business.

Agenda for Board Meeting

The ILCU suggests a model agenda including the credit union invocation (see page 263) and then the usual formalities such as ascertaining that a quorum is present, approving minutes, dealing with correspondence and reports of the treasurer and various committees, delinquency report, and also reports of delegates to chapters (the local grouping of credit unions), insurance, membership, accounts for payment and other business.

Removal of Director from Office

Section 56 and rule 72, enable a credit union to remove one of its directors from office with the agreement of a resolution of members present and voting at a special general meeting (SGM). To ensure fair procedures, the section was expanded at the Dáil select committee to give the director concerned a right to be heard. The right is qualified and the Registrar may curtail it if he considers that it would substantially diminish public confidence in a credit union. Directors must be given 21 days notice of the SGM and any written representations made by them shall be read out at the meeting, without prejudice to an oral hearing. The board may fill any casual vacancy arising from any removal from office.

Supplemental provisions on directors in section 57 and rule 77, include power for validation of acts of a director where defects are later discovered in his appointment as director.

OFFICER: PRINCIPAL POSTS AND THEIR FUNCTIONS

In accordance with section 63 and rule 89, immediately after the organisation meeting of a new credit union, or in an existing credit union after an annual or special general meeting at which an election for directors was held, the board of directors shall elect directors to fill the principal posts which are vacant: chairman (or president), vice-chairman (or vice-president), treasurer and secretary. A member of the Supervisory Committee must preside at that board meeting and the election shall be by secret ballot. The interval of seven days between the election of the board and the officers, allowed under section 18(1) of the 1966 Act, has been eliminated.

"Chairman" is construed in accordance with statutory interpretation to include chairwoman, chairperson, chair and cathaoirleach, terms which are not used in the legislation or rules. Gender inclusiveness is a fundamental co-operative concept since the pioneering days of Nora Herlihy, and many women serve in senior posts.

Chairman

His or her duties include the usual functions in accordance with common law procedures for meetings including presiding at meetings and cover such functions as the board may direct. Such functions must not be inconsistent with legal provisions or the rules. Rule 90 also provides that, if there is equality of voting at a meeting, the chair shall have a second or casting vote. The vice-chairman under rule 91 shall exercise the chairman's functions during absence or inability to act.

Treasurer

Section 64 and rule 93, set out in detail the functions of the treasurer, including:

- Submitting unaudited up-to-date financial statements monthly;
- Safeguarding the funds and having custody of all funds, securities and documentation relating to the assets;
- Preparing and maintaining accurate records and financial reports;
- Ensuring that cash is deposited in accordance with the board's instructions. (Personal depositing of cash is not required and security companies are often engaged to do so in banks.);
- Reporting to the members at the AGM;
- Complying with the board's instructions.

In accordance with section 64(4) and rule 93(3) & (4), a director designated to act as assistant treasurer to perform specific functions shall comply with the treasurer's instructions, limitation and control as approved by the board.

Neither the treasurer nor any assistant treasurer shall be eligible to serve on committees on credit, credit control, or membership. Unlike the position under the 1966 Act, the same person cannot be both treasurer and secretary.

Treasurers are Managing Directors but Specific Functions may be Delegated to Managers

Section 64(1) and rule 93(1), provide that the treasurer shall act as managing director. Nevertheless, section 64(6), reflected in rule 93(6) inserted at the Dáil select committee stage following comment by the Credit Union Advisory Committee (CUAC), makes it clear that managers who are not directors may be employed to carry out specific functions as decided by the board. That reflects the actual position and increasing trend, especially in large credit unions, to appoint professional managers. While the manager could attend board meetings, exclusion from board membership could cause anomalies if more junior staff members were elected as directors. Provision for conflicts of interest, however, would apply under section 69 and rule 118.

With regard to the treasurer's functions, other areas of this book, especially Chapter 7 and 8 on financial transactions and wider operations and Chapter 10 on accounts and audits, are also relevant.

Secretary

Minutes of Board Meetings: Secretary's Functions

In accordance with section 54(2), expanded in more detail in rule 74, the secretary shall keep minutes of all meetings. Particulars required by rule 74 include: date and place of meeting, names of members present, name of presiding member, short statement of all matters discussed, resolutions proposed and decisions made, and whether made unanimously or by a majority. Minutes must be maintained in a bound minute book.

The secretary shall also keep a register of directors and of the Supervisory Committee members who must sign the register.

The secretary must notify the Registrar and the Supervisory Committee if all the board members/directors intend to resign on the same date or if their number falls below a half of the number specified in the rules.

Terms of Office

The maximum statutory period of office for principal posts is three years under section 63(2), unless the registered rules provide otherwise, but ILCU rule 89 provides for periods of one year which was in the old rule 113. Outgoing members are eligible for re-election although section 63(2) stipulates a year's gap after a three-year period of office unless the registered rules of the relevant credit union provide otherwise.

SUPERVISORY COMMITTEE

This is a vital body required in each credit union by statute, section 58, reflected in rules 78 to 84. The general duty of the Supervisory Committee, which must have three or five members, is to oversee the performance of functions by the directors. The first committee is elected from among the members by secret ballot at the organisation meeting. Subject to section 62(4) and rule 82 (regarding a discontinuity because of resignations), subsequent vacancies on the committee shall be filled from among the members by secret ballot. Different persons shall be chosen from the committee as chairman and secretary.

To ensure independence and objectivity, section 58(6) and rule 84, makes ineligible to be members of a Supervisory Committee specific categories who are otherwise connected with the credit union: Members under 18, directors, employees (full or part-time), persons who perform any other function in the credit union, or a body corporate. (ILCU also has a supervisory board and a board of directors as part of its structure.)

Procedural Provisions

Section 59, reflected in general but not in identical detail in rule 85, requires the Supervisory Committee to meet at least once a month and to meet with the board of directors at least four times a year to review the directors' performance of their functions, having in advance submitted a report to the board on that performance.

Supervisory Committee members, often referred to as supervisors, have the right but are not required to attend all meetings of other committees and of the. Following a unanimous vote, the Supervisory Committee may notify the Registrar of any concerns it has about the proper conduct of the credit union. The committee's secretary shall notify in writing the Registrar and the board of any intention by all members of the Supervisory Committee to resign on the same date. The committee secretary's failure to comply with that requirement is an offence under section 59 (6).

Functions

Section 60 and rule 86, without prejudice to the general overseeing duties in section 58(1) and rule 78, set out the Supervisory Committee's functions for which purpose it shall have access to the credit union records at all times. The main functions are:

- Keeping minutes of its meetings;

- Examining, or having examination made, at least twice yearly of the books and documents, including securities, cash accounts and loan records;

- Comparing with the credit union records the pass-books or statements of a random sample of at least 10% of members;

- Ascertaining that all the relevant acts of the officers are in accordance with law and the registered rules;

- Furnishing a report of the results of its examination and enquiries to the next AGM or, if the committee considers it appropriate, to a SGM.

Term of Office

The term of office of Supervisory Committee members begins at the conclusion of the meeting where they are elected and under section 58(4) and rule 81, may extend for a period not exceeding three years, rather than one year as under the previous rule 62. The longer period will help continuity and maintain expertise. If there are three members, one shall retire at each AGM but in a five-member committee, two shall retire at each AGM. The longest serving member shall retire first but lots are drawn where members have equal service. Retiring members are eligible for re-election or appointment unless the rules otherwise provide. ILCU rule 81(3) provides for such re-election or appointment.

A Supervisory Committee member may be removed from office under section 61 and rule 87, by special resolution passed by a majority of members present and voting at a special general meeting (SGM). As a safeguard, the board does not have power to remove Supervisory Committee members. Following representations by the ILCU, and to ensure fair procedures, the section was expanded at the Dáil select committee to give Supervisory Committee members the same rights as a director in respect of removal from office, including a right to be heard. Such members must be given 21 days notice of the SGM and any written representations made by them shall be read out at the meeting, without prejudice to an oral hearing. The committee may fill any consequential vacancy.

Supplemental provisions, in section 62 and rule 88, include the keeping of a register of Supervisory Committee members by the credit union's secretary and notification to the Registrar and the board if certain events occur. The board, or by default the Registrar, must call a SGM to elect a Supervisory Committee in certain circumstances. The credit union shall meet the committee's reasonable expenses.

Power to Suspend or Remove an Officer

What happens if the Supervisory Committee considers that an officer (other than an employee) has acted in breach of the rules or the law? Suspension of an officer under section 66 and rule 115, in certain circumstances is a vital power of sanction. Safeguards and fair procedures include: Unanimous vote by the committee at a meeting called for that purpose; calling a SGM to consider the removal of an officer and the filling of any vacancy, and to vote on the matter by secret ballot; giving the officer an opportunity to be heard in accordance with fair procedures as discussed in chapters 10, 11 and 12 in Hogan and Morgan (1998). It is remarkable that there was no debate about this important section 66 at the Dáil select committee stage.

Dismissing an Employee

Employment law and unfair dismissal procedures would apply to the suspension or removal of employees by the board.

There are special considerations about dismissing an employee (also defined as an officer) and legal provisions on employment and unfair dismissals would be relevant.

In *Frizelle* v. *New Ross Credit Union Ltd.*, a case, about withdrawal of bonding and subsequent dismissal of a manager, arose under section 10(4) of the Unfair Dismissals Act, 1977 Flood J in the High Court on 30 July 1997 set out legal principles of natural justice including:

- The complaint must be *bona fide* unrelated to any other agenda of the complainant;

- Where the complainant is a person of intermediate authority, it should state the complaint, factually, clearly and fairly without any innuendo or hidden inference or conclusion;

- The employee should be interviewed and his version (of events) noted and furnished to the deciding authority contemporaneously with the complaint and again without comment;

- The deciding authority's decision should be based on the balance of probabilities flowing from the factual evidence and in the light of the explanation offered;

- Any dismissal decision should be in proportion to the gravity of the complaint and of the effect of dismissal on the employee;

- It is clear from the above case that boards should have fair procedures in place to deal with complaints against managers and other employees. Suspension and dismissal are potential minefields. Therefore, specialised training for officers and access to appropriate legal advice are essential.

OTHER COMMITTEES

There are (a) mandatory committees (credit, credit control and membership) appointed by the board of directors and not by members, which are now statutory requirements under section 67 of the 1997 Act and (b) optional committees appointed by the board under rule 114 for matters such as planning and development, and also education to inform members and potential members about credit unions. They are important areas and many credit unions appoint such committees.

At least one member of each mandatory committee and also of the planning and development committee must be a director of the credit union. Each committee must have at least three members except the membership committee in which one member satisfies the statutory requirement. There are some divergences in details between the 1997 Act and the ILCU rules. For example, under the Third Schedule to the Act each mandatory committee shall meet as often as necessary to carry out its functions and report in writing to the board and comply with its instructions. Rules 96 and 106, however, require at least monthly meetings of the credit and credit control committees in addition to written reports.

Credit Committee

This committee's functions and procedures are governed by detailed provisions in section 67(1) of the 1997 Act and the Third Schedule to it, and also rules 94 to 103 inclusive. The committee decides on loan applications in accordance with section 36 and rule 45, but section 36 also allows the board or the credit officer to decide on loan applications but that would depend on the relevant rules and loans policies.

Credit Control Committee

Its main function, under section 67 and rule 104, is to ensure the repayment of loans by members in accordance with their loan agreements.

There are exclusions from eligibility for committee membership of persons who connected with the financial operations such as credit officers and treasurers or their assistants.

At the Dáil select committee stage, section 67 and the related provisions of the Third Schedule were amended to prevent an overlap between the activities of the credit committee and the credit control committee. The Registrar had advised that some unwise decisions had been made in approving loans with subsequent reluctance to pursue such cases. A member of a credit control committee cannot now be a member of a credit committee and vice versa. Clear demarcation lines between loan approval and loan repayment functions, however, may cause practical difficulties in some smaller credit unions with limited voluntary resources.

Membership Committee

This is appointed by the board and operates under the procedures in section 67, the Third Schedule and rules 109 to 113. One member is the minimum statutory requirement but the rules envisage a larger membership. A single member committee would be known as a membership officer. Each month the committee must notify the board of new members whose applications have been approved and submit doubtful applications to the board for decision.

ILCU standard rule 112 contains detailed practical requirements including:

- Ascertaining and determining that an applicant is eligible for membership;

- Explaining membership requirements to applicants and assisting them with forms;

- Issuing numbered passbooks or other evidence of membership;

- Delivering copies of the rules to members who require them, on payment of a nominal fee.

In practice, the manager, other staff member or voluntary assistant deal with some of the above details.

GENERAL

Confidentiality: Written Declaration of Secrecy

Persons dealing with officers or voluntary assistants may fear that their personal business might be disclosed to other persons in circumstances other than those required for the proper conduct of the credit union under the law and the rules. Section 71, rule 120, tightened up the confidentiality procedures. The prohibition does not apply to disclosure of information in any court proceedings, a wide term clearly intended, as a result of a Ministerial amendment made at the Dáil select committee, to include, for example, family law as well as criminal proceedings.

All officers and voluntary assistants must be informed of, and acknowledge under signature, their obligations on taking up office. In any proceedings for an alleged offence, the onus of proving that a disclosure was permitted shall be on the person who made or permitted the disclosure.

Officers' Liability and Indemnity

Section 177 and rule 124, allow a credit union to indemnify an officer or voluntary assistant against any liability incurred in defending proceedings:

- In which judgment is given in his favour; or

- in which he is acquitted; or

- in connection with an application under section 178. That section provides that the court may relieve, partly or wholly, an officer or voluntary assistant. Such relief would be given only where the court considered that the individual acted honestly and reasonably and ought to be excused for allegations of negligence, default or breach of duty or of trust.

Payments to Directors and Committee Members Generally Prohibited

Although directors of some types of co-ops may be paid fees for their services, payment of remuneration directly or indirectly to members of boards or various committees of credit unions for any service in that capacity is not permissible. In section 68(1) (c), if and when commenced by Ministerial order, there is a similar prohibition on payments to credit officers or credit control officers. Section 68 of the 1997 Act and rule 117, allow payments or reimbursement of expenses which are necessarily incurred by a director or committee member in the course of performing any service on behalf, or for the benefit of, the credit union. Approval of a majority of the board of directors would be required for such payments.

As an exception to the general prohibition, treasurers may under section 68(4) and rule 117(4), be paid remuneration, whether described as a honorarium or otherwise, as approved in advance by the members in general meeting, provided that the amount does not exceed that recommended by the board of directors. Officers or voluntary assistants, acting not as such but in their professional capacity, may tender for and supply goods or services to credit unions. In such circumstances, however, it would be advisable to have regard to transparency and to avoid conflicts of interest by following the procedures in section 69 and rule 118 and making the necessary declarations.

In general, in line with the co-operative ethos, people contribute time and expertise to the management of credit unions for the service and satisfaction, not for personal profit.

Officers: Required Signatories

Section 70 and rule 119, provide that to legally bind a credit union, two officers (one of whom shall be a director) must sign specified documents: Conveyances or transfers of property and documents by which a credit union enters into obligations, except those referred to in section 55(k) — depositories for the funds designated by the board and signatories to cheques, drafts or similar documents drawn on a credit union's account. Because of that exclusion, each cheque would not necessarily have to be signed by a director and the board would have discretion.

Compliance with section 70 does not render invalid any documents which fail to comply with the provisions of the registered rules as to the signing of such documents. That provision is to ensure that, if there is a conflict between the rules and section 70, the latter will prevail.

The requirements of section 70 and rule 119 are without prejudice to any additional provisions as to signatories imposed by the Registrar as a condition under section 49 (regarding approval of additional services).

Rule 119(4) imposes detailed requirements for the disbursement of funds by cheque or other written instrument signed by any two officers, authorised to act for them by the board. The officers' signatures may be written autographically or printed by the use of various methods including photographic or electronic process, subject to safeguards decided by the board.

Security and Duty to Account

In a updated version of section 47 of the Industrial and Provident Societies Act, 1893, section 73 of the 1997 Act and rule 122, includes detailed provisions requiring officers and voluntary assistants who have receipt or charge of funds to give security in a form required by the board. Section 74 and rule 123, requires every officer and voluntary assistant who has receipt or charge of credit union funds to account for and to pay all such money and property under their control to the credit union or its board of directors.

DISQUALIFICATION OF PERSONS FROM BOARD OR OTHER FUNCTIONS

Section 72 of the 1997 Act and rule 121, provide that a person adjudicated bankrupt and whose bankruptcy still subsists, or who has been convicted of an offence in relation to a credit union or an offence involving fraud or dishonesty shall not be involved in the formation, management or operation of a credit union. Statutory exclusions include acting as a director, member of the Supervisory Committee or other principal committee, voluntary assistant, auditor, receiver or liquidator, or putting their name forward for election or appointment to any of those positions. Prohibited persons cannot directly or indirectly take part in the management or operation of a credit union. Persons adjudicated bankrupt or convicted of the specified offences while serving on the board or committee must resign forthwith and any casual vacancy shall be filled as appropriate.

The statutory exclusions follow the precedents in section 26 of the 1966 Act, updated in section 31 of the Industrial and Provident Societies (Amendment) Act, 1978 and in the Companies Act, 1990 (No. 33), referred to as the "Cowboys Act" because it tightened up restrictions on rogue operators. Chapters 2 and 3, sections 159-169, of the 1990 Act define "company" widely to include every company and body which may be wound up under the Companies Acts. Therefore, credit unions would come within the definition, resulting in persons convicted in respect of credit unions being excluded from acting as company directors.

The exclusionary provisions outlined above are complex with serious implications for officers and others involved in credit unions. Professional advice may be required before persons are nominated to specified positions or during their terms of office. In considering the legal requirements in respect of credit unions, it may be necessary to refer to the Companies Acts, 1963–1990, as amended from time to time, standard textbooks on company law and judicial interpretation of the relevant statutes. Acts by individuals in contravention of the exclusionary provisions would be an offence under section 72(4) of the 1997 Act incurring penalties under section 171(2).

Fiduciary Duties

Based on company law precedents as suitably adapted, directors and committee members and also other officers of a credit union occupy a fiduciary position. That means that they must always act in good faith towards the credit union as a whole. The principles in the company law case *Re City Equitable Insurance Co. Ltd* [1925] 1 Ch. 407 (CA) would apply, suitably adapted having regard to statutory requirements.

For example, in discharging their duties, directors must as a minimum (a) act honestly and (b) exercise such degree of care as would amount to the reasonable care that an ordinary person might be expected to take in the circumstances on their own behalf. Directors need not exhibit in the performance of their duties a greater care than might be expected of a person of their knowledge and experience. Continuous attention need not be given to the credit union's affairs but duties of an intermittent nature should be performed at periodical board and committee meetings. Attendance at such meetings as often as possible would be expected. Having regard to the exigencies of business and the requirements of the rules and statutes including the functions of the Supervisory Committee, duties may be properly left to another officer who could be expected, in the absence of grounds for suspicion, to perform such duties honestly.

PRACTICAL ISSUES

Strict requirements in respect of boards, committees and officers under the 1997 Act are understandable from the prudential aspects, especially with the growth in credit unions. Practical problems may result, however, especially in smaller credit unions. Despite the best efforts of the nomination committee, some credit unions may find it difficult to find and motivate sufficient suitable nominees for election to the board, committees and officer positions. Potential talent should be identified and encouraged to participate in training courses organised by the ILCU and to study specific materials for the various functions.

There are horses for courses and individuals may be more suited to one function rather than to others. For example, while informed enthusiasm and constructive commitment are common requirements for all credit union activity, Supervisory Committee members must specifically exercise independent judgement, be objective and avoid all conflicts of interest. Regulatory and also accountancy and auditing experience would be desirable but not essential. As an unduly suspicious approach could inhibit the smooth functioning of a credit union, tact in dealing with people is essential.

Importance of Quorum

After their election, members of the board and committees should participate actively to ensure effective functioning of the credit union. Specifically, it is necessary to attend regularly at meetings so that there is a quorum — the minimum number which must be present to ensure a valid formal meeting. ILCU standard rule 69 provides that a majority of the number of directors, the board members, specified in the rules (including any vacancies) shall constitute a quorum for transacting any business of the meeting of the board. The statutory requirement in section 53 of the 1997 Act is that there must be an odd number on the board, at least seven but not more than fifteen. The actual number is included in the rules.

If fewer than a quorum attend a meeting, the business cannot lawfully proceed and the meeting may (with adequate notice) be adjourned to any date not less than two more than thirty days from the date of the adjourned inquorate meeting. The quorum for an adjourned meeting shall be five or such greater number as the board has decided previously by resolution. A simple majority of members would constitute a quorum for the Supervisory Committee or other committee, in the absence of any specific rule.

Decision Making

Effective decision making is vital, as highlighted in the quotation at the start of this chapter. Officers, especially chairmen and also members of the board and committees should actively improve decision making by using specific techniques as taught during ILCU training courses.

Professional Managers

The trend, especially in larger credit unions, is for managers (who are not directors) to be recruited to perform specific functions mainly in the day-to-day financial operations as decided by the board of directors, in accordance with section 64(6), rule 93(6). Computer and financial expertise are essential and studying for the Diploma in Credit Union Studies from the National University of Ireland — Cork would be desirable. Specialised training through the ILCU and the Institute of Credit Co-operative Administration is also available.

As indicated in Parnell (1995, pp. 148–9) co-op managers need all of the usual managerial skills, a high degree of empathy with the aspirations of the cardinal stakeholders and also communication ability to undertake "management with explanations", explaining and justifying plans and actions to the board and members. The main stakeholders (using the term in a wide sense) in a credit union are the members who save and borrow money. Other interests are also relevant: the State as supervisor and regulator in the public interest, management and employees, the wider community, the ILCU and the credit union movement.

The relationship between voluntary staff and paid staff in voluntary organisations was examined with reference to a case study in credit unions in a MA thesis by Mary Phelan, for the National College of Ireland (NCI), formerly the National College of Industrial Relations (NCIR), Dublin in 1998. Good working relations between volunteers and paid staff are vital to the smooth running of credit unions.

Managers' Specific Duties

Subject to statutory requirements, especially the duties of directors and other officers, managers' duties may include, for example:

- Preparing financial and other reports for the board;

- Attending board or other meetings as required;

- Keeping the board informed of relevant developments;

- Dealing with correspondence and drawing it to the attention of the board and officers as appropriate;

- Supervising staff;

- Arranging for adequate insurance;

- Conducting research;

- Dealing with members as requested;

- Dealing with regulatory matters;

- Ensuring that audits and annual reports are dealt with on time;

- Dealing with the ILCU and supplying necessary information;

- Working closely with and presenting financial reports to the treasurer;

- Dealing with the auditor;

- Safekeeping of chequebooks, promissory notes, contracts, documents including those on loans and nominations;

- Managing filing systems;

- Managing computer systems;

- Supervising office administration;

- Working within budgets when required;

- Supervising daily cash balancing, lodgements and bank reconciliation, and also posting of journals;

- Dealing with staff salaries;

- Being responsible, as key holder, for the alarm system of the offices;

- Ensuring knowledge of, and compliance, with wider statutory requirements, including health and safety, and also taxation, money-laundering and employment law;

- Alerting the officers and board to problems arising, especially where professional advice on legal, insurance and accountancy matters may be desirable.

CONCLUSION

The main source of authority for the governance of a credit union derives from the members in general meeting in accordance with the democratic nature of co-operatives. Members elect from the membership the board of directors to govern, subject to statutory checks and balances including those operated by the Supervisory Committee which the members also elect.

Subject to maintaining the voluntary ethos, functions are delegated to various officers, other committees and to professional managers. They are likely to have an increasingly important role subject, however, to governance by the board and officers. At all levels, a vital element is efficient decision-making.

Chapter 7

FINANCIAL TRANSACTIONS: MEMBERS' SAVINGS, LOANS AND INSURANCE

"A credit union is a form of brotherly love. You simply take
what extra money you have — the savings in your sock —
and let your neighbours use it for a while, only you won't
demand their right hands for security."

Rev Dr James Tompkins,
Antigonish, Nova Scotia, Canada.

The above quotation, from the writing of an eminent authority on
financial co-operatives, may sound naïve, too idealistic and
simplistic. "Brotherly" should be understood in a gender-inclusive
way to mean closely united in fellowship. A model based on the
above system does function, however, when checks and balances
are added to the system and extra precautions are taken at
operational and official supervisory levels to ensure the safety of
savings and loans.

The model must be adapted to practical situations. Savers may
wish to diversify and place at least some of their spare money in
insurance-linked schemes or in banks or building societies
depending on trends in interest rates. Members' right hands will
not be required as security but prudence requires reasonable
assurance that monies owed to credit unions will be repaid.

Credit unions are mutual self-help societies but they are not
charities. Fundamental to successful financial operations is the
virtuous cycle of members saving money which is loaned out to
other members, thus earning interest for the credit union.

The motto is "What I save today may help you to borrow tomorrow". Members are encouraged to continue saving while they are borrowing.

If individuals do not save within the credit union system, finances for loans at favourable rates would be not be available.

MEMBERSHIP

As outlined in Chapter 3, people wishing to become involved usually join one or more existing credit unions in which they are eligible to be members. Another option is to take the longer route by forming a study group leading to a new credit union being registered with the Registrar of Friendly Societies.

Individuals or groups with the required common bond and who are otherwise qualified to join as new members apply by completing an application form under rule 15, in the format shown in appendix II to the ILCU standard rules.

Relevant requirements for membership detailed in section 17 of the 1997 Act, reflected in rules 14–18, include: paying an entrance fee to a maximum £1; holding fully paid-up shares of a £1 denomination, to the value of a £1 minimum and £10 maximum or such larger figure as the Minister may prescribe; application for membership must be approved by the affirmative vote of a majority of the board of directors or by a duly appointed and authorised membership committee present at a meeting at which the application is considered. If membership is refused, an appeal may be made under section 18, rule 19 to the District Court for the district where the registered office of the credit union is situated.

Other Legislation does not Apply to Credit Unions

As explained in the introduction to this book, legislation on financial institutions — the Central Bank Acts, 1942–1997, the Building Societies Act, 1989 and the Consumer Credit Act, 1995, do not apply to credit unions. Such exclusion is controversial and subject to criticism by the financial institutions. Members depend on the Credit Union Act, 1997 for statutory protection in their transactions.

SHARES

Sections 28, 29, 30, 32 in part III (Operation of Credit Unions) of the 1997 Act and rules 33, 34, 35, 36, 38, 39, (with some overlapping in respect of deposits) contain the main provisions on shares. They are a basic unit of savings in credit union and differ from shares in commercial limited companies which may be transferred to other people on a less restrictive basis. There is no provision for preference shares.

Under section 28(2) and rule 34(2), a credit union shall not issue to a member a certificate denoting ownership of a share. There is no limit to the number of shares in a credit union in accordance with members' wish to save through shareholding. Shares in a credit union are comparable with those in the traditional mutual building society as explained in the case of *Irvine & Fullerton Building Society* v. *Cuthertson* (1905) 45 SLR 17, quoted in Murdoch (1993, p. 489).

Fully paid-up bonus shares may be issued from reserves (other than statutory reserves) under section 28(5) of the 1997 Act and rule 34(5), mirroring section 8(7) of the 1966 Act. That procedure could be criticised as a tax avoidance measure.

Passbooks and other records are noted to show the value of shares and other financial transactions. An important distinction is that the co-operative principle of one-member-one-vote at meetings, irrespective of the value of shareholding or number of accounts in a credit union, applies in accordance with section 82(2) and rules 131(1) and 138. People who are members of other credit unions, however, would qualify for further voting rights in those other credit unions.

Shares may be withdrawable or non-withdrawable and equal rights would attach to shares within the respective categories. Withdrawable shares comprise the traditional form of savings in credit unions to preserve the capital base. Non-withdrawable shares are unusual. Members may generally withdraw shares and thus access their savings, subject to any relevant restrictions.

Shares Transfer

Section 29 and rule 35, set out the requirements for transferring shares within statutory limits without charge to another member subject to certain restrictions including: the board of directors, if it so requires, must approve the transfer; the number of shares held by that other transferee member does not exceed the statutory limit on individual shareholding. There is an appeal system to the District Court if share transfers were refused. It is important to note that shares cannot be transferred or sold outside the membership who would be qualified and hold the common bond. Those restrictions preserve the co-operative ethos and prevent demutualisation or sale of shares on the stock exchange following the trend in some building societies. Section 185 exempts from stamp duty instruments for share transfers and also instruments for mergers by transfer of engagements or amalgamation.

Dividends

Section 30 of the 1997 Act and rule 36, provide that on the board's recommendation, a dividend up to a maximum of 10% of the nominal value of the credit union's shares (or such other percentage as may be prescribed) may be declared on all shares for the preceding financial year at each general meeting. The dividend may only be paid out of either the surplus (as ascertained under section 45 and rule 54(2), after allowing for operating expenses and depreciation) or a reserve set aside for dividends in previous years. Proportionate dividends may be paid on shares held for less than a year. Fully paid-up bonus shares may be issued from reserves (other than statutory reserves) proportionate to the dividend entitlement.

Dividends are vital to members and enhance the attraction of credit unions. In recent years during an era of falling interest rates, many credit unions have paid higher rates than would be available from banks or building societies in respect of comparable savings. A balance has to be maintained so that large dividends on shares are not paid at the expense of unduly high or uncompetitive rates of interest on loans borrowed from credit unions. Lower investment income and the need to ensure a stable savings base are causing pressure to reduce the rates of dividend.

DEPOSITS

Section 27 of the 1997 Act and rule 33, allow funds to be raised by accepting deposits from members who have a minimum share balance of £1,000. Prior to the 1997 Act, the position on deposits was unclear and confusing. Diverse views will remain on the desirability of deposits as a form of credit union savings but if deposits are being accepted, a clear policy should be formulated and publicised by individual credit unions. In a rapidly changing financial market, however, it is vital for members and credit unions to have the option of deposits of one or more classes and earning interest. Interest rates on deposits, however, should not exceed the return received by the employment of the credit union funds generally (and not only deposits) in loans or investments.

Restriction on Shareholding and Deposits

Financial limits on members' financial interest in a credit union were the most controversial area of the 1997 legislation during the parliamentary process. The original proposal to increase the old threshold of £6,000 to a new ceiling of £10,000 met with disappointment and strong resistance from the ILCU and large credit unions which considered the new ceiling to be too low. Effective lobbying of politicians across the political spectrum resulted in higher thresholds and more flexible restrictions in section 27 and rule 33, summarised as follows:

A member, with a balance in shares valued at not less than a £1,000, may hold up to £20,000 on deposit but the aggregate value of the individual's shares and deposits may not exceed the greater of £50,000 or 1% of the total assets of the credit union. That latter provision would prevent undue dominance by individual members and spread any risks.

The aggregate liabilities of credit union in respect of deposits shall not exceed 75 per cent of its aggregate liabilities in respect of shares, unless the Registrar grants a dispensation. The financial and percentage limits may be increased from time to time by Ministerial order and there were transitional arrangements on commencement of the Act. The higher limits would be mainly relevant to large credit unions.

Restrictions on Withdrawal of Shares and Deposits

Section 32, rule 38, allow a credit union to require a member to give not less than 60 days' notice of withdrawing shares and not less than 21 days' notice for withdrawing deposits. Discretion is used and shorter periods of notice may be applied depending on liquidity, and withdrawal on demand is generally allowed in practice by many credit unions.

Withdrawal of shares is prohibited while a claim due on account of deposits is unsatisfied. Applications for withdrawal of either shares or deposits by a member who has an outstanding liability to the credit union shall not be permitted unless:

- The balance of a member's savings after the requested withdrawal would remain equal to or higher than the amount of that member's outstanding liability; or

- The withdrawal is approved, in accordance with the registered rules, by a majority of the board of directors. Such approval may not be given if the balance of the member's savings after the requested withdrawal would be less than 25 per cent of the member's outstanding liability (or such other percentage as the Registrar may have applied to the specific credit union.) For members, the lower threshold is more favourable than the restrictions applicable before the 1997 legislation, assuming that members can ultimately meet their liabilities.

The Minister of State explained at the Dáil select committee stage the prudential nature of the restrictions. A minimum threshold is provided. For example, a member with £10,000 savings and a loan of £6,000 who wished to borrow the remainder against the deposit could not go below savings of £1,000 or 25 per cent of the outstanding loan liability.

Under section 32(5) and rule 38(4), a credit union may withdraw any shares or deposits and set them against amounts owed to the credit union by a member who has agreed to the set-off in writing. Promissory notes signed by the member on receipt of a loan authorises the treasurer to apply all the shares and deposits in payment of loans in cases of default.

Records of Shares and Deposits

A record must be kept of shares held by each member in a share register which must contain particulars such as names, addresses and occupations of members, numbers of shares held by them, amount paid, date of entry on register.

A permanent record shall also be kept of deposits made by each member, of any withdrawals, and the dates of such deposits and withdrawals (rule 33(4)).

Joint Accounts

Rule 39 provides for joint accounts in both shares and deposits from two or more members. Following relevant legal principles on rights of survivorship, when one account holder dies the account becomes the property of the remaining joint tenants. There are restrictions on them: only the first-named joint tenant (as defined in law) may vote unless the other joint tenant nominates one of the other joint tenants to cast the vote. Tenants in a joint account are not eligible to hold office unless they own a separate account or unless all tenants to the joint account agree in writing to the nomination to office. Only joint tenants designated by the others are entitled to obtain loans by virtue of a joint tenancy. In joint accounts, only the first-named person in the membership application would benefit under the loan protection and loan savings schemes.

Receipting for Money

Numbered passbooks or statements of accounts shall be issued to members in accordance with the details in rule 40. Money paid in or out on account of shares, deposits, loans, interest, and entrance fees shall be evidenced by an appropriate voucher or receipt or by entries in a member's passbook. Each voucher, receipt or entry in a passbook shall identify the person receiving or paying out monies on the credit union's behalf. Members' records of transactions shall be the entries in passbooks when they are used, or otherwise statements of accounts itemising all transactions. Balances shall be issued quarterly to members and itemised statements issued on request.

Passbooks, when used, are the member's own personal record for retention by the individual member and not by the treasurer or other credit union personnel. Members should submit their passbook during transactions and to the Supervisory Committee if required for checking.

Loss of passbooks or other receipts should be notified to the treasurer or other relevant officer and the credit union may take reasonable precautions to indemnify itself against loss.

Due to computerisation, statements of account are replacing passbooks but they may be used in conjunction with computers, for example, by inserting printouts.

The emphasis on members' retaining their own passbooks is a reasonable precaution to avoid abuse which arose in other areas such as illegal moneylending.

Money-laundering

Potential savers in shares or deposits with large unexplained sums of money will be subject to money-laundering precautions as outlined in Chapter 6 on credit union Governance and Chapter 9 on the Registrar's functions. Each credit union must appoint a money-laundering officer in accordance with rule 116. A notice should be displayed in the public offices. Suspicious activities must be reported to the Garda Síochána under section 32 of the Criminal Justice Act, 1994.

LOANS

One of the main advantages of joining a credit union is the facility to obtain loans at terms including interest rates which have traditionally been favourable compared with banks and building societies and other financial institutions. Sample loan application forms are in appendix II to the ILCU standard rules and copies are available as stationery from the ILCU's office.

Restrictions on Loans

The ceiling on loans was a controversial aspect of the 1997 legislation. Effective lobbying of politicians by the ILCU and large credit unions resulted in the proposed limit of £20,000 being increased substantially. The Credit Union Advisory Committee (CUAC) was also consulted. Under section 35(3) as enacted, rule 44(3), a credit union may make loans to a member provided that the member's outstanding liability (including contingent liability) as borrower, guarantor or otherwise, does not exceed whichever is the greater of: £30,000 or 1.5% (adapting a UK formula) of the total assets of the relevant credit union. The limits may be increased by Ministerial order. The maximum period of loans were increased conditionally from the five years in the 1966 Act to longer periods as explained below.

During the Dáil select committee debate, Pat Rabbitte, TD, Minister of State, explained that in 1995 only about 0.2% or 1 in 500 of borrowers had loans of or above £20,000. In theory, 1.5% of total assets means that a very large credit union may loan about £1 million to an individual member. As that would be a very generous amount, the Minister hoped that there would be many small loans, a number of medium-sized loans of over £30,000, rather than a few very large loans to a few individuals. While flexibility is important, the preservation of the co-operative ethos is an argument against very large loans.

Detailed Provisions on Loans

Sections 35 to 38 and rules 43–47, contain the main conditions. It is an offence to breach any of the statutory conditions regarding loans.

- Loans may be made only to members and may be secured or unsecured.

- Security may take the form of a guarantee by a member or a pledge of shares or deposits but in some cases an insurance policy or title deeds to property may be required.

- Loans are made, on such terms as the rules may provide, for provident and productive purposes. The term "provident" derives from the Victorian ethos of self-help industrial and provident societies in the sense of prudent and thrifty provision for the future. "Provident" is unfashionable and was deleted from the name of a commercial insurance company. "Provident" may be interpreted widely to include loans for household and personal requirements, including home improvements, holidays and visits abroad to soccer matches.

- A loan to a member who has the legal status of minor, that is under 18 years of age (who neither is nor was married) is not permitted unless an indemnity is given by the member's parent or guardian or by a person approved by the board.

- The relevant provision in section 35(1) of the 1997 Act was amended at the Dáil select committee stage to substitute indemnity for guarantee as that latter might not be enforceable according to legal advice. The general position on enforceability of loans to minors was discussed by Bird, in his annotations on section 35 in ICLSA R62, and in Clark (1990 pp. 366-373).

- Guarantees from an officer for loans to another member cannot be accepted unless that other member is the officer's spouse, child or parent.

- Loans are prohibited:
  - ◊ If the member's liability to the credit union, as borrower, guarantor or otherwise, would exceed the greater of £30,000 or 1.5 per cent of the total assets, as explained in more detail above;
  - ◊ For a period exceeding five years if the total amount outstanding to such loans would exceed 20 per cent of all outstanding loans;
  - ◊ For a period exceeding ten years if the total amount outstanding to such loans would exceed 10 per cent of all outstanding loans.

  The period of a loan is measured from the date the loan was made or the first instalment paid.

  The above arrangements are more flexible than the previous five-year limit on the terms of loans but it is expected that most loans will still be made for periods up to five years. Longer terms will facilitate larger commitments such as farm machinery and also house extensions and improvements.

- Loans to persons who cease to hold the common bond, described as non-qualifying members in sections 17(4) and 35(4) of the Act, shall not exceed 10% (or such higher percentage as may be approved by the Registrar) of the total amount outstanding on all loans.

- Each loan application must be in writing, stating the purpose for which it is required and any security offered.

- Interest rates must meet the strict conditions specified in section 38 and rule 47, explained below.

Pre-enactment loans are not prejudiced but they would be included in calculating statutory ceilings and limits.

Approval of Loans

Under section 36, rule 45, loans to members must be approved in accordance with the rules, either by a designated officer or by a majority of the credit committee members, or by a majority of the board of directors voting in secret ballot. The functions of those and other bodies are described in more detail in Chapter 6 on Governance. Credit unions usually have a loans policy to facilitate members and officers in deciding on applications. A loan to a non-qualifying member which exceeds the value of that member's savings must be approved by secret ballot by two-thirds of the members of a special committee consisting of a majority of the board, at least one member of the credit committee and at least one member of the Supervisory Committee.

Appeal against Refusal of Loan

To ensure fair procedures, section 37 and rule 46, provide for a right of appeal against a refusal decision of the credit committee or credit officer, to an appellate body, comprising the directors (except any director who was a member of the credit committee dealing with the relevant loan application) and members of the Supervisory Committee. The quorum for the appellate body is a majority of the relevant directors plus at least one member of the supervisory committee.

Interest on Loans

Under section 38 and rule 47, interest may be charged on loans to members subject to strict conditions by which the interest rate must:

- not exceed 1% per month on the amount outstanding, that is on a declining balance (actual rates may be less than the maximum);

- include all of the charges in making the loan;

- be the same for all loans of the specific class granted at a particular time;

The interest rate charged on any class of loans granted at a particular time shall be the same for all loans of that class. That new flexible provision in section 38(1) (c) and rule 47(1) (c), was inserted at the Dáil select committee stage in response to comments from the ICLU that it may be unduly restrictive to require the same rates of interest on secured and unsecured loans. Credit unions for prudential reasons may tailor arrangements to suit the circumstances. Terms will be flexible to match the higher risk of large loans.

Interest charged or accepted at a rate exceeding the statutory limit will result in the interest being waived and the member may recover interest already paid which may be recovered summarily as a simple contract debt.

It is now an offence to knowingly charge or accept interest at a rate greater than that permitted.

Interest rates are vitally important to credit unions in terms of returns and to individual members in terms of cost. The limited rates allowable by statute are presented as a vital part of transparency and truth in lending with no hidden costs. If loans are repaid early, the cost is reduced without the type of penalty operated by some financial institutions. Tables are available to members to illustrate the amounts payable. For example, 1 per cent per month represents less than £6.50 on a loan of £100 repaid in 12 equal instalments.

The credit union annual percentage rate (APR), simply explained as the total cost of credit expressed as an annual percentage of the amount of credit extended, of about 12.67 per cent was very low when compared with 20 per cent to 30 per cent for commercial lending institutions during the exceptionally high interest rate regime in 1992/93. Commercial rates fluctuate with market forces. The effect of the downward trend in the current European Monetary Union (EMU) climate is that credit union interest rates are not as favourable as in the past, compared with those charged by banks and building societies. Rate reductions and interest rebates or refunds under rule 36(6) (a) and (b) are now being applied to maintain the comparative attraction of credit union loans in a low interest rate climate.

Criticism of Interest Rates

Critics often argue that the real rate of interest in credit unions is inflated by the requirement, now modified, to hold specified levels of savings before loans are granted. As such savings would be effectively frozen and lack liquidity, they could not be used to finance expenditure, thus increasing the amount of loan required.

On the other hand, not everyone would have the option of borrowing in the commercial financial institutions. Criteria such as an individual's track record in a neighbourhood or employment, need and personal integrity are relevant in a credit union. Access to credit is facilitated. If there were problems with repayments, it could be easier to deal with credit unions although they also have to take tough measures including court action to recover outstanding debts. Loan protection insurance, as explained under insurance on the opposite page, is an added attraction.

Promissory Notes and Bills of Exchange:
Section 39, Rule 48

A promissory note, simply explained, is a legally binding promise in writing between two parties that one will pay the other a stated amount on demand or at a fixed or determinable future date. Sample promissory notes forms are in appendix II to the ILCU standard rules and copies are available as stationery from the ILCU's office. Formalities, including a Revenue stamp and signatures, must be complied with.

Most of the rules applicable under the Bills of Exchange Act, 1882 apply to promissory notes. The main difference between them is that a bill of exchange is an order to pay and a promissory note is a promise to pay. In practice, promissory notes are used commonly by credit unions when granting loans but their use in the commercial world has declined.

Section 39 and rule 48 provide that a person acting under a credit union's authority may make, accept or endorse a promissory note or bill of exchange in the credit union's name and on its authority. Section 33 of the Industrial and Provident Societies Act, 1893 was the model but an innovation in section 39(2) of the 1997 Act allows the Registrar to appoint a person to act on behalf of a credit union where no such authority exists.

REMEDY FOR DEBTS FROM MEMBERS

Section 20 and rule 26 provide that all money payable to a credit union shall be recoverable summarily as a civil debt, that is through the normal court procedures governed by rules of court. The appropriate court would depend on the amount of debt due and the relevant jurisdiction limits which may be varied from time to time. For example, the Circuit Court may give summary judgment where the claim is for a debt or liquidated sum (at present up to £30,000) and the plaintiff proves by affidavit that the defendant has no *bona fides* defence to the claim and that the appearance or any defence was entered solely for the purpose of delay. The Master would have relevant jurisdiction in the High Court.

A credit union would have a lien on, and may set off against a member's shares, deposits, dividends and interest in respect of any debt due. A lien is the right to hold the property of another as security for performing an obligation. Credit unions will listen sympathetically to members with problems in paying monies owed and may make suitable arrangements including rescheduling loans. Nevertheless, the ultimate sanction of court action may be necessary to recover debts and protect the credit union and its wider membership.

INSURANCE

General

Savings and loan balances of eligible members are automatically covered (up to specified limits and subject to certain conditions which may vary from time to time) at no extra cost to individual members as credit unions pay the premiums. Credit unions affiliated to the ILCU may avail of schemes arranged by it and other credit unions arrange their own cover. Some mainstream financial institutions may also have protection schemes for commercial consumers. Members and consumers should enquire about the precise details of available schemes which vary from time to time. Individual policies may not be available but members can seek to inspect group policies.

The basic loan and savings insurance is provided by ECCU Assurance Company Ltd, which was specifically established to provide savings and loan protection for credit unions affiliated to ILCU at the lowest cost consistent with sound principles. As an independent insurance company, ECCU comes within the statutory supervision of the Department of Enterprise, Trade and Employment but those arrangements may change if a new financial services authority is established. The ILCU administers ECCU schemes on an agency basis and re-insurance was negotiated with CUNA Mutual, part of the international credit union movement.

The ECCU system may be criticised as restrictive and large credit unions may seek alternative insurance cover. There are economies of scale from the large volume of business generated by the nationwide credit union movement and, after providing for claims, commission and reserves, monies are returned to credit unions.

Loan Protection Insurance

Under this basic scheme on members' lives, if a member (or in the case of joint accounts, the first-named member) eligible for insurance cover dies the outstanding loan balance subject to any limits in the cover, is fully paid by insurance. This gives members the confidence that their dependents will be protected against outstanding debt. Eligibility depends on the member having signed a promissory note and being engaged in normal duties of livelihood, or, if not working, being in good health. Cover ceases on the member's 70th birthday but may be extended up to 80 years by effecting cover under the over-70 rider. Total disability is usually but not always covered but that cover would cease when the member reaches 60.

Life Savings Insurance

As another basic incentive, life insurance cover is provided for eligible members, (or in the case of joint accounts, the first named member), that is those aged 70 and under who are actively at work, or, if not working, in good health. Benefits payable on death vary. For example, for every pound saved, insurance cover is provided on a sliding scale depending on a member's age when lodging the monies, ranging from 100 per cent, that is £1 for £1 for members under 55, 25p for those aged 65 to 70. When earned, the insurance stays in force as long as savings remain. On death, the insurance in addition to the sum saved, is payable to the beneficiary. In joint accounts, the member whose name appears first on the ledger records is eligible for cover.

An increasingly sophisticated insurance service is provided by the ILCU in association with the insurance industry to cover risks outside the normal basic range of loan and savings cover. Some of the new insurance products would come within the category of additional services, covered by sections 48 to 52, rules 58 to 63, as explained below.

Health insurance through the VHI and BUPA may also be arranged through group schemes. Household insurance may also be arranged at favourable rates. Members must be alert to the basic insurance principle of *uberrimae fidei*, the utmost good faith, which requires full disclosure of material facts, such as those concerning health.

SAVINGS PROTECTION: SECTION 46, RULE 55

How safe are my savings? That fundamental question naturally concerns members. To underpin existing safeguards, a savings protection scheme was introduced in 1989 following discussions between the Registrar, the ILCU and other interests, and launched by the then Minister for Finance, Albert Reynolds, TD. The Registrar's report of 1987–89 explained the background.

The scheme is essentially a financial support system for credit unions experiencing financial difficulties. A pool of money, initially 1% of the movement's total savings, was set aside. It is not an insurance scheme but rather a copper-fastening of the various levels of support to protect members' savings up to specified limits, at present £10,000 for an individual member.

Under section 6(1) (f) of the 1997 Act, credit unions seeking registration must participate in an approved savings protection scheme.

Section 46 of the 1997 Act provides that a credit union may incur expenditure by participating in a savings protection scheme approved by the Registrar. The purpose is to protect, in whole or in part, members' savings (including shares, deposits and other funds held on behalf of members) in the event of insolvency or other default by a credit union. The Registrar shall be entitled to inspect, under sections 90 and 91, the books of an approved scheme and the authorised representatives of a scheme shall be entitled to inspect a participating credit union's books.

Rule 55 requires credit unions affiliated to the ILCU to participate in its savings protection scheme. ILCU's authorised representatives shall be entitled to inspect credit union books.

From experience, the schemes outlined above may be used only infrequently but the extra safeguard is important.

TRANSFER OF A MEMBER'S FINANCIAL INTEREST UPON DEATH

Under a procedure, inherited from the Victorian era and peculiar to mutual and other small savings schemes, monies, within specified limits, may be passed to beneficiaries when a saver dies. The intention was to bypass the normal procedures for wills and probate and thus to cover costs of death and funerals. The basic provisions in sections 25 and 26 of the Industrial and Provident Societies Act, 1893 have been continued in the Credit Union Act,

1997, sections 21 to 23, reflected in rules 27 to 29. The system is open to criticism as it is outside the normal succession procedures for passing property on death. Care is essential to comply with procedures as disappointed people may challenge the validity of payments. Particular care is necessary in sensitive family situations and second relationships.

Nominations

Section 21 and rule 27 provide that members may nominate in writing to the credit union any person or persons to become entitled to the whole or specified parts of their property (shares and deposits and also insurances with specified exceptions such as a death benefit rider) in the credit union when the member dies. There are restrictions: a person under 16 cannot make a valid nomination; to prevent abuse or undue influence, an officer cannot be a nominee unless that person is a member of the nominator's family; if the amount of the relevant property exceeds £10,000, the nomination is valid only up to a value of £10,000; during their lifetime, members may revoke or vary a nomination but amendments to a nomination in a member's will or codicil to a will shall be ineffective. Consequential provisions include: a requirement on credit unions to keep up-to-date records of members' nominations; protection of a credit union, which transferred property in accordance with a nomination while unaware of the member's marriage and defining circumstances, for example member's marriage, which operate to revoke a nomination. The latter provision in section 21 (6) was based on a precedent in the Credit Unions (Northern Ireland) Order, 1985.

Nomination forms, available from the ILCU, must be signed by the relevant member and witnessed by a person, other than a nominee. A sample is included in appendix II to the standard rules.

Section 22 and rule 28 set out detailed procedures and conditions for payments of property by a credit union following the death of a nominating member, including: satisfactory proof of death, validity of nomination, and payment in trust to a guardian or parent of a nominee who is under 16 years of age.

Provision for Small Payments on Death

Section 23 and rule 29 provides that: on death of a member who has not made a nomination under section 21, rule 27, and whose property in the credit union does not exceed £5,000, the board may without any letters of administration or probate of any will, distribute that property to such persons as appear to the board to be entitled by law to receive it. The board should be careful and seek satisfactory evidence before making any payments. This could be a problematic area.

The £5,000 limit for small payments and apparently also the £10,000 limit for nominations (although section 21 does not so specify, general regulations on altering financial limits under section 182(1) (i) seem relevant) may be increased by Ministerial regulations made under section 182. It also provides for prior consultation with the Registrar, CUAC — the advisory body, and other expert bodies which would presumably include the ILCU.

Preparing Wills

A will is a disposition by which the person making it, the testator/testatrix, provides for the distribution or administration of property after death. Certain procedures are required including that the will must be in writing and be properly witnessed.

Credit unions are now permitted to have wills prepared and to take instructions for grants of probate or letters of administration under the Solicitors (Amendment) Act, 1994, No. 27 of 1994, amending the Solicitors Acts, 1954–1960. The Succession Act, 1966 gives a surviving spouse a legal right to a share in an estate and allows children of a testator, who makes the will, to apply to the court to have just provision made for them. Credit union officers should be aware of the fundamentals and seek legal advice where necessary.

Payments in Respect of Mentally Handicapped Persons

Section 24 and rule 30 provide that the board, after considering medical evidence, may make a payment of any property held by or on behalf of members who are incapable by reason of a mental condition to manage and administer their own property. The provision would not apply, however, where persons have been duly appointed to administer a member's property, whether by a court pursuant to part II of the Powers of Attorney Act, 1996 (No. 12 of 1996) or otherwise. That Act was referred to because it is very relevant and it was considered desirable to alert credit unions to it. Safeguards are necessary, including a statement from the proposed recipient of a duty to administer the property in the best interests of the owner. As explained in ICLSA, August 1998, in which the 1997 Act was annotated by Bird, section 24 as amended reflects the new definition of mental incapacity in section 4(1) of the Powers of Attorney Act, 1996.

Validity of Payments

Section 25 and rule 32 provide that payments under section 23 or 24, rules 29 or 30, to any person appearing at the time of payment to be so entitled, such payments shall be valid and effectual against any demand which any other person may make against the credit union. This protects the board of directors against demands by other persons.

ADDITIONAL SERVICES TO MEMBERS

Section 48 and rule 59 permit a credit union to provide, as principal or agent, additional services for its members. The provision of additional services, other than those in earlier provisions of the Act or those excluded by Ministerial regulations must meet specified conditions including:

- Must be passed by a resolution of not less than two-thirds of the members present and voting at a general meeting;

- Must be subsequently approved by the Registrar under section 49 (in accordance with his regulatory powers as explained in Chapter 9);

- Must be permitted by the rules of the relevant credit union.

Therefore, providing additional services is an optional extra which only some credit unions, especially the larger ones, may wish to offer.

The Registrar, under section 48(7) and (8) and rule 59(6) and (7), may stipulate the requirement considered necessary for credit unions providing additional services and, if those requirements are not met, or if the credit union does not begin to provide the services within twelve months of approval by the Registrar, the credit union shall not provide the specified services.

Registrar's Approval of Additional Services

Section 49 and rule 60 specify the information to be contained in an approval application. The Registrar shall have regard to specified matters in deciding whether to approve (on such conditions which he considers appropriate) or to refuse to approve the application.

There is a four months' time limit on the Registrar in making the administrative decision or requiring additional information where a credit union applies to provide additional services as a principal. On receipt of any such additional information, the Registrar has another four months to decide. Where the credit union intends to provide the additional service as an agent, there are similar obligations but the time limits are reduced to two months.

Section 49(4) places the matter in context by providing that in making a decision, the Registrar shall have regard to the interests of the public and the members and to the orderly and proper regulation of credit union's business and such other matters as he thinks proper.

Additional services were not specifically defined but they would be those outside the primary and traditional role regarding savings, loans and related insurance. Services involving no risk to funds, such as advisory and budgetary services would be excluded. Cheque books, foreign exchange, ATMs and also additional insurance products and mortgages would be examples of additional services.

Some credit unions were offering extra services in advance of official sanction. To cover the situation where additional services were being provided before the relevant provisions of the Act were commenced by Ministerial order, transitional arrangements allow the services to continue pending the Registrar's decision on an application for approval. The relevant sections on additional services were not commenced with the main sections of the Act in October, 1997 under SI No. 403, Credit Union Act, 1997 (Commencement) Order, 1997, pn. 4459, published in *Iris Oifigiúil*, (October, 1997).

Supplementary Provisions

Section 50, reflected in rule 61, provides that in exercising powers under sections 48 to 50, the Registrar may consult with the Advisory Committee (CUAC) and other expert bodies and may also commission an independent assessment of the capacity to provide the additional services. Further consultations between the Registrar and the ILCU will be necessary. The Registrar may withdraw an approval or revoke or vary any conditions on an approval or impose new conditions on an approval.

Section 51 and rule 62 prohibit a credit union from offering or making loans on condition that a member shall avail of another service provided. For example, a car purchase loan cannot be made conditional on the borrower insuring the car with a insurance company for which the credit union acts as agent. Services may only be made in terms which distinguish the cost of each service. The constraint on linking loans to providing additional services to members is akin to consumer protection in section 127 of the Consumer Credit Act, 1995 as explained in Bird (1998, pp. 532–539).

Court Review

Under section 52, rule 63, there is a right of appeal to the High Court against the Registrar's decision to:

• Refuse to approve an application;

- Withdraw approval;

- Vary or impose a condition on an approval to provide additional services.

The High Court may give such directions as it thinks appropriate, if it considers that the Registrar's decision should not be confirmed. T.C. Bird in his annotations in ICLSA, R 62, 1998, considers that the wording of section 52(1) (c) is inconsistent with that of section 50(3) (b) as the word "revoke" seems to have been inadvertently omitted from section 52(1) (c).

TAX

This complex area, including reporting to Revenue, provoked controversy when the Minister for Finance proposed changes in the tax treatment of credit unions during the debate on the Finance Bill, 1998. The basic position when this book was being written was that credit unions were not required to deduct deposit interest withholding tax (DIRT) on dividends or interest paid to members but those individuals could be taxable depending on their own liability and other income. Credit unions have traditionally not been liable to corporation or income tax. They, and individual members, should be aware of their own tax position which may change depending on circumstances and legislation.

The future depends on government reaction to, and decisions on, the report of a special committee set up in 1998 to consider taxation and credit unions. The report recommended that only dividends of over £375 annually would be taxable. DIRT at 20 per cent would apply to dividends and deposit interest above £375. The Credit Union movement, fearing that higher taxation could be proposed by the European Commission, favours the committee's recommendations.

Chapter 8

WIDER OPERATIONS BY CREDIT UNIONS: CONTRACTS, INVESTMENTS, SPECIAL FUNDS AND BORROWING CONTRACTS

"Credit Unions should bear in mind that even where a particular investment is legally permissible prudential considerations also have to be taken into account."

Report of the Registrar of Friendly Societies, 1997

Following the model in section 35 of the 1893 Act, section 40 of the 1997 Act and rule 49 set out the conditions in respect of legally binding agreements — contracts: their making, varying and discharge by or on behalf of a credit union. Section 35 of the 1893 Act is followed generally but an innovation in section 40(3) gives the Registrar power to appoint a person to act on behalf of a credit union. The thrust was to follow general law governing contracts. Some require a seal, for example those conveying property; some must be in writing, while others may be parol — verbal or oral. Signatures shall be taken to be those of relevant officers unless proved to the contrary. If authority no longer exists for discharging a contract, the Registrar may appoint a person to act with appropriate powers on behalf of the credit union. Relevant contracts shall be effectual in law and bind the credit union, its successors and all other parties to the contract. Officers should be aware of basic contract law and seek professional advice if in doubt.

LAND: ACQUISITION, HOLDING AND DISPOSAL

This can be a controversial and confusing area as property speculation by credit unions is often considered to be undesirable in the interests of members and the wider public. The 1997 Act facilitates the holding of property subject to specific safeguards.

Section 41 and rule 50 provide that a credit union may acquire and hold in its own name any land for the sole purpose of conducting its business, including erecting a building on the land for that purpose. Land may be disposed of, and shall be disposed of as soon as practicable, where a building ceases to be occupied entirely for the purpose of its business or where the Registrar so directs as not being in the best interests of the credit union, in accordance with section 41(5) which as a regulatory provision is not reflected in the ILCU rules. The Registrar has complete discretion in making a direction under subsection 5 because regulations under the Statutory Instruments Act, 1947 are not necessary as section 3(3) of the 1997 Act does not apply.

As explained and clarified by the Minister of State during the Dáil select committee stage, section 41, enacted as amended, allows credit unions which occupy part of their premises to lease on a commercial or other basis, that part of the property which it does not use. Section 41(4) makes it clear that where a building it owns becomes empty, a credit union must sell its entire interest in it. Section 41 does not deal with use of, or funding for, existing or other property for community development coming within section 44 and rule 53.

INVESTMENTS: SECTION 43, RULE 52

Credit unions earn interest from their basic function of providing loans to members out of members' savings but there is scope for wider investment. Section 43 and rule 52 contain detailed provisions of the ways in which credit unions may invest their surplus funds in:

- Authorised trustee securities, which are wider in scope under the Trustee (Authorised Investments) Order, 1998;

- Shares of or deposits with or loans to a credit union;

- Shares of a society registered under the Industrial and Provident Societies Acts, 1893 to 1978. (Most, but not all such societies, would be co-operatives.);

- Such other manner as may be prescribed, being in a manner appearing to the Minister to be beneficial to the credit union.

Surplus funds, not invested as above, or not kept as cash by the officers in the credit union shall be kept on current account with, or on loan to, credit institutions. They are defined in section 2 of the 1997 Act as:

a) A recognised bank within the meaning of the Central Bank Acts, 1942 to 1997;

b) A trustee savings bank;

c) The Post Office Savings Bank; or

d) A building society within the meaning of the Building Societies Act, 1989.

If a institution ceases to be a credit institution as defined, practicable steps must be taken to call in and realise the loan within three months or as soon as practicable. There are transitional arrangements to validate investments not permitted prior to the commencement of the statutory provisions but which would now be within them. Temporary loans may be made to another credit union and there may be petty cash and change funds.

As explained in Chapter 9 on the supervisory and prudential functions of the Registrar, in his annual statutory reports he has stressed the need for a cautious approach to investments.

The Registrar's general cautionary approach is still relevant despite the wider choice of investments allowed under section 43 and rule 52 and the Trustee (Authorised Investments) Order, 1998.

The ILCU, conscious of the need for a professional approach to investments, has arranged for the services of Davy Stockbrokers to advise credit unions about investments through Central

Investment Management. The flexible service providing for security, liquidity and flexibility will be subject to independent audit established by the ILCU.

Special Funds for Social, Cultural or Charitable Purposes (Section 44 and Rule 53): Background

This is an important area on which there are diverse views. There are social and economic arguments for credit unions becoming involved in wider co-operative and community enterprises: relatively small amounts out of the extensive volumes of community-based savings could stimulate enterprise and help towards solving problems such as long-term unemployment. Some co-operative activists feel strongly about that thrust.

On the other hand, wider involvement outside the core business of credit unions could expose members' savings to risk and loss.

Expertise in evaluating projects for local enterprise may be lacking. It may be difficult to keep credit unions at arm's length from local enterprises because in many towns the same personalties tend to become involved in a range of voluntary and community activities. Thus, even though credit unions are legally separate from other community enterprises, the public may associate them because of the common personalties involved. Financial problems in a local community co-op or other project may indirectly cause problems for a credit union. The basis for such problems may be lack of confidence due to the interlocking of personalities in various local enterprises, rather than any real difficulty with credit unions.

Under the law prior to the Credit Union Act, 1997, limited access to credit union funds was available to community groups which qualified for credit union membership through the common bond. Members as individuals could borrow to finance local enterprise. Those general arrangements would still apply but section 44, rule 53, makes specific provisions for funding community and related enterprise, subject to prudential safeguards:

1) By a resolution passed by a majority of members present and voting at a general meeting, a credit union may establish a special fund to be used by the credit union for such social, cultural or charitable purposes (including community development) as have been approved, either generally or specifically, by a similar resolution; and any such fund shall be maintained separately from the rest of the credit union finances.

2) Subject to point 4 below, the monies may be paid into a special fund established under this section only out of the annual operating surplus. No monies may be paid unless the directors are satisfied that:

3) Adequate provision has been made to cover all current and contingent liabilities and maintain proper reserves; and

4) The payment of the monies into the special fund will not affect the financial stability of the credit union.

5) Annual payments into the fund shall not exceed 0.5 per cent of the value of the credit union's assets as shown in the latest annual accounts.

6) An amount not exceeding 2.5 per cent of the accumulated reserves of the credit union, excluding the statutory reserve, may be paid into the special fund in the year of its establishment.

7) A higher ceiling than the 0.5 per cent specified at 5 above, may be approved by the Registrar and agreed by a resolution passed by two-thirds of the members at a general meeting.

8) The social, cultural or charitable purposes of the fund may be varied by a further resolution under 1 above. (The purposes would, however, still have to be within those parameters.)

9) On the board's recommendation, a general meeting by a majority of members present and voting may pass a resolution to wind-up the fund. Then the monies standing to the credit fund shall be transferred to the general funds and the special

fund shall cease to exist. (That provision facilitates the establishment of funds for temporary purposes.)

Section 44(7) ensures that if a special fund runs into difficulties or completes its social or charitable work, the funds can be transferred back into the general funds.

Rationale for Special Funds Provisions

At the Dáil select committee, the Minister of State, Pat Rabbitte, TD, explained the rationale for section 44, as amended at the committee stage: the relevant purposes cover credit union support for developing business enterprise or community centres to improve the local economic and social infrastructure of communities. Following representations from the ILCU, the legislation was amended to allow individual credit unions to contribute a lump sum of up to 2.5 per cent at the fund's initial stage. Promotional costs would be met from the general funds, not from the special funds. The special funds would be of specific interest in deprived communities where social and economic stimulation was required but the relevant local credit union would require adequate resources.

BORROWING BY CREDIT UNIONS

Section 33, reflected in rule 42, allows a credit union subject to its rules to borrow money on security or otherwise, and to issue debentures. They are simply explained as fixed interest bonds issued by the borrower to medium- or long-term investors, with a promise to pay the amount mentioned on it. A debenture usually gives a charge over the assets (facilitated by section 34 below) or some form of security. Under general principles of company law which would apply to credit unions, debentures are not part of the capital. Debenture holders are creditors, not shareholders.

Limitations on Borrowing in Section 33 Include:

- Total borrowing, excluding members' shares and deposits and any temporary bank loan cannot exceed 50 per cent of aggregate shares and deposits balances, but lenders who are unaware of any breach of the 50 per cent limit would be protected by section 33 (5).

- Unless the lender was aware in advance by actual notice, a transaction involving lending funds to a credit union in excess of the 50 per cent limit shall not be invalid or ineffectual. (The intention is to protect the lender in accordance with general principles but the notice must be actual not constructive.)

- The Registrar's prior approval is required for a proposal to borrow money which would raise total borrowing in excess of 25 per cent of aggregate shares and deposit balances. 28 days' notice of intention to apply must be given to the Registrar.

Under section 33 (6), a credit union borrowing in excess of the statutory limit of 50 per cent or failing to give notice to the Registrar of a proposal to borrow in excess of 25 per cent, shall be guilty of an offence.

At the Select Committee stage, a reference to approval by the Registrar of sources of funds borrowed was deleted because the issue could be dealt with in the registered rules which the Registrar would have to approve.

Charges on Assets: An Important Reform

Section 34 and rule 41 provide that an instrument executed by a credit union constituting a charge on its assets shall not be a bill of sale under the Bills of Sale (Ireland) Acts, 1879 and 1883, nor be invalidated by those Acts where the charge is recorded with the Registrar. There are specified procedures for notifying charges, and recording, acknowledging, filing and making information available for public inspection. The model was section 31, Credit Unions (Northern Ireland) Order, 1985. Regulations may provide for notifying the Registrar of any release, discharge or other transaction. Under section 34(5), the High Court on application by a credit union or other person claiming the benefit of the instrument, may make an order amending the time for the applicant to have the charge recorded, or rectifying any omission or misstatement.

The above provisions are a vital and long-awaited law reform because credit unions classed as industrial and provident societies, were (unlike registered companies) not exempted from the Bills of Sale legislation. The lack of exemption effectively inhibited the raising of funds by debentures and the creation of floating charges on the assets. The Dáil select committee agreed to section 34 without debate or discussion despite the importance of the reform being made in the law.

Although the system in section 34 of the 1997 Act differs from that in part IV of the Companies Act, 1963, the considerable body of jurisprudence in company law should provide precedents.

INSURANCE

Insurance is also necessary to cover risks incurred by credit unions, as distinct from their members, for example, in respect of premises and employment under rule 57 and also fraud by officers under section 47 of the 1997 Act and rule 56.

Some insurance cover is a statutory requirement: section 47, rule 56, requires a credit union to insure itself, in accordance with any prescribed requirements, against loss suffered or liability incurred through the fraud or other dishonesty of its officers and voluntary assistants. Failure to comply is an offence. Evidence of such cover must be submitted by the 1st December annually to the Registrar.

Judgments Against a Credit Union

Section 179 provides procedures for implementing court orders and judgments for its unpaid debts against a credit union. If it cannot pay its debts within 21 days or such time as the court may allow, it shall be deemed to be unable to pay its debts for the purposes of section 133 and rule 164 dealing with the Registrar's power to petition the High Court to wind-up the credit union. Chapter 12 on Termination deals with winding-up.

CUMIS (Credit Union Mutual Insurance Society) Bond

The wide range of cover available through the ILCU includes financial loss caused by embezzlement, fraud, dishonesty, failure by employees to do their duty, burglary and theft. Optional extras would cover additional audit expense and mysterious disappearance of cash.

Insurance, available through the ILCU, covers: fire and special perils; business interruption; plate glass breakages; motor contingency for claims against the credit union by a third party involved in a traffic accident caused by an officer or voluntary assistant of the credit union who is on its business when the accident occurred; public liability arising when a member of the public is injured as a result of the negligence of a credit union or its officials in the course of their duties; employers' liability for injury or damage to property; personal accident or assault arising from a burglary, robbery or hold-up while an officer or voluntary assistant is on credit union business; post-robbery trauma counselling; fixed benefits to officers who suffer personal injury from accidents arising any time, subject to some exceptions; motor vehicle extension to public liability to cover selected officials while using their cars on official business; engineering to cover central heating systems; financial loss due to the inability to collect loans because some records were lost; all risks following accidental loss of or damage to office equipment including computers.

Details of cover vary and should be checked by the manager and officers who should also shop around for the most suitable cover. The ILCU also seeks the most favourable terms in arranging cover.

ATMs and Computerisation

Automated Teller Machine (ATM)

Hole-in-the-wall machines are cash dispensers, operated through an electro-mechanical terminal. In the banks and building societies, customers with a personal identification number (PIN) may obtain cash from their accounts and access other services.

In recent years, to meet members' requirements a group of credit unions formed the CUTECH Society specifically to provide ATMs and ATM card facilities. Michael Woods, formerly manager of St Mary's Navan Credit Union Ltd, and CUAC chairman, was prominent in the initiative.

In 1996, the ILCU and CUTECH credit unions agreed to combine their efforts to provide one main ATM and electronic funds transfer (EFT) network and issue cards under the IQ Cash brand. It is proposed that the integrated IQ Cash service will be provided by ILCUtech, a limited company representing the ILCU and user credit unions.

Eventually, member and credit union financial transactions will be facilitated on a nationwide electronic basis. Initially, members of some credit unions will be able to withdraw cash through ATMs at financial institutions and selected credit unions. Some credit unions, while agreeing in principle with electronic systems, are cautious because of the high costs, especially of an extensive nationwide network.

Computers

Computers are a basic part of most credit union's operations. The long-term implications of these developments are dealt with in Chapter 16 on Future Trends and Developments.

In this advanced technological era, financial and related operations are now a long way from money in the sock, as quoted at the start of Chapter 7. Mutual savings, however, require adequate procedures to protect members' money.

Chapter 9

REGISTRAR OF FRIENDLY SOCIETIES: SUPERVISION AND CONTROL; COMPLAINTS AND DISPUTES

"The rules of the early friendly societies were allowed by Justices of the Peace and enrolled at courts of record called quarter sessions. In the early nineteenth century, barristers-at-law certified societies' rules. The barristers' certifying functions were assigned to a statutory officer constituted as the Registrar of Friendly Societies in 1846."

A.P. Quinn, (1989).

The above extract illustrates the long historical tradition of the Registrar as the officer for registration and control of mutual societies. The Registrar's functions evolved and developed over the years to cover, in varying degrees, industrial & provident societies (mainly co-ops), trade unions, savings banks, building societies (now supervised by the Central Bank) and credit unions.

When Ireland was part of the UK, the Assistant Registrar in Dublin was responsible to the Chief Registrar in London. After 1922, a separate Registry was established in Northern Ireland (dealt with in Chapter 15 on Northern Ireland) and an Irish Registrar was appointed in Dublin. The Friendly Societies (Amendment) Act, 1977 provided that the Minister for Industry and Commerce (now the Minister for Enterprise, Trade and Employment) appoints the Registrar. The current holder of that civil service office Noel Martin Sisk, solicitor, succeeded Eamon Carey, barrister, in 1985. Section 105 of the Credit Union Act, 1997 provides that in the absence of the Registrar, his functions may be exercised and performed by such person as the Minister may from time to time authorise.

The Registrar of Friendly Societies is legally independent in the exercise of his statutory functions, and is distinct from the Registrar of Companies but depends on the relevant Department, currently of Enterprise, Trade and Employment, for staff and finance. The Registrar was defined and interpreted as the Registrar of Friendly Societies under the relevant Acts: The Industrial and Provident Societies Act, 1893 as amended, especially by the Industrial and Provident Societies (Amendment) Act, 1978 (No. 23), and the Credit Union Act, 1966 (No. 19) as repealed and replaced by the Credit Union Act, 1997 (No. 15). The Registrar's supervisory and control powers were considerably strengthened by the 1978 Act, replaced by the Credit Union Act 1997 to provide more extensive powers for the Registrar. The ILCU revised standard rules for credit unions do refer to the Registrar's powers but do not include all of the Act's detailed provisions, such as the sanctions for non-compliance.

MISSION STATEMENT

According to his annual report for 1997 (incorporating proceedings to 31 December 1997), the Registrar's mission statement includes ensuring that the various mutual entities registered at the Registry comply with their statutory obligations, and to maintain an up-to-date record of those entities. The Registry's role within the Department is to complement its objective of providing and enforcing a modern legal framework facilitating the start up and proper operation of enterprises through clear compliance requirement by (a) clear and simple compliance requirements and (b) effective regulatory arrangements. Specific objectives include the efficient and effective registration and prudential supervision of credit unions and providing an efficient and effective service to the public.

REGISTRATION

The Registrar's basic control functions relate to registration and filing records. Societies, including credit unions, have a statutory duty to submit to the Registrar, rules and amendments, annual returns and accounts and also information about registered office and officers. As explained in Chapter 10 on Accounts and Auditors, the Registrar's office checks annual accounts and returns and may pursue aspects with specific credit unions having regard to prudential considerations.

Registration of existing credit unions is continued by virtue of section 5 of the 1997 Act, including a few promoted by the Community Development Movement of Ireland and registered under the Industrial and Provident Societies Acts, 1893 to 1936, between 24 January 1962 and 31 August 1966.

For new credit unions, two copies of the printed rules and formal application signed by 15 members (not 7 as previously) who have a common bond, are submitted under section 7 to the Registrar. The common bond must also be shown in the rules (standard rule 14). Section 8(1) of the Credit Union Act, 1997, (part II), provides that the Registrar, on being satisfied that the appropriate statutory provisions have been complied with, has a duty to register a society as a credit union. That means that a society which fulfils the conditions specified in section 6 shall be registered.

Those conditions include (a) that the society is formed for the (core) objects specified in paragraphs (a) to (c) of section 6(2) and for no other purposes beyond those (extra objects) specified in paragraphs (d) to (g) of that subsection. The essential core objects as specified at paragraphs (a) to (c) of section 6(2) are promoting thrift among members by the accumulation of their savings, creating credit for mutual benefit of members at a fair and reasonable rate of interest, and the use and control of members' savings for their mutual benefit.

The extra and optional purposes in section 6(2) include at (d) to (g): purposes as defined relating to training and education of members in the wise use of money, education of members in their economic, social and cultural well-being as members of the community and the improvement of the well-being and spirit of the members' community; and also the provision to its members of such additional services for their mutual benefit, subject to section 48 of the Act, (which gives the Registrar discretion regarding sanctioning additional services). Terms such as community, well-being and spirit are not defined precisely and would be interpreted according to their normal meaning but in the context of the 1997 Act and the co-operative ethos of credit unions.

Essential registration conditions also include those at section 6(1) (b) to (g) which in summary are: restriction of membership to those within the common bonds specified at section 6(3), minimum membership of 15 persons of full age, rules complying with section 13 (which refers to the First Schedule to the Act and the content of rules) and having a registered office in the State. Rules shall be in such form as the Registrar shall require and including matters specified in the First Schedule to the Act and possibly also other additional matters as the Registrar may determine under section 13(1) (b) of the 1997 Act. In that context, the Registrar's powers to determine the form of rules is enabling, not mandatory.

On registration, a credit union would be required to participate in a savings protection scheme approved by the Registrar under section 46(1) and have a policy of insurance as required under section 47 (as a protection against loss due to fraud or dishonesty of officers or voluntary assistants). Section 8 provides for acknowledgement or refusal of registration. When all the required conditions have been met to the Registrar's satisfaction, he issues an acknowledgement of registration which shall be sufficient evidence that the credit union was registered. If the Registrar refuses to register a society as a credit union, he shall notify the society accordingly. If the society is aggrieved by the Registrar's decision, it may apply to the High Court for a review of that decision. If the Court considers that the Registrar's decision should not be confirmed, it may give directions as it thinks appropriate, to the Registrar or otherwise, to resolve the matter.

That implies that the High Court may impose its own decision which could overrule that of the Registrar.

Although not specifically stated in the Act, there is scope for a further appeal to the Supreme Court on a point of law. The High Court procedure and jurisdiction, a type of judicial review, replaces the less expensive system in the District Court under section 2(4) of the 1966 Act regarding review of the Registrar's refusal of registration.

TIME LIMITS ON THE REGISTRAR

There is no time limit in respect of decisions on registration applications under section 8. At the select committee stage of the Dáil debate on the Credit Union Bill, the then Minister of State, Pat Rabbitte, TD, rejected an opposition amendment which would have an imposed a deadline on the Registrar. The legal advice from the parliamentary draftsman and the Attorney General, based on parallels with courts of justice, was that time limits would be inappropriate where the Registrar was discharging judicial functions such as deciding whether a separate corporate entity, such as a credit union, should be established. It would be desirable, however, that a code of good practice should require decisions on registration to be made within a reasonable time.

Statutory time limits are appropriate, however, where the Registrar discharges administrative functions. For example, section 14(5) (a) provides for a three months' time limit (reduced from six months as originally proposed in the Bill) on the Registrar in respect of applications to register amendments to rules. Section 14(5) (b) provides for review by the High Court of refusals to register amendments to rules.

Section 8(5) provides that the Registrar shall enter the names of every credit union in a register maintained for the purposes of the Act, as a continuation of the register kept for the 1966 Act.

CANCELLATION OF REGISTRATION

The Registrar's control and supervisory functions in part VI of the Act, include in section 97 his power to cancel registration of a credit union in specified circumstances: reduction below 15 of numbers of members, original registration obtained by fraud or mistake, or when the credit union had not commenced business within six months of registration, or had suspended its business within 12 months of registration, or that it had ceased to function. Other grounds for cancellation include illegality of purpose, violation of the Act's provisions or cessation of the common bond, dissolution under sections 128, 129 or 135, or winding-up under section 133 or 134. Chapter 12 on Termination refers.

Two months' prior notice of a proposed cancellation is usually required except in winding-up or dissolution. Section 98 provides for suspension of registration for up to three months. Suspension of registration may also apply where a credit union appeals against cancellation of registration. Notices of cancellation, suspension and renewal of suspensions must be published in *Iris Oifigiúil*, the official gazette. Cancellation and suspension result in cessation of privileges of the Act, without prejudice to the enforcement of any liability incurred before such cancellation or suspension.

LIMITS TO REGISTRAR'S FUNCTIONS

In the case of *The Prison Officers' Credit Union* v. *Registrar of Friendly Societies*, reported at [1987] ILRM 367 and discussed by Bird in the annotations in ICSLA R62 on section 14 of the 1997 Act, the High Court defined the limits of the Registrar's jurisdiction and functions in deciding or refusing to register credit union rules or any amendment to them. The credit union appealed to the District Court under section 2(4) of the 1966 Act, against the Registrar's decision not to register an amendment. The District Justice stated a case to the High Court on points of interpretation of the Industrial and Provident Societies Acts 1893–1978. Barrington J in the High Court on 26 June 1986, held that the

Registrar's sole function (in the context of rules and registration) was to enquire whether or not a proposed amendment would result in breach of the Acts. Barrington J concluded that where the Registrar was satisfied that no breach would occur he was under a mandatory duty to register the proposed rules' amendment.

In the Prison Officers' case, the proposed amendments related to definition of officer in standard rule 1 and the deletion of the requirement, in the then rule 138, that the treasurer or assistant treasurer should sign cheques. The Registrar considered that there was no conflict between the definition of officer in standard rule 1 and section 1 of the 1966 Act. In the Registrar's view, the requirement for the treasurer's signature on cheques was a desirable prudential check which should not be lightly set aside. The details of the scenario outlined in the *Prison Officers' Credit Union* case would be altered by the 1997 Act and revised standard rules, for example in the definition of officer (section 2 of the 1997 Act and rule 1) and the treasurer's functions (section 64 of the Act and rule 93). The general principles set out by the High Court regarding the Registrar's functions are still relevant, subject to the enhanced supervisory powers under the 1997 Act. Section 14 (4) of the 1997 Act refers to the Registrar being satisfied that proposed amendments to rules would not be contrary to the provisions of the Act. The High Court judgment used similar wording as to whether or not proposed amendments would result in breach of the Acts.

PRUDENTIAL ROLE

The Registrar's prudential functions were contained in Part III of the Industrial and Provident Societies (Amendment) Act 1978 (No. 23). Although that statute was to a large extent enacted to control and wind down the undesirable activities of deposit-taking industrial and provident societies, it also included specific extra provisions on credit unions.

McMahon v. *Ireland, Attorney General & Registrar of Friendly Societies*, High Court 1987, reported at ILRM 198, Blayney J, held in a case stated from a District Judge dealing with industrial and provident societies that there was a limit to the Registrar's duties. There was not a sufficient relationship of proximity between the Registrar and the plaintiff, a depositor in an industrial and provident society, as to place the Registrar under a duty of care towards her. That case is useful as a guideline on the Registrar's duties towards credit union members, even allowing for substantial changes contained in the 1997 Act enhancing the Registrar's prudential powers and especially section 84(3) indemnifying the Registrar and the State from liability in respect of losses due to the insolvency or default of a registered credit union.

CONTROL AND SUPERVISION OF CREDIT UNIONS BY THE REGISTRAR

Part VI of the 1997 Act, sections 84–106 inclusive, increase considerably the Registrar's powers of control and supervision, including regulation and inspection. The Registrar's role was subject to much debate and some criticism. It was argued that the Registrar's enhanced powers would be too intrusive. The additional powers given to the Registrar, however, are an essential element to ensure that an adequate regulatory framework balances the increased functions and wider role of credit unions. Protecting credit union savings is important not only for members but also in the wider public interest having regard to the extent of the credit union movement in Irish society.

Section 84(1), on the Registrar's general functions, provides that he shall administer the system of regulating and supervising credit unions to protect members' funds and maintain the financial stability and well-being of credit unions generally. Section 84(2) provides wide general powers to do anything necessary to facilitate the exercise of the Registrar's functions. He may also consult the Credit Union Advisory Body (CUAC) and other expert bodies. Under section 84(3), neither the State nor the Registrar shall be liable for any losses incurred through the insolvency or default of a society which is registered as a credit union. (In that context, the *McMahon* case above is relevant.)

Assets and Liabilities, Ratios and Structures

Section 85(3) and (4) underpin the requirement in subsections (1) and (2) that credit unions must keep a minimum proportion of their assets in liquid form to meet its liabilities as they arise, by giving specific powers to the Registrar to assist his supervisory functions. Standard rule 141 reflects section 85 and provides in rule 141(3) that credit unions shall maintain the assets and liabilities, ratios and structures required from time to time by notice from the Registrar or the ILCU. The Registrar may require by notice in writing one or more credit unions to comply with a specified asset/liability ratio or with specified requirements for the composition of its assets or liabilities. The power to give notice shall be exercisable by rules.

Liabilities are defined to include contingent liabilities as the Registrar may specify. He may also specify liquid assets by notice in writing and, until he does so, liquid assets include assets held in a form provided for by section 43 which provides for the types of investment which credit unions may make. It should be noted that the Trustee (Authorised) Investment Order, 1998 facilitates a wider range of investments than previously.

A reference, in section 85(6) (b) in an earlier version of the Bill, to the exclusion of reserves required by section 45 on statutory reserves was deleted at the select committee stage. That deletion brought section 85 provisions nearer to the precedent in section 39(9) of the Building Societies Act, 1989, on which section 85 was modelled.

Control of Advertising

Section 86 of the 1997 Act provides that the Registrar may give directions regarding the content and form of advertising, including the withdrawal or amendment of such advertising. The general purpose was to ensure that credit unions would be subject to controls similar to those imposed on other financial institutions under consumer credit legislation. The Registrar's powers are generally similar to those of the Director of Consumer Affairs under the Consumer Credit Act 1995, and echo those of the Central Bank under section 42 of the Building Societies Act 1989. Amendments at the select committee stage, however, widened the scope of section 86 to include groups or associations of credit unions as well as individual credit unions. That ensures that standard advertising criteria apply to the ICLU or other bodies when they promote savings, loans and interest rates of the credit union movement in general.

Advertisement is defined widely in section 86(3) (a) to include films and electronic communication as well as traditional forms of advertising. Failure to comply with directions under section 86 is a criminal offence, generally dealt with in part XIII of the Act.

REGULATORY DIRECTIONS

The circumstances in which the Registrar may give regulatory directions to a credit union are specified in section 87(1). Circumstances include: a credit union's inability to meet its obligations to its creditors or members; lack of adequate capital resources and, in particular, lack of adequate security for funds entrusted; non-participation in an approved savings scheme or failure to manage such a scheme satisfactorily, and dominance or likely dominance by a member or group. A vital wide-ranging provision in section 87(1) (b) allows regulatory directions to be given if it is expedient to do so in the public interest or in the interest of the orderly and proper regulation of the credit union's business or to protect its members' savings.

The Registrar may also give regulatory directions that a registration application would be refused if it appears to him that a credit union failed to comply with requirements under the Act or was convicted of specified offences, or if circumstances changed since the registration of the credit union,.

The Registrar's directions may include a temporary prohibition on credit unions from raising funds, making payments, acquiring or disposing of assets or liabilities, and also requiring that certain investments be realised within a defined period. Directions may also include specific requirements on loans, including maximum amounts and ratios of loans to savings. The procedures reflect the general thrust but not all the details of banking control legislation, especially section 21 of the Central Bank Act, 1971 as substituted by section 38 of the Central Bank Act, 1989. Despite the regulatory directions, credit unions would still be permitted under section 87(5) to receive funds as voluntary non-repayable donations from its members or other persons approved by the Registrar, or to set-off a member's share capital against his indebtedness to the credit union. Such a set-off would be regarded as a repayment of share capital.

As the Dáil select committee agreed sections 87 and 88 without effective debate, detailed arguments are lacking. The general purpose of the sections, however, is to provide further protection for members' savings and to facilitate the rescue and survival of credit unions experiencing financial difficulties.

Procedural Requirements for Regulatory Directions

Section 88 specifies the procedures for the Registrar when giving regulatory directions under section 87, especially serving the directions at the credit union's registered office. A notice should also be sent to each director and all members of the supervisory committee but failure in that respect shall not affect the validity of the directions. The Registrar has discretion to publish relevant notices in *Iris Oifigiúil* or elsewhere.

A credit union for which the regulatory directions are in force may not be wound up, put into receivership, or have its property attached, sequestered or restrained upon, unless the High Court so orders. This provides a breathing space which may allow the credit union to be rescued from its difficulties. The court may, in the interests of justice, order that the whole or part of the relevant proceedings be held otherwise than in public, that is *in camera*. That would an exception to the general principle of rights arising from article 34.1 of the Constitution of Ireland which provides for the administration of justice in public. Only very limited exceptions to that principle would be allowed, as indicated in the Supreme Court's decision on 2 April 1998 in an appeal case by *The*

Irish Times and other media organisations against a ban on contemporaneous reporting of court proceedings, [1998] 1IR 359.

Failure to comply with the Registrar's regulatory directions is a criminal offence and credit unions convicted shall be liable to fines as specified in section 88(6): £1,000 on summary conviction and £25,000. Fines for breaching regulations may be specified by Ministerial regulations, under section 182, to maxima of £1,000 and £10,000. On the Registrar's application, the High Court has extensive powers under section 89 to prohibit contravention of the Act, including failure to comply with a condition imposed on granting an approval application in respect of additional services under section 49, or failure to comply with regulatory directions. The court may make interim or interlocutory orders.

At the select committee stage, section 89 was amended following representations from the ILCU to delete, in the context of the Registrar's application to the court, the words 'in a summary manner'. That amendment made it clear that the Registrar could not apply *ex parte* to the court and ensured that other relevant parties, especially the credit union, would be notified and given an opportunity of being represented in court.

The Fourth Schedule to the 1997 Act includes extensive supplementary provisions on regulatory directions. A credit union may appeal to the High Court against the making of a regulatory direction. The Registrar may request the court to confirm, extend, revoke or terminate his direction. Under 6 of the Fourth Schedule, where the Registrar forms the opinion that a credit union, to which a regulatory direction was given, is unable to meet its obligations to its members and creditors, and the circumstances giving rise to the direction are unlikely to be rectified, he shall apply forthwith to the High Court. It may order the credit union, in consultation with the Registrar, to prepare a scheme for the orderly termination of its business and discharge of its liabilities under the Registrar's supervision. The court may make any order which it deems fit, including an order to a have a scheme prepared for court consideration for the orderly termination of the credit union affairs. The court may require that the scheme be submitted to it within two months for approval. If regulatory directions are in force, the credit union shall take all necessary steps including those to ensure that its assets are not depleted. The court may make further orders including an order to wind up a credit union.

A practical measure under 10 (c) of the Fourth Schedule to the Act to facilitate members and retain confidence, requires a credit union, for which regulatory directions are in force, to make reasonable arrangements for using its funds to meet members' applications for refunds of monies which they subscribed or deposited.

The elaborate procedures under sections 87–89 and the Fourth Schedule should ensure that the Registrar has effective powers, while protecting credit unions and their members by fair procedures in accordance with the principles of natural justice.

INSPECTION

Section 21 of the 1978 Industrial and Provident Societies (Amendment) Act, part III, provided for the inspection of books and other documents of a credit union by an authorised person, defined as any person or any body of credit unions authorised by the Registrar for the purposes of section 21. Inspections should be distinguished from investigations which require more detailed and searching procedures as outlined later in this chapter.

The thrust, but not all the details, of the earlier provisions of on inspections are contained in an enhanced form in sections 90– 91 of the 1997 Act which also permits an authorised person to remove documents for examination.

The Registrar may set limits and conditions on the inspector's scope and section 90 sets out the powers of an authorised person in relation to an inspection and copying of books and documents of a credit union or associated body. The Registrar could authorise a body such as the ILCU to carry out an inspection. A report of such inspection shall be made to the Registrar by the relevant authorised person.

The Registrar's statutory report for 1981 referred to discussions held with the ILCU about the possibility of its carrying out inspections on the Registrar's behalf. The League was not prepared to undertake that role on terms acceptable to the Registrar. That report referred to the good relations between the Registrar and the ILCU and emphasised that the supervisory activities of the Registry were not intended to diminish the degree of self-supervision exercised by the credit union movement through the League. Standard rule 126(1), reflecting section 76 (1) of the 1997 Act, states that, except, as provided by the 1997 Act or any other enactment, for example, officers, auditors or the supervisory committee, no one (whether a member or not) shall have the right to inspect the books of a credit union. That indicates the importance of confidentiality, except in special circumstances including inspections or investigations. Members have limited rights of access as indicated in section 76(2) (a) and (b) and rule 126(2) (a) & (b) to inspect registers and their own accounts.

In practice, officers of the Registry are authorised to act as inspectors and that procedure is likely to continue. In recent years, professional accountants on the Registry staff have added expertise to the inspection process.

Extensive powers are given in section 91 to a person authorised under section 90 and also to the Registrar, to serve notice on a credit union, its officers and other relevant persons. Such notice would require books and information to be furnished to the Registrar. The notice may require that relevant items be furnished within a period, or at a time and place specified in the notice or that any information be verified by statutory declaration. Section 91(6) provides, under legal professional privilege, for exemption from disclosure requirements for barristers and solicitors.

The Registrar may determine that the officers or former officers of the credit union, or the funds of the credit union, shall bear all or any of the expenses incurred in exercising his functions under section 91(1) in respect of notices to furnish books and other information. Sums required to be paid shall be recoverable summarily by the Registrar as a civil debt in the court of relevant jurisdiction, depending on the amount due.

Accounts and Other Records

Under section 90(3) of the 1997 Act, an authorised person may at the Registrar's request, and on production of his authorisation to any person concerned, at all reasonable times inspect and take copies of or extracts from accounts, deeds, books, records or other documents relating to the business of a credit union. For any of those purposes, the authorised person may enter any premises where such documents are kept.

An inspection may be extended, with the Registrar's approval, to include an inspection of any other society or body corporate which is or has been associated with the credit union being inspected. What precisely constitutes "association" has not been defined but would depend on the facts of the case, company law precedents and a reasonable interpretation of what the authorised officer considered necessary to find out the relevant facts in the credit union being inspected.

STATUTORY REPORT AND WEAKNESSES OBSERVED DURING INSPECTION

The Registrar's statutory reports, available from the Government Publications Sales Office, include in part I on Credit Unions, general information about inspections. Section 106 of the 1997 Act provides for an annual report not later than the end of September each year by the Registrar to the Minister who shall lay a copy of the report before each House of the Oireachtas. The report for 1994-96, under previous legislation, stated that the principal weaknesses observed during those years were very similar to previous years.

The Main Weaknesses Were:

a) Inadequate performance of their statutory duties by the Supervisory Committee. The Registrar recommended that the relevant manual issued by the ILCU be regarded as essential reading;

b) Inadequate control of expenses;

c) Imprudent lending policies which do not take into account the borrower's ability to repay the loan within the specified time;

d) Inadequate procedures relating to loan approvals and inadequate completion of promissory notes;

e) Inadequate monitoring and control of arrears and inadequate review of dormant accounts;

f) Inadequate, or non-existing, financial planning. This can result in lending levels not being determined by means of cash flow projections which, in turn, can lead to excessive bank borrowing by credit unions;

g) Inadequate internal control systems and undue reliance on individual officers for management of the credit union;

h) Inadequate knowledge of the principles of bookkeeping combined with inadequate performance of their statutory duties by Treasurers;

i) Personality differences between Board Members which at times seriously interfere with the proper management of the credit union and which, if allowed to fester, can lead to damaging long-term implications for credit unions;

j) The non-participation in the running of the credit union by some directors who leave the work to a small number of their colleagues;

k) A lack of foresight and effort on the part of some Boards to ensure that there are suitable members available to replace outgoing directors;

l) Loan policies and other directives being passed by word of
    mouth, leading to misunderstandings, although the same
    policies and directives may have been previously noted in
    minutes. Boards of directors should ensure that all policies
    and directives are documented and reviewed annually.

Despite those weaknesses, the Registrar's report states that
inspections indicate that most credit unions carry on their
business in a competent and prudent manner. A policy of random
inspection of a wider range helps to ensure the monitoring of a
cross-section of credit unions, rather than just those with
problems. Additional staff will allow for a substantial increase in
inspections and monitoring compliance with the stricter requirements of the 1997 Act.

REGISTRAR'S FOLLOW-UP ACTION

As explained in his annual reports, the Registrar sometimes finds
it necessary to take serious action following inspection. Repeated
inspections may be made where specific problems and weaknesses
are identified. The Registrar may have detailed discussions with
boards and supervisory committees and he may attend AGMs or
preside over special meetings. Usually such serious action results
in a considerable improvement in the position of credit unions
which have problems.

INVESTIGATIONS

Following precedents for other registered societies, power to
appoint inspectors is vested in the Registrar and not in the courts
as for registered companies. The general procedures differ in some
ways from those in company law. Courts have some specified
functions. For example, inspectors may apply to the High Court
for an order that a person be examined under oath.

Section 92 of the 1997 Act allows the Registrar to take the
initiative in inspections rather than relying on members to
request the Registrar to appoint inspectors. That latter procedure

for members to request an investigation is common to most categories of societies. It derived from section 18 of the Industrial and Provident Societies Act, 1893, and is continued in section 92(1) (a) of the 1997 Act (standard rule 142) with some changes. A minimum of 30 qualifying members of a credit union is now required in a members' application to the Registrar to appoint an inspector to investigate the affairs of a credit union.

The Registrar has discretion in deciding whether or not to appoint such an inspector. Before acting on an members' application or deciding to appoint an inspector on his own initiative, the Registrar shall notify the credit union and its associated bodies, if he is of the opinion that this would not prejudice the interests of members or creditors. He must also consider any explanations received within 14 days of such notification.

Investigation Procedures

Section 92(1) (b) of the 1997 Act provides that when the Registrar is of the opinion that is necessary to do so in the interest of the orderly and proper regulation of the business of a credit union, the Registrar may appoint one or more inspectors to investigate the affairs of the credit union (or may call a special meeting.) For that purpose, the inspector could require the production of all or any of the books, accounts, deeds, records or other documents of the credit union and may examine on oath its offices, members and agents in relation to its business, and may administer an oath to any such person. The Registrar, not the High Court, appoints the inspectors. Extension of the investigation to include societies or bodies corporate associated with the credit union is provided for in section 92(4). Association is not defined and would depend on the circumstances and interpretation.

Supplemental Provisions

Section 93 contains detailed supplemental provisions to ensure effective action and fair procedures during investigations. Subsection (2) requires all persons who are or have been officers, members, voluntary assistants, or agents of a credit union being investigated to produce to the inspector all books, accounts, deeds, documents or other records (in whatever form) relating to the society which are in the power, possession or procurement of such a person. "Agent" has the same meaning as in section 91 and includes bankers, accountants, solicitors, auditors and financial and other advisers.

Sanctions for Non-compliance

The officers and others are otherwise required to give to the inspector concerned all assistance in connection with the investigation which such a person is reasonably able to give.

Under section 93(4), if any relevant person fails, without reasonable excuse, to produce relevant books or documents which it is his duty to do so, fails to attend before an inspector when required to do so, or fails to answer any question put to him by the inspector with respect to the affairs of the credit union or other body, that person shall be guilty of an offence. As the penalty is not specified, the general provisions in part XIII of the Act would apply and, in particular, section 171(2) which provides for penalties not exceeding £1,000 or three months' imprisonment on summary conviction or both, or £5,000 or two years' imprisonment on conviction on indictment, or both.

Examination on Oath by Court

If the inspector thinks it necessary for the purpose of his investigation that a person be examined on oath, he may, under section 93(5), apply to the High Court which may order that person to attend and be examined on oath before it on any matter relevant to the investigation. On any such examination, the inspector may take part by solicitor or counsel (barrister); the Court may put such questions to the persons examined as it thinks fit; the person examined shall answer all such questions as the Court may put to him. He may also at his own cost employ a solicitor (with or without counsel) who may put such questions as the Court may think fit for the purpose of enabling him to explain or qualify any answers given by him.

Notes of the examination shall be taken down in writing, and shall be read over to or by, and signed by, the person examined and may be used in evidence. There is also provision for an interim report to the Registrar by an inspector.

Elaborate procedures were included in the 1978 Act and enhanced in the 1997 Act to ensure that fair procedures and natural justice are observed having regard to the case of *In re Haughey* [1977] IR 217 and rights under the Irish Constitution, especially Article 40 (personal rights) and Article 38 (trial of offences) as discussed by Kelly in Hogan and Whyte (1997).

Company Law Comparisons

The inspection and investigative procedures for credit unions under 1997 Act are in general comparable to, but different in detail from, those under the Companies Acts. Having regard to effectiveness and personal rights, the relevant procedures for credit unions are an improvement on sections 165–173 of the Companies Act, 1963, as repealed by the 1990 Act. Part II of that Act, however, contains very elaborate provisions for investigations. Inspectors for companies are now appointed by the High Court rather than as previously by the Minister. For credit unions, however, the Registrar of Friendly Societies continues to be the appointing authority. Section 9 of the Companies Act 1990 provides for power to extend company investigations into the affairs of related companies and other bodies corporate, which could include industrial and provident societies and also credit unions. Thus company law may be still be relevant to credit union inspections. Court cases on company law may be helpful as precedents for credit unions.

Irish Commercial Society case, unreported judgments of Barron J, High Court, 13.5.1986 and Finlay, CJ, Supreme Court, 16.6.1986 covered areas of the Industrial and Provident Societies (Amendment) Act 1978 on inspections and investigations of societies.

Those cases are a useful reference for credit union law because they deal with the Registrar's regulatory powers, which are comparable to those for credit unions, may provide precedents for credit unions. An outline of such cases is included in the Registrar's annual reports. The Registrar's power to require the society to pay costs of the investigation was challenged in court proceedings in *Irish Commercial Society Ltd.*

Costs of Investigation

The High Court may allow a person examined by it under section 93 such costs as, in its discretion, it may think fit, and any costs so allowed shall be paid as part of the expenses of the investigation. The credit union which was investigated, or persons who sought the investigation, may be required to pay the costs of the investigation in such proportions as the Registrar may direct under section 93(8). That ensures a penalty for bodies or individuals who cause problems by their negligence or other bad behaviour. Courts may also order convicted persons to pay expenses.

Follow-up on Report of Investigation

Section 94(2) (b) provides that the Registrar shall send the report to the High Court where an application had been made under section 93 for examination on oath. A copy must also be forwarded to the Minister who may lay the report before each House of the Oireachtas (Dáil and Seanad) and such publication shall be privileged. If a report is not so laid, the Registrar may have it printed and published. He may also send a copy to the credit union and other specified persons in specified circumstances.

The Registrar may also bring proceedings in the name of the credit union for damages in respect of fraud, misfeasance or other misconduct in a credit union's affairs. The Minister may indemnify the credit union against any costs or expenses incurred in connection with any proceedings brought under section 94(7). Section 94(4) provides that the Registrar shall also refer to the Director of Public Prosecutions (DPP) if an offence involved criminal liability is apparent. Credit unions and their officers must co-operate with any such proceedings under section 94(5).

The Registrar may, under section 92(1), if he is of the opinion that it is necessary to do so in the interest of the orderly and proper regulation of the business of a credit union, call a special general meeting of the credit union, with full powers of a meeting in accordance with the rules. The Registrar has powers on directions for such a meeting, appointing a chairman and levying the expenses on the credit union, officers and members (or former members).

Following an inspection or investigation, the Registrar may, under section 95, appoint a person as a director of a credit union, for such a period and on such terms as he may specify. He may also direct the manner in which the expenses of such an appointment shall be defrayed. Specified persons must co-operate with the appointee, who shall report to the Registrar on the credit union's affairs.

INVESTMENTS

The Registrar's statutory reports for 1994–96 and 1997 pointed out again that the huge inflows of savings in recent years resulted in many credit unions accumulating funds which are surplus to lending requirements. The Registrar warned that a small number of credit unions invested imprudently in equities (shares, quoted on the stock exchange, which may fluctuate in value), by investing through brokers who promised high returns without guarantees of solvency, and by investing in very long-term investments which may not be available to meet urgent demands for liquid cash. Although some investments were legally permissible, prudential requirements have to be taken into account. The Registrar stressed the need for caution when considering the increasingly sophisticated investment products on the market. The Registrar's cautionary approach remains relevant despite the wider choice of investments allowed under the Trustee (Authorised Investments) Order 1998. ILCU arranges specialised advice on investment.

Specific and enhanced provisions on investments, contained in section 43 and section 44 (standard rules 52 and 53), allow for special funds for social, cultural or charitable purposes. These are dealt with in more detail in Chapter 8 on wider operations.

Directions Regarding Interest in Land including Buildings

As pointed out by T.C Bird in his annotations on the 1997 Act in ICLSA R.62, August 1998, the Registrar has untrammelled discretion in respect of a direction, under section 41(5), to a credit union to dispose of an interest in land. Such directions are an exception to the general provision in section 3(3) which provides as follows: any power which the Act confers on the Registrar to give directions shall be exercisable by rules and, for the purposes of section 2 of the Statutory Instruments Act 1947, any rules made by the Registrar under the 1997 Act shall be taken to be of a character affecting a class of the public.

Exemptions deal with situations where regulations are of local interest and thus publication in *Iris Oifigiúil* would not be necessary in such exceptional cases.

Money-laundering

The Registrar's statutory reports for 1994–96 and 1997 referred to the Criminal Justice Act, 1994, relating to the offence of money-laundering and the State's power to confiscate monetary proceeds of criminal activities. The Registrar, after consulting the ILCU, issued to credit unions guidance notes setting out procedures to prevent money-laundering. The Registrar will use those guidance notes as criteria against which he will assess the adequacy of a credit union's internal controls, policies and procedures to counter money-laundering.

Standard rule 116 requires boards of credit unions affiliated to the ILCU to appoint a money-laundering reporting officer to whom all reports of suspected money-laundering offences will be directed, assessed and passed to the Garda, in accordance with the Criminal Justice Act 1994. Section 32 of that Act requires all financial institutions to report suspicious activities to the Garda Síochána. In general, financial institutions are legally required to train their staff to prevent money-laundering.

DISPUTES AND COMPLAINTS: SETTLEMENT AND ARBITRATION

Sections 125 and 126 (rule 158) deal with settlement of disputes and arbitration procedures, some of which relate to the Registrar. Disputes between a credit union and specified persons: members, in their capacity as members, former members or persons claiming through such members or former members or under the rules, shall be settled either:

1) In accordance with the rules;

2) By the Registrar with the parties' consent, unless the rules expressly forbid that course. (Under an old arbitration procedure common to mutual societies, members could refer disputes to the Registrar for adjudication. Under section 126(3) of the 1997 Act, rules may provide that disputes may be determined by the Registrar and such rules will constitute an arbitration agreement under the Arbitration Acts);

3) By the District Court, where the rules do not contain any directions regarding disputes, or where, on the application of a party to the dispute, no decision has been made within 50 days of the dispute being notified to the credit union.

Applications for enforcement decisions under section 125(2) and (3) may be made, under section 125(4) (b), to the District Court and not the Circuit Court, as proposed in earlier drafts of the 1997 Act. In contrast, the High Court has the relevant jurisdiction under the Arbitrations Acts.

Under section 126, where the rules provide for arbitration or settlement of disputes by the Registrar, the relevant legislation applies — the Arbitration Acts 1954 and 1980 as amended by the 1998 Act. The Registrar shall be deemed to be a single arbitrator for the purposes of the Arbitration Acts and his arbitration functions may be devolved to an adjudicator appointed by the Minister under section 127, or by an adjudicator appointed under a non-statutory scheme.

A scheme for investigation of complaints, a type of ombudsman, may be established under Ministerial regulations following consultation with the Registrar, CUAC and other relevant expert bodies. Ombudsman schemes in the insurance and financial services would not normally apply to disputes or complaints arising from the usual credit union activities but could apply to related insurance services. ILCU standard rule 158 contains detailed procedures for settling disputes and complaints.

The general thrust of the above is to provide modern systems for solving credit union disputes and complaints in accordance with arbitration and ombudsman schemes in other spheres. The ILCU rules, as distinct from the standard rules for credit unions, provide for a system of arbitration for settlement of disputes arising within the credit union movement.

ADMINISTRATIVE FUNCTIONS

The Registrar's administrative powers and duties in respect of records, inspection fees, information and reports are set out in sections 100–106 of the 1997 Act. In accordance with the usual requirements for registered companies and societies, a file on each credit union must be kept for public inspection and should include relevant documents and records of matters required under the Act to be kept in such public file. Section 100(2) lists other documents, copies of which are required to be placed on the public file, including all special resolutions, transfer of engagement documents, winding-up or dissolution orders, administration orders, court orders under section part XII of the Act which deals with the appointment of an examiner, and also any other prescribed document. Members of the public may inspect the public files and obtain copies of relevant documents.

Requirements for delivery of required documents including periodic accounts, statements and returns to the Registrar in both legible and non-legible form (by electronic means or otherwise) are dealt with in sections 103 and 104. Section 186 of the Act provides that records additional to those under section 108 must be maintained, as the Registrar may specify by directions.

CONCLUSION

This chapter concentrates mainly on the Registrar's control and supervisory functions. Some of these are also considered in other parts of the book as they relate to the operations of credit unions. For example, the Registrar's powers to remove or suspend members of the board of directors or the supervisory committee are considered in Chapter 6 on Governance. Some functions of the Registrar are dealt with as appropriate in other chapters, for example regarding auditors in Chapter 10. In particular, the Registrar has power under section 113(9), rule 149(9), to order a credit union not to elect or re-elect a particular person as an auditor.

A useful analysis of the Registrar's role and functions, together with an interview with him, were included in a dissertation by Daniel M. O'Leary, in 1988 for the National Diploma in Business Studies, NIHE, now the University of Limerick. Since then, improved facilities are available to the Registrar's Office, especially in the accounting and computer areas. There is scope for even further improvements following the 1997 Act and increased staffing and other resources.

It is evident from the detailed provisions outlined above, that the Registrar has considerable powers in the control and supervision of credit unions, considerably strengthened by the 1997 Act. Many of those powers, such as investigations of affairs, are in reserve to be used in extreme cases. Other powers, such as inspection of books rather than the more extensive investigation of affairs, are used frequently as a check to protect credit union members.

The supervision of credit unions on an all-Ireland basis in the context of the Belfast Agreement, as suggested by Noel Treacy TD, Minister of State at the Department of Enterprise, Trade and Employment, in his speech at the annual dinner of the ILCU in

1998, would have fundamental implications for the Registrar's role.

The Registrar is influential when making critical statements, as in his report for 1997, for example, about auditing standards in credit unions and on the need for prudence by credit unions. The views have to be taken seriously by relevant parties who should be alert to problems and seek relevant professional advice on legal and accountancy matters.

The credit union movement is, to a large extent, self-regulatory through active members, officers and managers, combined with the League's system of support and supervision. The Registrar keeps in touch with this voluntary role by attending meetings of local chapters and also the ILCU's AGM. His office provides an important supervisory framework to protect credit union members in the public interest. The supervisory functions may change in the future if the government establishes a single regulatory authority for all financial bodies including credit unions.

In summary, at this stage the Registrar is the official watchdog with sharpened teeth who has been endowed by the new credit union legislation of 1997.

Chapter 10

ACCOUNTS, AUDITORS AND WATCHDOGS

"It is the duty of an auditor to bring to bear on the work he
has to perform that skill, care and caution which a
reasonably competent, careful and cautious auditor would
use. An auditor is not bound to be a detective.
He is a watchdog, not a bloodhound."

Lopez LJ — Re Kingston Cotton Mills (No.2)
([1896] 2. Ch. 279 at 288/9)

The above quotation from a company law case in the English
Chancery Court is a starting point for auditing requirements. As
law and practice have evolved since the Victorian era, more
exacting standards would now be required.

In common with companies and other bodies registered in
accordance with specific Acts, credit unions are required by law to
keep books of account. These must be audited by qualified
auditors who examine and adjust accounts to ensure that they are
correct and in accordance with law. The detailed requirements for
accounts and audits vary according to the specific type of company
or society.

The basic provision on societies' auditors was in section 13 of
the Industrial & Provident Societies Act, 1893, as amended by
section 2 of the 1913 Act which provided that public auditors
would be mandatory, and by section 7 of the Credit Union Act,
1966. Sections 29 of the Industrial and Provident Societies
(Amendment) Act, 1978, applied also to credit unions. Sections 29
and 30 of the 1978 Act repeated, with some improvements, the
requirements of section 7 of the 1966 Act and applied higher
standards, including the true and fair view, to all societies. The

Minister could make regulations specifying the form and content of income and expenditure accounts and balance sheets.

Part VII, sections 107–124 of the Credit Union Act, 1997, as reflected in rules 143–157 of the ILCU revised standard rules, provide modern consolidated provisions on accounts, audits and auditors.

BASIC REQUIREMENTS

Section 108 of the 1997 Act and rule 144 (reflecting provisions of the Building Societies Act, 1989) include comprehensive provisions. In summary, they require every credit union to establish and maintain in the State proper accounting records and control systems and to take adequate precautions to ensure the safe keeping and storage of the accounting records, so that they may be available readily for inspection by the directors and the Supervisory Committee members. Such books of account shall be a correct record and explanations of the credit union's transactions, receipts and expenditure, and also the assets and liabilities. Proper accounting records shall be deemed to be kept if they comply with the specified requirements in respect of accurate recording, including a record of services provided and transactions in respect of new services under section 48 of the 1997 Act, rule 59, and give a true and fair view of the state of the credit union's affairs and explain its transactions.

True and Fair View

The true and fair view accounting requirement is required under sections 108(4) and 111(1) (b) and (c) of the 1997 Act, [rules 144(4) and 147(1) (a), (b) and (c)]. The courts have not defined comprehensively the true and fair view concept which is a basic element in company accounts. Described as a term of art, it is an elusive concept which is difficult to define but is useful in practice. The true and fair view, in essence, requires that accounts reflect the actual financial position and give a clear overall picture.

Compliance with required technical rules does not necessarily mean that a true and fair view is shown. Some accounting rules and conventions may, if rigidly applied in specific cases, give a distorted picture. Therefore, allowance has to be made for the size, materiality and relevance of specific figures. Accounts should contain sufficient information in quantity and depth to satisfy the reasonable expectations of readers to whom they are addressed, especially the members.

ACCOUNTS AND RECORDS

Before considering auditing aspects in more detail, it is necessary to highlight some specific requirements on accounts and records.

Books and records must be kept at the registered office or such other place as the board considers suitable and be at all reasonable times open to inspection by directors and the supervisory committee. Records must be kept for a period of not less than six years under section 108(6) of the 1997 Act and rule 144(6), but, as rule 166(1) points out, some records must be retained permanently including: receipts for securities held; various registers including those of shares, deposits, loans, nominations, members and officers' loans; registered copies of rules; annual returns and applications and promissory notes for outstanding loans. Section 186(1) of the 1997 Act and rule 166(2) provide that in addition to records required under section 108, credit unions shall maintain other records as may be specified by the Registrar's directions.

Section 109 of the 1997 Act and rule 145, specify that control systems under section 108(1) and rule 144(1) are those for the control of the conduct of affairs such that accurate information is delivered regularly and promptly to enable officers, the auditor and the Registrar to discharge their functions. A system for safe custody of all documents of title must also be established.

Section 110 of the 1997 Act and rule 146 set out the accounting principles to be followed by a credit union in preparing its accounts, including the presumption that the business is carried on as a going concern with consistency in its accounting policies.

Any decisions by directors to depart from those principles must be justified in a note to the accounts.

Section 111 of the 1997 Act and rule 147 require the directors to prepare or cause to be prepared annual accounts, comprising an income and expenditure account, balance sheet, any auditor's statement, and such supplementary information as is required by or under the Act, so that they give a true and fair view of the state of affairs for each financial year. Unless the Registrar allows otherwise, accounts shall include corresponding particulars for the preceding financial year. Accounts shall not be published unless they were audited and contain the auditor's report. Specified officers must also sign the accounts before publication.

Section 112 of the 1997 Act and rule 148 require credit unions to keep a copy of the latest audited balance sheet, and also a copy of the auditor's report on the balance sheet, available for inspection by members at all reasonable times. A notice must be displayed at all times in a conspicuous position at the registered office informing members that those documents are available. That replaces the previous requirement that financial information be displayed publicly in credit union offices.

TREASURER'S FUNCTIONS

Section 64 of the 1997 Act and rule 93 provide details of the treasurer's functions regarding books of accounts including:

- Not later than the last day of each month the treasurer must submit to the board of directors an unaudited financial statement (and described as such) showing the income and expenditure for the period from the beginning of the current financial year to the end of the preceding month, and a balance sheet for the same period. In summary, a type of running commentary up-dated each month is required;

- Report to the members at every general meeting;

- Prepare and submit to the auditor such financial reports and returns as the auditor may require;

Under section 108(7) of the Act and rule 144(7), where accounting records are kept at a place other than the registered office, the treasurer shall be responsible for keeping a written record of their location. Further information about the treasurer's functions is given in Chapter 6 on Governance.

AUDITING AND AUDITORS

As provided by section 113 and rule 149, the members at each AGM shall elect, by a majority of members present and voting, an auditor who shall hold office from the conclusion of that meeting until the next AGM. The previous procedure for appointing an auditor at the organisation meeting of a new credit union has been replaced by section 113(3) and rule 149(3), providing for the first auditor to be appointed by the directors before the first annual general meeting. Such first auditor shall hold office until the first AGM when he shall be eligible for re-election.

Under section 113(8) and rule 149(8), the election of a firm by its name to be the auditor shall be deemed to be an election of those persons who from time to time during the period of appointment are the partners in that firm as from time to time constituted and are qualified to be auditors of the credit union. The partners in such firm may be qualified to act as auditors only if they have practising certificates and fulfil the statutory requirements including section 187 of the Companies Act, 1990.

The board may fill any casual vacancy, for example if the auditor retires or vacates office due to disqualification or is removed from office during the year: section 113(7) of the 1997 Act and rule 149(7). While such vacancy continues, the surviving or continuing auditor or auditors may act. A general meeting may, by resolution, remove an auditor, despite any agreement he may have with the credit union, and without prejudice to any rights of the auditor under the Act.

The Registrar has extensive powers regarding auditors under section 113 and rule 149. He may appoint an auditor where none is elected at the AGM and may make a prohibitory order to a credit union not to elect, re-elect or appoint a named person as auditor, if he is of the opinion that it would not be in the orderly or proper regulation of business under section 113(9) of the Act and rule 149(9). The credit union may appeal to the High Court against the Registrar's decision under section 113(10) and rule 149(10), but subject to any direction or decision of that court, the credit union shall comply with the Registrar's order.

STATUTORY REQUIREMENTS FOR AUDITORS

Acts under which companies and societies are registered require in the public interest that accounts be audited by suitably qualified persons. This requirement is usually by satisfied holders of valid practising certificates who are members of recognised accountancy bodies traditionally recognised by the Minister under section 187 of the Companies Act, 1990: The Institute of Chartered Accountants in Ireland (and also in England and Wales), the Chartered Association of Certified Accountants, and the Institute of Certified Public Accountants in Ireland. A recent addition of the Institute of Incorporated Public Accountants was challenged by the Consultative Committee of Accountancy Bodies in Ireland (CCAB–I) through judicial review. Authorisation by the Minister as a public auditor under the Companies Acts also qualifies a person to audit credit union accounts.

Equivalent qualifications may also be recognised on the basis of reciprocity and European Community requirements. Qualifications for auditors of accounts of friendly and industrial & provident societies, however, were traditionally based on the concept of public auditors who were specially authorised by the Minister or other relevant authority. For industrial and provident societies, the public auditor requirement derives from section 2, Industrial and Provident Societies (Amendment) Act, 1913.

The modern trend, however, is to align the requirements for society and credit union auditors with those under company law. That trend was reflected in part X of the Companies Act, 1990, (No. 33) to ensure that high standards were met and that auditors were properly qualified and impartial. The consolidated modern provisions are in section 114 of the Credit Union Act, 1997, (as reflected in rule 150) which follows the company law principles but makes some changes, especially the inclusion of voluntary assistant as well as officers in the categories for exclusions from acting as auditor.

EXCLUSIONS

For the sake of impartiality and to avoid conflicts of interest, an auditor may not hold any other office in connection with the credit union. Section 114(2) of the Credit Union Act, 1997 and rule 150(2), exclude from appointment as auditor of a credit union specified categories such as:

a) A person who is, or at any time during the period of three years preceding the meeting at which the election is to be made has been, an officer or voluntary assistant of the credit union. In the 1997 Act, officers are defined in section 2(1) and rule 1 to include employees.

   The three-year period, suggested by the Credit Union Advisory Committee (CUAC), replaced a blanket prohibition in an earlier draft of the legislation. The Minister of State, Mr. Pat Rabbitte, TD, explained at the Dáil select committee stage that amendment to three years should allow for a situation where former voluntary workers could subsequently be appointed auditor after a three year gap;

b) Near relatives — parent, spouse, brother, sister or children — of officers;

c) A person who is a partner of, or in the employment of, or who employs, an officer or voluntary assistant of the credit union.

Elections in contravention of the above provisions shall be ineffective for the purposes of the 1997 Act.

"Partner" is presumably intended in the precise legal sense within a business partnership and not in the wider colloquial meaning of spouses or couples living together. Such situations could also give rise to conflicts of interest which may require disclosure and possible disqualification.

Under section 115 of the 1997 Act and rule 151, a person elected or appointed as auditor for a financial year and who continues to be qualified under the Act, shall be eligible at the date of the AGM for election, re-election or re-appointment unless there are specified circumstances such as incapacity or a prohibitory order by the Registrar under section 113 (9).

Section 116 of the 1997 Act empowers the Registrar to remove an auditor from office in the members' or creditors' interest or for the orderly or proper regulation of the business. There is no standard rule related to this regulatory provision. To ensure fair procedures and natural justice, an auditor may appeal to the High Court against his removal in accordance with procedures in the Fifth Schedule to the Act, adapted by substituting references to auditor for those referring to director or member. Court proceedings may be held *in camera* thereby excluding the public.

Requiring that auditors be appointed by the members is in accordance with company law practice of ensuring that primary consideration is given to members' interests and that auditors are not under directors' influence. In his report in 1997, the Registrar said that he referred to the appropriate authorities specific details about two auditors resulting in successful prosecutions for breaches of the law.

APPOINTMENT AND REMOVAL OF AUDITOR

Based on section 84 of the Building Societies Act, 1989, section 117 of the 1997 Act and rule 152 provide for at least 28 days' notice to the credit union, the auditor and the Registrar of resolutions at an AGM about removing the auditor early or affecting the retiring auditor. After seven days, the credit union must inform members of the proposed resolution, with notice of the general meeting or, if that is not practicable, by advertisement in at least two appropriate newspapers. The relevant auditor may require the credit union (unless the Registrar decides otherwise) to notify the members of any written representations which the auditor makes and to arrange that such representations be read out at the meeting. That procedure would not prejudice the auditor's right to be heard orally. As a further safeguard of fair procedures, an auditor removed from office shall be entitled to receive notice of specified general meetings and to be heard at them.

AUDITORS' DUTIES DISTINCT FROM THOSE OF CREDIT UNION

It is important, especially for boards and auditors, to be clearly aware of the distinctions between the duties of the credit union and those of the auditor. In summary, the credit union must keep proper accounting records (section 108 and rule 144), have proper systems of control (section 109 and rule 145) and also have an income and expenditure account and balance sheet prepared which give a true and fair view (section 111 and rule 147). It is also the credit union's duty to appoint an auditor (section 113 and rule 149). Section 110 (rule 146) contains the accounting principles for determining the amounts to be included in accounts, for example that the credit union shall be presumed to be carrying on business as a going concern and that accounting policies be consistent.

Auditors, when appointed, have their own distinct duties. The auditor's duties are set out in section 120 (rule 155) which are, in effect, the interface between the respective duties of the credit union and those of the auditor. The relevant provisions deal with the auditors' reports, right of access to books and documents and right to be heard at general meetings. Section 120(3), (4) and (5), reflected to some extent in rule 155, set out what the auditor must report on. In effect, that is the scope of the audit. The auditor must report to members on accounts examined and the annual accounts to be laid before the credit union. Before signing the report, the auditor shall meet with the directors and the Supervisory Committee and draw to their attention any relevant matter.

When preparing reports, auditors must include statements and opinions as specified in section 120(3) and rule 155 (3), about proper books and accounting records, conformity with statutory requirements and the true and fair view. The auditor must also state whether the accounts contain any statement required under section 111(1)(c) by the auditor's professional accountancy body. Under section 120(4) and rule 155(4), if an auditor's report relates to any accounts other than the income and expenditure account for the financial year for which the auditor was appointed, the report must state whether those accounts give a true and fair view.

Section 120(5) requires the auditor to investigate whether the credit union kept proper books and records and adequate control systems. Any failures must be stated in the report.

In accordance with section 120(6) and rule 155(5), the auditor must be given access to all books and documents and to information and explanations within the knowledge of officers and voluntary assistants. Under section 120(7) and rule 155(6), an auditor shall be entitled to attend any general meeting and to be heard on any relevant part of the business. The credit union must give the auditor notice of, and any communications about, the general meeting.

ACCOUNTING GUIDELINES

The professional accounting bodies, including the Institute of Chartered Accountants in Ireland and the Chartered Association of Certified Accountants, through the CCAB-I, issue various technical guidelines and other documents to assist accountants and auditors in their practices. Miscellaneous Technical Statements, M22 and M23, deal with credit unions in the Republic of Ireland and Northern Ireland respectively. Those comprehensive statements cover: the legal background, duties of officers and committees, including the supervisory committee, requirements for loans and other financial transactions, and accounting procedures in detail.

Document M 22, which is being up-dated to take account of the 1997 Act, explains duties of the auditors. They are required:

1) To express an opinion as to whether the income and expenditure account and balance sheet give a true and fair view of the credit union's result for the latest financial period and of its state of affairs as at the balance sheet date.

2) To report whether, in the auditor's opinion
   (i)   The credit union has kept "proper books" with which the accounts are in agreement, and
   (ii)   The credit union has complied with the relevant statutory provisions, and
   (iii) All the information and explanation which the auditor considers necessary have been obtained.

Auditors are also required to follow other general professional auditing guidelines, for example on planning, controlling and recording their work. The professional guideline, *Auditing in a Computer Environment*, is relevant as credit unions are becoming more computerised. The guidelines are revised periodically.

The professional bodies' requirements were backed by the statutory provision in section 120(3) (e) of the 1997 Act and rule 155(3) (e), by requiring auditors' reports to indicate whether any statements necessary under section 111(1) (c) and required under rule 147(1) (c) were included in the annual accounts.

The Minister, after consulting the CUAC and other expert bodies, may make regulations about annual accounts and their audit, under section 121. An additional provision empowering the Minister to specify a programme of audit procedures was deleted at the Dáil select committee stage, following objections from ILCU.

RESIGNATION OF AUDITORS

Under the procedures in section 118 (rule 153), an auditor may resign by serving notice on the credit union and the Registrar. Such notice would be effective from a date not less than 28 days after it is served. The notice must include either a statement that there are no circumstances connected with the resignation which must be brought to the notice of members or creditors, or otherwise a statement of such circumstances must be included. A credit union receiving such a statement of circumstances must send within 14 days a copy of the notice to everyone entitled to notice of a general meeting. The Registrar may decide, after an application by the credit union or aggrieved persons, that the notice would be likely to diminish substantially public confidence in the credit union or that the rights conferred are being abused to secure needless publicity for defamatory matter. In such cases, the notice need not be sent.

Based on section 86 of the Building Societies Act, 1989, section 119 of the 1997 Act and rule 154, add further safeguards of fair procedures by allowing a resigning auditor to requisition the convening of a general meeting by the directors. They must then within 14 days convene a meeting for a date not more than 30 days after the notice was served. Unless the Registrar decides otherwise, statements of circumstances notified by the auditor are also circulated to members. Persons who resigned as auditors shall be notified of subsequent general meetings and be permitted to attend them and be heard by the members.

Registrar's Warning

The Registrar, in his annual report for 1997, stated that, where it came to his attention that auditors failed to perform their functions adequately, he would take appropriate action. Details of unauthorised persons acting as auditors would be sent to the appropriate prosecuting authorities. Action will also be taken where persons are apparently acting as auditors in circumstances suggesting an attempt to circumvent the intentions of the legislation.

ANNUAL RETURN

Section 124 of the 1997 Act and rule 157, require each credit union to submit an annual return to the Registrar, not later than 31st March in each year. The return must contain specified material and be made up to the end of the latest financial year, unless the Registrar allows otherwise. The annual return, including accounts, should be accompanied by the auditor's report, in the required format as set out in Form AR 28, Credit Union Annual Return to Registrar. The relevant standard rule 157 also requires that the return be sent to the ILCU. The latest return must also be available without charge to members.

MONITORING OF ACCOUNTS

Annual accounts must be submitted by each credit union to the official supervisory authority: Registrar in Dublin or Belfast and also to the ILCU. The Registrars have a statutory responsibility for ensuring that required standards are met. There are also prudential considerations in the Registrar's examination of annual returns and accounts to ensure that credit unions do not put their members' savings at risk. In Dublin, information from the annual returns is input into computers and held on data base. The system is compatible with that of the League but there are differences of emphasis between the Registry and the ILCU. The Registry's specific functions in checking accounts include solvency and liquidity tests and also ratio analysis. The Registrar has to ensure that the ratio of statutory reserves is being maintained. Problem credit unions are highlighted and remedial action taken. There are follow-up visits by a professional accountant and other staff from the Registrar's office on both a targeted and a random basis. As explained in Chapter 9, the Registrar's annual statutory report also highlights accounting and auditing deficiencies.

The auditor must report to the Registrar in the circumstances specified in section 122, including any belief that there are material defects in accounting records or systems for control or safekeeping of important documents. The auditor must also report to the Registrar, on request, whether a credit union has compiled as specified with the Act.

It is an offence under section 123 if officers or voluntary assistants recklessly make statements which are misleading, false or deceptive in a material particular, or if an auditor fails to provide, within five days, information or explanations within his knowledge. Defences on the grounds of reasonableness are provided in section 123(4). Standard rule 156 reflects the purposes, but not all the details, of section 123 by requiring officers or voluntary assistants not to knowingly or recklessly make misleading, false or deceptive statements to auditors in respect of statutory requirements.

Monitoring by the League

As outlined in Chapter 12, the ILCU utilises its sophisticated computer system to monitor annual accounts and returns as a vital element of the savings protection scheme (SPS). The CAMEL score report system is used to rate the performance of each credit union in relation to other credit unions with comparable assets. Ratios are devised, for example, of net loans over thirteen weeks in arrears as a percentage of gross loans. Remedial action has to be taken by the League in a small number of cases and further monitoring may be necessary in other cases. The League's sophisticated system depends on the quality of the information furnished in accounts. Thus accurate and up-to-date accounts for each credit union are vital. Officers, especially treasurers, accountants and auditors, have a vital role to ensure a high standard of accounts.

RESPONSIBILITIES OF AUDITORS AND CREDIT UNIONS

The quotation at the start of this chapter should be considered and interpreted in the light of modern conditions and in relation to mutual societies such as credit unions where members have an active role. In *Irish Woollen Co Ltd* v. *Tyson* (1900) 26 *The Accountant Law Report* 13, Fitzgibbon LJ said that the earlier reference to the auditor being a watchdog not a bloodhound, was very unfair to the bloodhound who would be just as little likely to have his sense of suspicion aroused as the watchdog. Was the watchdog not bound to bark and thus follow up any trails discovered when sniffing? As in the case of the hound, the auditor will follow up the trail to the end. That stricter view of auditors' duties is more in accordance with company modern law, e.g., *Re Thomas Gerrard & Son Ltd* [1967] All ER 525 Chancery Division.

Although the relevant cases, quoted above, arose in company law, they provide precedents for credit union auditors because of the alignment of qualifications for auditors of companies and societies including credit unions.

Members and especially officers should be aware of the importance of effective audits of high standards. Credit unions should not be unduly influenced by cost, personal bias or local connections when choosing auditors. It is false economy for credit unions to skimp on audit fees at the expense of adequate audits. Many boards are relatively unsophisticated in financial matters and depend on good quality auditing to deter and detect financial irregularities. Officers should co-operate with auditors, for example by encouraging procedures such as issuing circulars to members to ensure that balances in accounts are correct. Audits during the year, and not only at the end of the financial year, are advisable.

The lack of accounting expertise within some credit unions places a greater onus on auditors to ensure adequate internal systems so that accounts meet proper standards and that the true and fair view can be confidently asserted. Outside their official duties, auditors should be helpful and supportive to credit unions. It should be especially noted, however, that sections 108 and 109 and rules 144 and 145, place onerous duties on credit unions to maintain adequate accounting records and also systems of control and safe custody.

There are heavy duties imposed on auditors by statute and professional standards but they cannot be expected to check every detail. Treasurers and other officers should carry out checks, and members, in the spirit of mutuality, take a keen interest in their credit union's accounts.

Adequate internal control procedures are vital to ensure efficient operation of accounting systems within a credit union. Such procedures should not depend on specific individuals but should operate objectively irrespective of the personnel who operate them. Control systems recommended by the ILCU should also be followed by the Supervisory Committee and other officers. To supplement the formal safeguards, which have been enhanced by the 1997 Act, officers and members should be their own watchdogs.

Chapter 11

EXAMINERS AND ADMINISTRATORS

"The principal function of the examiner is to investigate the
viability of the company, and where appropriate,
to formulate proposals for a survival scheme for presentation to the members and creditors, and ultimately to the
court . . . the examiner is given a wide range of powers to
assist him in carrying out his primary obligation.
The legislation also permits the court to grant further
powers to the examiner where necessary."

O'Donnell, *Examinerships*, Oak Tree Press, 1994.

EXAMINERS

The above extract was written in the context of the Companies
(Amendment) Act, 1990, as amended by section 180 and 181 of the
Companies (No. 2) Act, 1990, as construed with the other
Companies Acts. The quoted extract, however, may, with suitable
adaptations, be applied to credit unions having regard to
statutory differences.

Although it was an innovation in the Credit Union Act, 1997 to
apply the concept of examiners (and administrators) to credit
unions, there was very little parliamentary discussion on these
topics. The innovation recognised the complex nature of modern
credit unions and their extensive financial structures. The
provisions on examiners in part XII, sections 142 to 170 of that
Act, were mainly based on the principles in the company law
model, suitably adapted for credit unions. Changes, however, were
made to take account of recommendations in the first report of the

Company Law Review Group, December 1994, especially the following:

- Before appointing an examiner to a credit union the court must be satisfied that there is a reasonable prospect of the credit union surviving. That is a more onerous requirement than the company law model of facilitating the survival of a company;

- The general period for examinership is reduced from three months to 70 days;

- An independent accountant's report must accompany the petition for appointment of an examiner;

- Creditors have a statutory right of attendance at the court hearing of a petition to appoint an examiner.

Therefore, in the above respects, when this book was being written, credit union law on examiners was more advanced than company law but changes in that legislation were being considered.

The company law model was based in some respects on comparable American and English legislation aimed at rescuing companies in financial difficulties. An administrator under the UK Insolvency Act, 1986, has a role like a receiver, which in some ways is more akin to that of an administrator under part XI of the Credit Union Act, 1997, than to examiners under part XII of that Act.

Most credit unions have an excellent record of financial stability which is supported by the statutory scheme of prudential supervision under the Registrar of Friendly Societies. The enhanced regulatory framework under the 1997 Act is supported by the systems put in place by the ILCU, especially monitoring and savings protection schemes. Nevertheless, provisions for appointing examiners and administrators are a useful fallback in extreme cases where financial problems arise but rescue and restoration of viability is possible.

High Court's Power to Appoint Examiner

Section 142 of the Credit Union Act, 1997, provides that on the petition of specified persons, the High Court may appoint an examiner to a credit union to examine the state of its affairs. Appointment of examiners arises only where there are severe financial problems, that is in situations where it appears *inter alia* that the credit union is or is likely to be unable to pay its debts. The emphasis is on insolvency and the process cannot be abused as a method of enforcing debt collection. The court must also be satisfied that there is a reasonable prospect of the credit union's surviving as a going concern.

Under section 142(3), specified persons who may present a petition for appointing an examiner are the Registrar, or, with his consent, all or any of the following, together or separately: a credit union, its directors, a qualifying group of members of the credit union, and (unlike in current company law) a creditor, or contingent or prospective creditor, (including an employee of the credit union). A qualifying group comprises at least 30 members of 12 months' standing or, if less than 30, at least 10% of the members on the date of application for the Registrar's consent.

Section 142(5) states that a credit union is unable to pay its debts if it is unable to pay them as they fall due, or if the value of its assets is less than the amount of its liabilities, taking into account contingent and prospective liabilities. Section 142 is reflected in principle but not in detail, in rule 165 as the ILCU standard rules do not include all the statutory details on examiners that are included in the Act of 1997.

Petition for Protection of the Court

Section 143 of the Act specifies that the petition presented under section 142 shall nominate the person to be appointed examiner. Unlike in current company law, the petition shall also be accompanied under section 143(1) (b) by a report of an independent accountant (either the auditor or a person qualified to be auditor of a credit union) as specified under section 145 and also by a consent signed by the person nominated to be the examiner.

Section 143 sets out grounds on which a court shall not hear or may, at its discretion, decline to hear a petition, including requirements for security for costs and exercise of utmost good faith. The latter measure in section 143(2) is a deterrent to unwarranted petitions or abuse of the process.

The court, on hearing a petition, may dismiss it, or adjourn the hearing conditionally or unconditionally, or make any interim or other orders, including restricting the exercise of the powers of the directors or of the credit union.

When a order is made, a copy shall be delivered to the Registrar for placing on the public file. Further publicity is required under section 154 by requiring delivery to the Registrar of a copy of an order of appointment and by publication of the appointment in *Iris Oifigiúil* and two daily newspapers circulating in the area. The examiner's failure to comply with the requirement relating to publicity would be an offence.

Circuit Court's Powers

Under section 144, where a credit union's total liabilities (taking into account contingent and prospective liabilities) do not exceed £250,000, the High Court may order that the relevant matters concerning examinership may be remitted to the Circuit Court which shall have full jurisdiction to exercise all the powers conferred on the High Court. An advantage would be to reduce costs. The appropriate circuit would be that where the credit union's registered office is situated. A similar discretionary power in section 3(9) of the Companies (Amendment) Act, 1990, is rarely, if ever, utilised because, in practice, the assets of relevant companies would normally exceed the £250,000 threshold. The Circuit Court jurisdiction, however, may be more relevant for credit unions because of their wide geographical base but the low threshold of £250,000 in liabilities would exclude medium and large credit unions.

Independent Accountant's Report

Section 145 outlines the material, including a statement of affairs and an opinion whether the credit union would have a reasonable chance of survival as a going concern, which must be included in the report of independent accountant. An innovation in section 145(1) (j) requires details of the extent and sources of funding required to keep the credit union in existence during the examinership, the expenses of which would rank ahead of existing debts. That could affect existing creditors but they may make a submission to the court on the possible effects on their position. Under section 145(1) (k), debts incurred before the petition is presented may be recommended by the independent accountant for payment.

The independent accountant must supply a copy of his report to the credit union and the Registrar (but not for the public file) on the same day as he delivers it to the court. Upon written application members and creditors may also be supplied with a copy of the report. If the court directs, the report shall omit such parts as the court thinks fit.

Interim Protection Pending Report

Under section 146, in exceptional circumstances where the independent accountant's report is not available, the court may make an interim protection order for a period of grace of up to ten days. The directors shall provide all reasonable assistance in preparing the report. If it is not available after ten days, the court's protection ceases but without prejudice to a further petition being presented to the court.

Effect on Creditors and Others of Petition to Appoint Examiner

The fundamental provisions in section 147(1) state that a credit union shall be under the court's protection for the period beginning with the presentation of the report and ending after 70 days from that date, unless, in exceptional circumstances, the court extends the protection period under section 157(4) or (5) or unless the petition is withdrawn or refused. Section 147(2) of the Credit Union Act, 1997, reflecting the principles, but not all the details of section 5(2) of the Companies (Amendment) Act, 1990, defines the effect of court protection which includes that no proceedings for winding up may be commenced, no receiver may be appointed over the assets and creditors' rights are suspended. In summary, the main effect is to protect the credit union from its creditors and to provide a breathing space for formulating a survival plan.

As indicated by T.C. Bird in his detailed annotations on the examinership provisions of the Credit Union Act, 1997, in ICLSA, R62 August 1998, the company law concept of protecting minorities from oppression was excluded from the 1997 Act because it was unnecessary in view of the one-member-one-vote principle.

Effect on Receiver or Provisional Liquidator

Section 148 of the Credit Union Act, 1997, prevents conflicting situations between two court-appointed officers, such as an examiner and receiver operating at the same time. Reflecting the principles but not all the details of section 6 of the Companies (Amendment) Act 1990, section 148 provides that:

Where, at the time when an examinership petition is presented, a receiver or provisional liquidator stands appointed to the whole or part of the assets, the court may make such orders as it thinks fit, including the cessation of the receivership or liquidation. Where an examinership petition is presented under section 142 of the 1997 Act, after a winding-up petition has been presented but before a provisional liquidator is appointed or a winding-up order made, the court shall hear both petitions together: section 148(4) of the Credit Union Act, 1997, based on section 6(5) of the Companies (Amendment) Act, 1990.

Examiner's Powers

Section 149 of the 1997 Act, reflecting most of section 7 of the Companies (Amendment) Act, 1990, provides that the auditor's rights and powers, shall apply, with necessary modifications, to an examiner whose powers would include:

- Convening, setting the agenda for, and presiding at board meetings and general meetings;

- Entitlement to reasonable notice of, and to attend and be heard at, all such meetings;

- Halting, preventing or rectifying the effects of any act, omission, course of conduct, decision or contract by the credit union or its officers which in the examiner's opinion is likely to be detrimental to the interests of the credit union or any member or creditor;

- Applying to the court to determine any question arising in the course of the examiner's office. (The comparable provision in section 7(6) of the Companies (Amendment) Act, 1990, also provides for the exercise of powers, which a court could exercise upon the application of any member, contributory, creditor or director.)

- If directed by the court, ascertaining and agreeing claims against the credit union.

Unlike a liquidator or receiver, an examiner does not have power to carry on the business of a credit union or be involved in its management. The appointment of an examiner does not automatically suspend the directors' functions or powers. The court may in specified circumstances make an order that all or any of such functions or powers shall be performed or exercised only by the examiner: section 151(1) of the 1997 Act reflecting section 9(1) of the Companies (Amendment) Act, 1990.

Production of Documents and Evidence

Section 150 of the 1997 Act, reflecting with some variations section 8 of the Companies (Amendment) Act, 1990, requires all present and past officers, members, voluntary assistants and agents or any other persons to:

- Provide the examiner with all books and documents of the credit union;

- Attend before the examiner and to give all reasonable assistance in connection with his functions.

Such persons may be examined on oath and, if there is failure to co-operate, the examiner may refer the matter to court which may make such order or direction as it deems fit. This is an example of onerous responsibilities being placed on credit union activists. Barristers and solicitors, by implication in professional practice, may claim legal professional privilege.

With regard to sanctions under section 150(5), for failure to co-operate, T.C. Bird in his detailed annotations on the examinership provisions of the Credit Union Act, 1997, in ICLSA, R62 August 1998, comments on possible constitutional implications by reference to section 5 of the Consumer Credit Act, 1995.

Detailed Procedures

Following the general scheme but not all the details, in the Companies (Amendment) Act, 1990, sections 149 to 170 inclusive of the Credit Union Act, 1997, provide for the nuts and bolts of examinerships including: further powers of the court, incurring liabilities, power to deal with charged property, notification of appointment of examiner, general provisions as to examiners, court hearing where there is evidence of a substantial disappearance of credit union property or of serious irregularities in its affairs, examiner's duties on compromise or arrangement proposals for the survival of the credit union, content of examiner's report, repudiation of certain contracts, appointment of creditors' committee, proposals for compromise or scheme of arrangement, consideration of such proposals, confirmation by the court, ending of protection, disqualification to act as examiner, costs and remuneration, publicity and hearing court proceedings otherwise than in public.

Some points of special interest to credit union officers and members are:

- **Publicity** — Section 154 of the 1997 Act, following the scheme, but not the details, of section 12 of the Companies (Amendment) Act, 1990, requires notice of a petition presented under section 142 to be placed on the public file. The examiner shall arrange within the specified time limits for publication, in *Iris Oifigiúil* and in at least two daily newspapers circulating in the relevant district, of details of his appointment, and deliver to the Registrar a copy of the court order of appointment. All relevant documents shall contain a statement that the credit union is under court protection. Court orders relating to the scheme of arrangement or compromise must also be published in *Iris Oifigiúil* by the examiner or such other person as the court may direct. Relevant documents including invoices and letters shall contain the statement "under the protection of the court". It is an offence to fail to comply with the statutory requirements.

- **Consideration of Proposals by Members and Creditors** — Section 157 of the 1997 Act deals with the examiner's involvement in the survival of the credit union. It requires the examiner to convene and preside at meetings to consider compromise proposals or arrangements for survival of the credit union. The Registrar shall have the right to attend and speak at such meetings.

  Section 162 of the 1997 Act, adapted from section 23 of the Companies (Amendment) Act, 1990, provides detailed procedures for such meetings including voting by a majority of those members who are present and vote in favour of the proposals. The implications for officers, where their interests differ from those of other persons, must be indicated. Section

162 (4), exceptionally for credit unions, allows proxy voting and requires a majority in both number and value to prevent dominance by one creditor.

- **Court's Consideration of Examiner's Proposals** — Under section 163 of the 1997 Act, specified persons entitled to appear and be heard at the court hearing include the examiner, the Registrar, the credit union, the savings protection scheme in which a credit union participates, and also any creditor or member whose claim or interest would be impaired by implementation of the proposed compromise or scheme of arrangement. At the Dáil select committee stage, a Ministerial amendment suggested by the ILCU was agreed to include the specific reference to the savings protection scheme during the court hearing as the scheme's resources might be called upon.

Court Rules

The Rules of the Superior Courts, Order 75A, (SI 147 of 1991, amending SI 15 of 1986), regulate court procedures in examinership proceedings under the Companies (Amendment) Act, 1990. Amendments to the rules will be necessary in respect of examinerships for credit unions.

Ending and Outcome of Examinership

Under section 165 of the 1997 Act, court protection ceases when a compromise or scheme of arrangement comes into effect or on such earlier date as the court may direct. The examiner's appointment terminates on the date of cessation.

The main thrust is to try and ensure that the ailing credit union becomes viable and restored to a sound footing for survival, thus avoiding liquidation by winding up. Under section 164 of the 1997 Act, adapted from section 24 of the Companies (Amendment) Act, 1990, where the court confirms proposals for a compromise or scheme of arrangement (with or without modification) they shall be binding on the credit union, its members and on all creditors or class of creditors affected by the proposals and shall come into effect from a date fixed by the court. If the court refuses to confirm the proposals or the examiner concludes that it is not possible to reach agreement on a compromise or scheme of arrangement, the court may make any order it deems fit including a winding-up order which would terminate the credit union's existence. The general provisions on winding up are dealt with in Chapter 12 on Termination.

In summary, examinership may provide the credit union with a new lease of life but in extreme cases the outcome may be the termination of existence — death.

ADMINISTRATORS

The High Court, on the Registrar's application, may, in specified circumstances, make an administration order to enable a credit union to be carried on as a going concern with a view to re-establishing the proper and orderly regulation and conduct of the credit union and placing it on a sound footing. The administrator takes over the management of the credit union and shall have all necessary powers in relation to the credit union, including the sole authority over, and direction of, all officers and voluntary assistants. That means that the normal governance and management functions are suspended during the period of administration. The appointment of an examiner does not, however, automatically suspend the directors' functions or powers. The court, however, may make an order that all or any of such functions or powers shall be performed or exercised only by the examiner.

The administration procedures, which follow the general scheme but not all the details in the Insurance (No. 2) Act, 1983, No. 29 of 1983, are an innovative feature of credit union legislation.

Section 137(2) of the 1997 Act, adapted from section 2 of the Insurance (No. 2) Act, 1983, provides that, on the Registrar's application, the High Court may make an order if it considers:

a) that the manner in which the credit union business is being, or has been, conducted has failed to make adequate provision for its debts, including contingent and prospective liabilities; or

b) that the business is being or has been conducted as to jeopardise or prejudice the members' rights and interests; or

c) that the credit union has become unable to comply with the requirements of the 1997 Act in a material respect, and that the making of an administration order would assist in the re-establishment, in the public interest, of the proper and orderly regulation and conduct of the credit union. Provisional administrators may be appointed under section 138.

Effects of Administration

Section 139 of the 1997 Act, adapted from section 3(2) of the Insurance (No. 2) Act, 1983, provides that, during the appointment of the administrator, without the court's prior sanction:

- No proceedings or resolution for winding up shall be commenced or passed;

- No receiver shall be appointed over any part of the property;

- No attachment, sequestration, distress or execution shall be put in force against any part of the property of the credit union.

The net effect is to protect the credit union during an interim period when the administrator maintains the business as a going concern. Various procedures are provided for paying the administrator out of the credit union's assets, and for the administrator's calling a general meeting of members to report on work and plans. Section 141 provides that the whole or any part of the relevant proceedings may be heard otherwise than in public where the court considers that it would be so required in the interests of the credit union, its members, the creditors or the public. Unless the court otherwise directs, a petition for an administration order may be served only on the credit union, and only the Registrar and the credit union shall be entitled to be heard by the court.

Termination and Outcome of Administration

Section 140 of the 1997 Act sets out the grounds on which the administration of, and the appointment of an administrator to a credit union may be terminated, that is upon the making of an order: (a) for winding-up the credit union, or (b) for appointing an examiner, or (c) for termination of the administration but that would only be in specified circumstances where the members' interests would be protected and the credit union placed on a sound financial footing. The Registrar's regulatory role is ensured as an application for termination, if not made by the Registrar, must be approved by him.

CONCLUSION

In contrast to examinerships where there is a large body of court activity and legal precedent available for general guidance, administration under the Insurance (No. 2) Act, 1983, although an important safeguard for the public, has been used rarely. Some guidance, however, may be available from case law: in *Re PMPA Insurance Co.* [1986] ILRM 524, and [1988] ILRM 109. In the latter, the Supreme Court held on 5 November 1986 that the combined definition of "administrator" and "functions" conferred by the Insurance (No. 2) Act, 1983, must be construed as meaning that 'functions' include powers and functions conferred by the Act, but not those otherwise conferred. Thus, powers and functions of a receiver could not be described as powers or functions conferred by the Act on an administrator. It would be reasonable to assume that the powers and functions of an administrator under the Credit Union Act, 1997, would be similarly limited to those conferred by the statute.

It is unlikely that examiners or administrators will have a major role in the functioning of Irish credit unions as financial and related problems rarely arise. Established procedures would be generally sufficient to deal with such difficulties. Having regard to the large scale of credit union finances and operations, however, the additional statutory provisions in the 1997 Act are worthwhile extra safeguards to help ensure the viability of credit unions in the interests of members and the wider public.

Chapter 12

TERMINATION: WINDING-UP, DISSOLUTION, AMALGAMATION, TRANSFER OF ENGAGEMENTS AND CANCELLATION

"It is as natural to die as to be born."

Francis Bacon, *Essay on Death*

A credit union is born as a legal entity, a corporate body, when the Registrar completes the registration process by signing and issuing an acknowledgement of registry. Each credit union is a legal entity, distinct from any other credit union or representative body such as the ILCU. A credit union continues its legal existence as a corporate body distinct from its members until some event occurs which terminates such existence. The limitation on a member's liability to the amount of individual shareholding protects members from exposure in the event of a termination.

This chapter deals with the ways in which a credit union ceases to exist — its death. There may be various reasons for this, such as amalgamation with, or transfer of engagements (a type of merger) with another credit union. Or members may wish to discontinue or wind up the society because its aims have been achieved or the original need has declined or ceased. There are legal rules regarding the various ways of ending a credit union's existence. Some processes can be carried out by the members themselves, subject to complying with legal procedures. The agreement of another credit union is required before amalgamation. Other procedures may require decisions or guidance from outside bodies such as the courts or the Registrar. In the past, relatively few Irish credit unions have terminated their existence, but the procedures are relevant because there may be future trends towards mergers or alliances to facilitate expanded services as facilitated by the Credit Union Act, 1997. Part X of that Act, sections 133–136 and rule 164 deal with winding up.

WINDING-UP

Winding-up under the Companies Acts

There are distinct procedures, one under the High Court; and the other a voluntary winding up which may be by either (a) the members or (b) the creditors. The procedures are an expanded form of those in sections 58 and 60 of the Industrial and Provident Societies Act, 1893.

Section 134 of the Credit Union Act 1997 and rule 164(2) provide that a credit union may be dissolved by being wound up in accordance with the Companies Acts. Those Acts are defined in section 2 of the Credit Union, 1997, rule 1, as the Companies Acts 1963 to 1990, together with any enactment which is to be construed as one with those Acts.

The relevant provisions of the Companies Acts shall, subject to any necessary modifications, apply as if a credit union were a company limited by shares. References to articles of association shall be construed as references to rules and the Registrar as the Registrar of Friendly Societies. He shall have the right to attend and be heard in any proceedings relating to the winding up.

Where a credit union is wound up, the liability of present or past members for payment of debts and liabilities, expenses of winding up and the adjustment of contributories' rights among themselves shall be qualified on the basis specified in section 134(4). That provides a measure of protection and fairness so that, for example, persons would not be liable for any debt or liability contracted after they had ceased to be members.

Certain provisions of the Companies Acts relating to the liabilities of directors and officers shall apply with the necessary modifications to credit union officers, except employees (although they are generally defined as officers).

The relevant sections are sections 293 to 299 (as amended) of the Companies Acts, 1963 which deal with offences before or during the winding up and also criminal and civil liability for fraudulent or reckless trading, and sections 202 to 204 of the Companies Act, 1990, which deal with personal liability of officers where proper books of account are not kept.

The application of those provisions to credit unions could have serious personal implications for officers.

Winding-up by the High Court

The procedures in part VI (ii) sections 212 to 250 of the Companies Act, 1963, as amended, were designed for special circumstances where there are problems, for example when the companies affairs are not being properly conducted or the company is unable to meet its debts, or where the court considers that it is just and equitable that the company be wound up. These procedures, suitably adapted, apply to credit unions.

Based on section 33 of the Credit Union Act, 1966, section 133(1) of the Credit Union Act, 1997, which is reflected in general but not in detail in standard rule 164, gives the Registrar power to petition the High Court for an order to wind-up a credit union in specified circumstances as follows:

a) that it is unable to pay sums due and payable to its members or its creditors. (Where a judgment against a credit union is obtained under section 179, failure to satisfy claims within the specified period would be deemed inability to pay debts.);

b) or the credit union has, failed to comply with a provision made by, or under, or by virtue of the Credit Union Act, 1997, and the failure continued after notice from the Registrar;

c) less than one-half of the credit union's members have a common bond (and thus departing from its special nature) or (following company principles) in any other case where it appears to the Registrar that the winding-up is in the public interest or is just and equitable, having regard to the interests of all members.

Under section 133(2) of the 1997 Act, where such a petition to wind up is presented within one year after a credit union has changed its name, both the existing and former names shall appear on all notices and advertisements relating to the winding-up.

Voluntary Winding-up

Procedures for voluntary winding-up under the Companies Acts, sections 251 to 282, either by the members or by the creditors, may also be applicable to credit unions, as outlined below.

Members' Voluntary Winding-up

Members decide to initiate the process which is started by a special resolution of members. They control the process which would usually cost less than a winding-up by the court. A vital element is a declaration of solvency under section 256(1) of the Companies Act, 1963, amended by section 128 of the Companies Act, 1990. This requires a statutory declaration by a majority of the directors, after a full enquiry into the affairs of a company, that they have formed an opinion that the company will be unable to pay its debts, within a period not exceeding 12 months from the commencement of the winding-up. In credit unions, a majority of the board members would make the statutory declaration. If it were not made, the winding-up would proceed as a creditors' voluntary winding-up.

The Companies Act, 1990, strengthened the procedures which now require a report by an independent person stating whether in their opinion, and to the best of their information, and from explanations, the statements of assets and liabilities in the declaration are reasonable. The new section 256(8) and (9) of the Companies Act, 1963, substituted and amended by section 128 of the 1990 Act, provide for personal liability for debts on directors who signed the declaration of solvency without having reasonable grounds for their opinions. In credit unions, such personal liability would fall on the members of the board of directors.

Procedures to protect creditors include the right to apply to the court within 28 days after the passing of the winding-up resolution for an order that the winding-up continue as a creditors' voluntary winding-up. The court will only make such an order if it considers it unlikely that the company or credit union will be unable to pay its debts within a specified time.

Creditors' Voluntary Winding-up

This differs fundamentally from a members' winding-up. A declaration of solvency is not required. Procedures in sections 265 to 273 of the Companies Act, 1963, as amended, must be followed including holding a creditors' meeting and having a statement of affairs from the directors, with a list of creditors and estimated amount of claims. There is also provision for a committee of inspection consisting of not more than five persons appointed by the creditors.

General Procedures

In general, the appropriate procedures for winding up under the Companies Acts are set out in relevant Acts and statutory instruments including Rules of Court. With regard to winding up under the Companies Acts, Order 74, Rules of the Superior Courts, SI 15 of 1986, amended by SI 265 of 1993, would apply. The rules include provisions and time limits for placing advertisements in daily newspapers and in *Iris Oifigiúil*. The rules also include matters such as adjudication of debts, notice of winding-up orders and notice of appointment of a liquidator. Section 278 of the Companies Act, 1963, requires the liquidator to deliver to the Registrar of Companies notice of appointment within 14 days of appointment. For credit unions, suitable adaptations should be made to company law procedures. If a credit union were being wound up under company law, the required notice should be sent to the Registrar of Friendly Societies. Rules of bankruptcy may apply as appropriate to winding up under company law.

Liquidators and Liquidations

The liquidator is a person, usually a professional accountant specialising in insolvency, appointed to carry out the winding-up. The main duties are to get in the assets and realise them, pay or settle debts, and distribute any surplus to members. Section 231 of the Companies Act, 1963, amended by section 122 of the 1990 Act, contain the extensive powers and duties of a liquidator in a winding-up by the court.

An important difference between a liquidator in a voluntary winding-up and a liquidator in a court winding-up is that the latter must obtain the permission of the court or committee of inspection before exercising many of the powers of a liquidator. A liquidator appointed by the court is known as an official liquidator. There are detailed and complex procedures in company law with which a liquidator must comply. For example, section 129 of the Companies Act, 1990, imposes a duty on a liquidator in a members' voluntary winding-up to call a meeting of creditors if the liquidator considers that the company will not be able to pay its debts.

In liquidations, as well as the areas outlined above, many other legal aspects apply. For example, preferential creditors are entitled, under sections 283 to 285 of the Companies Act, 1963, as amended by section 10 of the 1982 Act, to payment of debts owing to them before other creditors are paid.

Winding up by Instrument of Dissolution

As this is a procedure peculiar to mutual societies and credit unions some explanatory background is necessary. Under section 58(b), as expanded by section 61, of the Industrial and Provident Societies Act, 1893, as amended by section 8 of the 1913 Act, and reflected in the old ILCU standard rule 186, a credit union could have been dissolved by the consent of three-fourths of its members, testified by their signatures (identified by the membership numbers) to an instrument of dissolution in the form required by law.

The voluntary dissolution could have been in accordance with the provisions of the Industrial and Provident Societies Act of 1893 or in the manner required, under the Companies Acts, for solvent societies only. Company law procedures in sections 251 et seq. in part VI of the of the Companies Act, 1963, were applicable with suitable adaptations, especially regarding the Registrar of Friendly Societies fulfilling the functions of Registrar of Companies. The process of dissolution by instrument is a procedure peculiar to societies and is not available to registered companies.

The option of voluntary dissolution by instrument, closed off to deposit-taking industrial and provident societies under section 19(5) of the 1978 Industrial and Provident Societies Act, continues to be available to credit unions. That option is now provided for in section 135 of the Credit Union Act, 1997. The detailed revised procedures of that section, however, are not included in the ILCU's relevant revised rule 164(3) on the various methods of winding up. That rule states briefly that a credit union may be wound up "by special resolution of the credit union under the Act resolving that it be wound-up by an instrument of dissolution in accordance with section 135 of the Act".

Detailed procedures for winding up by instrument of dissolution set out in the sub-sections of section 135 of the 1997 Act include:

1) A special resolution is required and the instrument of dissolution must be signed by the secretary and a member of the board of directors. The previous procedure which required signatures by three-quarters of the members no longer applies but not less than that proportion of membership would be required at a special general meeting (SGM) to pass the necessary special resolution in accordance with the definition of such resolution in section 2(1) of the 1997 Act, rule 1;

2) The instrument of dissolution must set forth certain information including liabilities and assets, the numbers of members and the nature of their respective interests, creditors' claims and provision for payment, and also the intended appropriation or division of any surplus or balance, as recommended by the board and approved by the Registrar;

3) Alterations to the instrument may be made by the consent of three-quarters of the members voting at a SGM, but such consent shall be testified by the signature of the secretary and a board member;

4) The instrument of dissolution shall be sent to the Registrar with a statutory declaration made by the secretary and three other members of the credit union stating that all relevant provisions of the Act have been complied with.
    A statutory declaration is a written statement of facts in which the person making it, the declarant, signs and solemnly declares, conscientiously believing it to be true. It is made before a notary public, a commissioner for oaths or a peace commissioner under the Statutory Declarations Act, 1938. Section 6 of that Act provides that it is an offence for a person to make a statutory declaration knowing it to be false or misleading. There is a heavy onus on the declarant to ensure that relevant statements are accurate;

5) When the Registrar has received the final annual return up to the date of dissolution, he shall register the instrument of dissolution (and any amendments to it). The effect is similar to an amendment of rules and shall be binding on all members;

6) The Registrar shall have notice of dissolution advertised at the credit union's expense in the official gazette, *Iris Oifigiúil*, and in any other manner considered necessary for bringing the matter to the attention of persons affected by the notice. The credit union is considered to be dissolved from the date of the advertisement of the dissolution or, if it is later, from the

date when a certificate under section 136(1) of the 1997 Act is lodged with the Registrar;

7) A credit union shall not be dissolved if the High Court sets aside the dissolution, following application, within three months of the dissolution being advertised, by a member or other person interested in or having any claim on the funds.

Restriction on Dissolution or Cancellation of Registration

To protect members' interests, there is a new provision. Section 136 of the 1997 Act provides safeguards by prohibiting the dissolution of a credit union in accordance with section 135(6) (or the cancellation of its registration under section 97(2) (a)) until specified procedures have been completed: A certificate, signed by the secretary or other officer of the credit union approved by the Registrar and stating that all property vested in the credit union has been duly conveyed or transferred to the persons entitled, should be lodged with the Registrar.

Administrators and Examiners : Effect on Winding-up

Innovative provisions in parts XI and XII of the Credit Union Act, 1997, sections 137–141 and 142–170 respectively, introduced the company law concept of administrators and examiners to credit unions. Chapter 11 of this book deals with the relevant procedures which provide a breathing space for credit unions experiencing financial problems, by the appointment of an administrator or examiner. It should be noted that in such circumstances, winding-up and appointment of a liquidator or a receiver would be affected. In cases of administration, court sanction would be necessary for winding up or appointing a receiver. Section 147 of the 1997 Act provides that when a credit union is under the protection of a court following the appointment of a examiner, winding-up proceedings may not be commenced and any receiver or provisional liquidator shall cease to act from a date specified by the court.

Amalgamations and Transfers of Engagements

Part IX, sections 128 to 132 of the Credit Union Act, 1997 and rules 159 to 163 and provide for the amalgamation and transfer of engagements of two or more credit unions after special resolutions have been passed and formalities complied with. The effects of amalgamation are that two or more societies disappear and a new society comes into existence. The property of the original societies becomes vested in the amalgamated credit union. No form of conveyance is necessary other than that contained in the special resolution amalgamating the societies, including credit unions. In contrast, a transfer of engagements means that another society undertakes to fulfil the engagements of the original society which then ceases to exist.

Amalgamation

In an expanded form of section 53 of the 1893, Act, section 128 of the 1997 Act and rule 159 provide for the amalgamation of two or more credit unions and state the conditions for the formation of a credit union as their successor, including agreement on the rules of their successor in accordance with the First Schedule to the Act. A formal statement must be issued to members in accordance with section 130 and rule 161, as explained below. Each credit union must approve the terms of amalgamation by special resolution. Where the Registrar confirms an amalgamation under section 131, he shall issue a certificate confirming his approval and also specify a date from which the registration of a successor credit union takes effect. On the specified date, all the property, rights and liabilities of each amalgamating credit union shall be transferred to and vested in the successor credit union and each of the amalgamating credit unions shall be dissolved.

Transfer of Engagements Between Credit Unions

Section 129 and rule 160 set out the conditions for the transfer of the engagements of one credit union to another one which, in accordance with procedures, undertakes to fulfil the engagements.

On the specified date, all the property, rights and liabilities of the credit union transferring its engagements shall be transferred to and vested in the credit union taking the transfer, and the credit union whose engagements are transferred shall be dissolved.

A decision by resolution of the board of directors of each relevant credit union may, if the Registrar has consented under section 129, suffice in a transfer of engagements (but not in an amalgamation), instead of a special resolution at a general meeting. In that case, there are safeguards for members because the boards' resolution and the statement with specified information, including that on financial matters, as explained below must be sent to members, and also the auditor, within seven days of the board meeting.

Statement for Members about Proposed Amalgamation or Transfer of Engagements

Section 130 and rule 161 require that members and the auditor must be notified in accordance with specified procedures in a statement which the Registrar must approve. Members must receive such a statement, with detailed information about the amalgamation and the relevant credit union, including the financial position, not later than the date on which they receive notice of any resolution in favour of a proposal to be moved at a relevant general meeting.

Confirmation of Amalgamation or Transfer

Section 131 and rule 162 provide that an application for confirmation by the Registrar of an amalgamation of credit unions or transfer of engagements shall be made in such manner as the Registrar may specify. Under section 131(2) and rule 162(2), within seven days of making an application, each credit union shall publish a notice giving particulars of the application and stating that representations may be made to the Registrar within a period of not less than twenty-one days. The Registrar may specify the form of the notice, which shall indicate that a copy of the statement may be obtained on demand at the registered office of the credit union during its ordinary office hours. The Registrar shall allow the relevant credit union(s) an opportunity to comment on any representations before deciding to confirm the amalgamation or transfer, or if he is satisfied that certain conditions prevail, before refusing to confirm it.

Section 131(7) and rule 162(7) permit some flexibility in procedures by allowing the Registrar to confirm amalgamations or transfers even if some non-material, that is unimportant requirements under the Act of the rules were not fulfilled.

Section 131(8) provides that a credit union or person who fails to comply with a requirement of the relevant part IX of the Act (on amalgamations or transfers of engagements) shall be guilty of an offence. Such penalty provisions, however, are not included in the ILCU standard rules as they are official regulatory matters.

Distribution of Funds to Members

Section 132 and rule 163 provide that the Registrar's consent must be obtained where the terms of an amalgamation or transfer of engagements involve a distribution of funds among any members of participating credit unions. A distribution must be approved by special resolution at a general meeting under the provisions of section 128(2) (b) and rule 159(2) (b) or section 129(2) and rule 160(2) (b). If the Registrar agrees, a resolution of the board of directors under section 129(2) and rule 160(2) (b) may suffice.

CANCELLATION OF REGISTRY OF SOCIETY

Section 97 (1) of the 1997 Act provides that the Registrar (as part of his supervisory powers described in Chapter 9 of this book) may, by writing under his hand, cancel the registry of a society in certain specified circumstances:

a) Proof to the Registrar's satisfaction that

    (i)   The number of members has been reduced below the statutory minimum of fifteen, or

    (ii)   An acknowledgement of registry has been obtained by fraud or mistake, or

    (iii)   The credit union had not commenced business within twelve months of registration, or

    (iv)   The credit union has suspended its business for a period of not less than six months or has ceased to function;

b) If the Registrar thinks fit, at the request of the credit union, to be evidenced in such manner as he shall from time to time direct;

c) On proof to the Registrar's satisfaction that the credit union exists or is being used for an illegal purpose or has wilfully and after notice from the Registrar violated any of the provisions of the Act. (A previous requirement of the Minister's approval has been deleted.);

d) Where it appears to the Registrar that the members no longer have a common bond.

Section 97(2) provides that the Registrar shall cancel the registration of a credit union where it has been dissolved by virtue of section 128 or 129 (amalgamation or transfer of engagements outlined above); or wound up under section 133 or section 134, or dissolved under section 135 by instrument of dissolution.

Where a credit union's registration is being cancelled otherwise than in the circumstances in section 97(2) outlined above or at its own request, section 97(3) of the 1997 Act provides for safeguards including a two months' notice to the credit union. There is provision for an appeal. Publication of a notice of cancellation in the official gazette, *Iris Oifigiúil*, provides further safeguards. From the date the notice is published, the credit union shall cease to be entitled to any of the privileges of the Act, without prejudice to the enforcement of any credit union liability incurred before its registration was cancelled.

Section 99 of the Credit Union Act, 1997, provides credit unions with a right of appeal to the High Court against the Registrar's proposal to cancel registration under section 97(3) or to suspend, or extend suspension, of registration under section 98(3).

Credit Union Cannot Convert into a Company

Industrial and provident societies have traditionally had, under section 54 of the 1893 Act, the option of converting into companies registered under the Companies Acts. That option is not available to credit unions under the 1997 Act, thereby giving further protection for their mutual status. In contrast, when the building societies legislation was being revised and modernised in the 1989 Act, the demutualisation option of converting from the traditional mutual society status to that of public limited company, plc, was facilitated.

CONCLUSION

The complexities in the various options outlined above, and especially the interface between company law and credit union law, illustrate the need for professional accountancy and legal advice.

Compared with small business trading as companies or co-ops, there are few terminations of credit unions. During the first decade of the Irish League's existence, there were about six credit unions wound up. The general pattern, however, is for credit unions to continue to exist when they become firmly established. Trends in unemployment and business closures were reflected in the cancellation of some credit unions, for example, Gateaux Employees' Credit Union and that in the *Irish Press*.

Future rationalisation may result in smaller credit unions, especially in urban areas transferring their engagements to, or amalgamating with, larger ones, to obtain advantages of scale and thus be able to provide a wider range of services for members, as facilitated by the Credit Union Act, 1997.

Marriage and partnership by alliances, rather than death, may be the way ahead for many Irish credit unions.

Chapter 13

IRISH LEAGUE OF CREDIT UNIONS

BY WHAT MAGIC?

"Critics profess to be surprised that a movement of this
character and magnitude should be possible in Ireland . . .
They ask with surprise by what magic this phenomenon
has been brought about . . . It has been accomplished by the
familiar magic of common sense . . . We assured them
(the Irish people) that their fortunes are absolutely in their
own hands."

Rev T.A. Finlay, SJ, Vice-Chairman,
Irish Agricultural Organisation Society (IAOS), 1902.

The words quoted above, spoken with reference to the Irish
agricultural co-op movement at the turn of the century, are apt in
the context of the Irish credit union movement as the next new
century approaches. The magic and common sense in the context
of credit unions are based on the enthusiasm, solid achievements
and effectiveness of the Irish League of Credit Unions (ILCU).

There are about 540 credit unions, including over 100 in
Northern Ireland and over 430 in the Republic, affiliated to the
League which is a representative and service body supplying
educational and other support services. Membership is open to
every credit union in Ireland which accepts and adopts the
standard rules of the ILCU, as agreed by its AGM. The rules for
the Republic of Ireland were revised in 1998 to reflect the
provisions of the Credit Union Act, 1997. Standard rule 169
provides that credit unions affiliate with ILCU and adopt the
standard rules as its registered rules and shall not unilaterally

amend them. Co-operation with the ILCU as specified in rule 169 is also required. Standard rules, with discretion in some matters such as numbers of board and committee members, encourage cohesion and administrative efficiency. There are separate standard rules in respect of Northern Ireland, reflecting its distinct legal framework.

Affiliated credit unions account for about 2.2 million members representing personal savings of about £2.8 billion Irish pounds and over £3 billion in assets. As some individuals may be members of more than one credit union, it is difficult to give precise figures of membership. In the movement, there are over 16,000 active volunteers and almost 2,000 employees.

In the Republic of Ireland some credit unions, including that representing prison officers, are outside the ILCU. Most credit unions south of the border and a large proportion of Northern Ireland credit unions are affiliated to the ILCU.

A useful analysis of the ILCU and an interview with Mr J. Murphy, then general secretary, was included in a dissertation by O'Leary (1988).

FORMAT AND HISTORY OF THE LEAGUE

The ILCU is a non-statutory body organised voluntarily from within the credit union movement. The ILCU is not registered under any legislation as a company, industrial and provident society nor as a credit union of credit unions. As an unincorporated association, the league lacks a formal legal status and cannot sue or be sued. Following legal advice, however, a subsidiary company wholly owned by the ILCU, was established in 1995/6 to facilitate the acquisition of new premises and the operation of revised security arrangements relating to member loans. There are also other associated companies serving specific functions, such as information technology, within the overall structure.

The ILCU's lack of legal status has been criticised. The then Minister of State, Pat Rabbitte, TD, referred to it as causing difficulties, during the Dáil select committee debate on the 1997 legislation. The feeling within the movement has been that registration within one jurisdiction, either in Dublin or Belfast, could be divisive as the movement is non-political and non-sectarian. Limited companies have been registered for specific purposes such as insurance or overseas development assistance.

The general background to the origins of the ILCU was traced in Chapter 1. The seeds, sown at an evening Diploma course in Social and Economic Science at UCD, 1948–51, led to action. The founders of the Irish credit union movement and thus of the League in 1960 — Seán Forde, Nora Herlihy and Séamus MacEoin — were commemorated in 1992 by a special ILCU medal, silver replicas of which are on the chains of office worn by current chairmen of chapters, the local groups of credit unions.

SPECIFIC HIGHLIGHTS

1957	Credit Union film, *King's X* was shown at the Folk School, organised by the National Co-operative Council (NCC) at Red Island, Skerries, Co. Dublin. The credit union pioneers, however, were active before this Folk School was held. NCC and a core group of Dublin Central Co-op had led to Credit Union Extension Service.
1958	First Irish credit unions formed without formal legal basis: Cumann Muíntir Dún Óir (Donore Credit Union, Dublin 8) led by Eileen Byrne, and also Dun Laoghaire Credit Union connected with the local grocery co-op.
1959	Seminal meetings in Monaghan and O'Lehane Hall, Cavendish Row, Dublin, addressed by Olaf Spetland, director of world department of Credit Union National Association (CUNA). Seán Healy, National Farmers' Association, (NFA, later IFA), provided a recording machine.
1960	Clones Credit Union Ltd was the first to take out loan protection and life savings insurance.

1960	Credit Union League of Ireland formed in old Jury's Hotel, Dame Street, Dublin, later a Telecom Éireann building. The League's first officers were: Rev. Paddy Gallagher president; Seán Forde, vice-president; Nora Herlihy, secretary, whose home Loyola, 50, Shandon Park, Phibsboro, Dublin 7 served as first offices; PRO and editor of first magazine *Creidmheas*, was Séamus MacEoin. Early loans were for consumer needs, paying bills and renovating houses.
1961	League's first AGM held in Dublin. First set of standard or model rules adopted.
1962	First chapter, or regional group, set-up in Dublin.
1963	Part-time managing director appointed.
1966	First full-time employee, field officer of League. General manager appointed, office in 22, North Frederick St. Dublin. Credit Union Act, 1966, enacted in Ireland
1968	The League, with Philip Ryan as general manager, was appointed European agent for the USA-based Credit Union National Association's CUNA Mutual Insurance Society.
1969	League headquarters moved to 9, Appian Way, Dublin 6. Movement had spread to Northern Ireland, led by John Hume, later MEP, MP and SDLP leader. The growth was facilitated by legislation, the Industrial & Provident Societies (NI) Act, 1969.
1972	New name, Irish League of Credit Unions (ILCU), and also new rules adopted at special convention (AGM).
1973	General Secretary, Michael O'Doherty, appointed. Central Financial Service established. Central Agency Agreement established.
1980	ECCU Assurance Co. Ltd registered.
1981	League headquarters moved to 68, Merrion Sq. Dublin 2.

1984	New purpose-built offices opened in Castleside Drive, Rathfarnham, Dublin 14, aptly near the Castle, which had been the home of the Jesuits, the religious order which included co-op leaders and inspirers: Fr Tom Finlay, SJ, Fr Edward Coyne, SJ, Fr E. Kent, SJ. (The Jesuit tradition of communal initiatives, outlined in *To the Greater Glory: A History of the Irish Jesuits*, L. McRedmond, Dublin 1991, has been continued by Fr John Brady, SJ and Fr Dermot McKenna, SJ.)
1984	*Statement of Credit Union Operating Principles* adopted at AGM, founded in the philosophy of co-operation and its central values of equality, equity and mutual self-help. The Statement, at Appendix 2 to this book, was based on the International Co-operative Principles.
1987	AGM at City Hall, Cork, adopted a policy of encouraging community developments and group employment initiatives, including the formation of worker co-operatives.
1988	International Credit Union Day, 20 October, at Rathfarnham offices: The President of Ireland, Dr Patrick Hillery, unveiled a portrait in oils of the late Nora Herlihy, first secretary of League, who died in Dalkey, Co. Dublin on 7 February, 1988. Tom Ryan, RHA, was the artist.
1992	AGM approved a new model rule providing for credit unions to conduct their affairs within the framework of the Operating Principles as adopted in 1984.
1992/3	Plan to restructure organisation and administration.
1993	President of board: Tom McCarthy, Cork. Thirty-third AGM, Killarney, Co.Kerry

1993	Death of Séamus MacEoin, last surviving founder member of the Irish credit union movement and former League director, who had been honoured with a special founders' gold medal.
1994	Mary Robinson, President of Ireland, opened an international Credit Union Forum in Cork, at which the keynote speaker was Michael D. Higgins, TD, Minister for Arts, Culture and the Gaeltacht. Gus Murray, Irish president of World Council of Credit Unions (WOCCU) dies. Memorandum of understanding signed by the Registrar and Frank O'Kane, then League president, placed on a formal footing the good working relationship between ILCU and Registrar.
1995	Fr Paddy Gallagher, first League president, dies.
1996	Tony Smyth appointed general secretary in place of Jim Murphy. Gerry Foley elected secretary of WOCCU executive.
1997	Credit Union Act, 1997, enacted after effective lobbying by ILCU under Norman Murphy, president. Death of former general secretary, Jim Murphy, in whose memory awards for excellence in Diploma in Credit Union Studies, NUI — Cork were named.
1998	New offices, 33–41 Lower Mount St, Dublin 2, officially opened by Mary McAleese, President of Ireland. Attendance included Tánaiste, Mary Harney, TD, Minister for Enterprise, Trade and Employment and the Lord Mayor of Dublin, John Stafford, a former activist in North William Street Credit Union; and also John Hume, MP, MEP, a pioneer of the movement.

1998	AGM at Limerick, chaired by Frank Lynch, vice-president and subsequently president, adopted revised standard rules for Republic of Ireland, reflecting relevant provisions of the 1997 Act. AGM also adopted the interim report of the youth policy task force (YPTF). Noel Treacy, TD, Minister of State, speaking at the annual dinner, paid tribute on the government's behalf to the commitment of the dedicated volunteers within the credit union movement.

League's Status Recognised

The status of the ILCU as the pre-eminent association representing credit unions was officially recognised under the Credit Union Act, 1997. Section 12(4) (b) formally allowed the use of its name by the unincorporated association known as the ILCU, as an exception to the general prohibition in section 12(3) on the use of the title of credit union otherwise than by a registered credit union. Section 181 requires the Minister and the Registrar to consult the ILCU on the implementation of the new legislation, with specific reference to consulting expert and knowledgeable bodies. Such references occur in section 13(1) (b) regarding rules, section 50(1) dealing with additional services, section 84 on arrangements for control and supervision by the Registrar and section 182(1) on preparing ministerial regulations under the Bill.

LEAGUE RULES

For the purpose of organising and managing ILCU business, there are extensive League rules which are distinct from the standard rules for use by individual credit unions. The League rules include objects, membership, meetings, elections and voting, board of directors, supervisory committee, standing orders for meetings, officers, committees and sub-committees, chapters (local regions), finance, expulsions, amalgamations.

OBJECTS

League rules in section 1.3, detail the objects for which the League was formed. These objects, in summary form, include:

1) Promoting fraternal and co-operative relations with credit unions, leagues and councils in other countries for furthering common interests;

2) Fostering the organisation of new credit unions;

3) Contributing to developing higher standards of credit union management, operation and supervision by advice and direction in the interests of members and membership of credit unions;

4) Conducting such central services or otherwise as may be deemed necessary or expedient for and on behalf of its members;

5) Maintaining the unity of League membership;

6) Ensuring and maintaining the movement's non sectarian and non political character, by fostering the ideal of total community and voluntary effort;

7) Representing members in contact with Government and its agencies, and with other bodies, and dealing with legislative problems of credit unions;

8) Maintaining the individual and collective autonomy of credit unions in Ireland;

9) Encouraging members to operate in accordance with the *Operating Principles*, set-out in Appendix 2 to this book and in Appendix 1 to ILCU standard rules, and based on the International Co-operative Principles.

There is also a catch-all general objects clause covering all other things permitted by law and not inconsistent with the rules. In interpreting the rules, it should be borne in mind that the ILCU, an unincorporated body, is not registered as a company, credit union or as an industrial and provident society.

VISION AND MISSION STATEMENT

Reflecting its traditional philosophy and its rules, the ILCU have recently formulated a vision that credit unions will satisfy the social and economic needs of their members, with dignity and integrity, by offering, in the co-operative manner and on a not-for-profit basis, full financial services for everyone in the community who wishes to join. The League states that it will achieve the above vision through:

- Providing leadership for the movement in philosophy and services;

- Fostering and maintaining unity and co-operation between credit unions;

- Developing, and making available to credit unions and their members, a full range of the highest quality financial products and services;

- Recognising the dignity of credit union members and their value in the community by their contribution to the social development of communities in Ireland and other countries.

Guidance notes issued to credit unions by the ILCU deal with specific points which directors and supervisors are asked to consider carefully. The guidance notes outline the policy of the ILCU's monitoring service on steps to be taken where fraud or embezzlement is discovered. Those steps include: informing the League office, seeking suspension or resignation of the individuals involved and an independent investigation. The monitoring department of ILCU arranges a meeting with the board of directors and supervisory committee, informs the Registrar and informs CUMIS through the insurance department. An investigation, by the monitoring department or an independent investigation, follows.

ANNUAL CONVENTION/AGM AND ELECTIONS TO BOARD

The ILCU is governed by a board of directors of 16 persons, including the officers. Directors serve in a voluntary capacity but expenses may be paid. Directors have traditionally been elected by keen competition on the proportional representation system at the League's AGM, an elaborate and well-organised event, the largest of its kind in Ireland. The AGM is also called the convention. Following a review of procedures, it was recommended that postal voting would replace the direct voting system at the AGM/convention. Such a change would require further debate and a change of rule. Held in major centres which have adequate conference and hotel facilities, the convention is the parliament of the credit union movement and may be attended by two delegates (plus two alternates) from each affiliated credit union. Each credit union has two votes, whether one or two delegates are present. Entitlement to vote is confined to credit unions which meet specified conditions including being up-to-date with insurance reports and also annual returns, accounts and auditor's report and payment of affiliation fees to the ILCU. There are special sponsorship arrangements for newly formed credit unions.

Directors normally serve for a period of three years, subject to a maximum single continuous period of nine years when they must stand down for at least two years. To encourage new nominees for board membership, a third of the directors must retire from the board each year but are eligible for re-election.

The board provides the voluntary input into League administration and decision making. As stated in the ILCU rules, the board's functions, under its chairman, include general control, direction and management of the League's affairs, funds and records and determination of policy. Executive functions may be delegated to the general secretary and reporting systems established. The rules also includes procedures for meetings and voting, vacating and removing directors from office, and also filling casual vacancies. Changes in both the ILCU rules and the standard rules are made by vote at the AGM/convention.

SUPERVISORY COMMITTEE OF ILCU

This comprises three persons, elected by the annual convention. There is a general parallel with the supervisors' system for individual credit unions. Regular terms of office for supervisors shall be three years and one supervisor retires each year. There is a chairman and secretary. The committee's duties include: ensuring the preservation of the credit union movement's integrity and philosophy; ascertaining that the board's actions and decisions are in accordance with the rules and decisions of AGM/convention; and ensuring that resolutions passed by any AGM are examined and acted upon as ordered.

The ILCU annual reports include its Supervisory Committee's report. Examples of the committee's work include supervising the election of board officers, attending meetings of ECCU Assurance Co. Ltd., and the International Development Foundation Co. Ltd, watching trends in financial markets, checking on funds investments and criticising undesirable practices among some credit unions.

OTHER COMMITTEES

There are three standing committees of the ILCU board: administration (responsible for the monitoring area), audit, and also planning and development. From time to time ad hoc committees are formed to deal with such key matters as new legislation and rules. Additionally the board can appoint committees which include representatives and specialists from the movement as a whole. Such committees include the AGM review committee and the youth policy task force.

INELIGIBILITY

Under ILCU rule 7, certain persons shall be ineligible to hold office as a director of the League board, supervisor or member of standing orders committee (dealing with procedures) or nominating committee. There are the usual exclusions of bankrupts and persons of unsound mind. Also excluded are: employees of a local chapter, the ILCU or its associated bodies; subject to thresholds, persons earning under specified annual amounts; members of any legislature or parliament having jurisdiction in Ireland; a member of the Credit Union Advisory Committee (CUAC) to the Minister under the Credit Union Act (the CUAC is dealt with in more detail in Chapter 14); members of credit unions which already have representatives as ILCU directors, supervisors or members of a standing orders committee. The thrust of the exclusions is to avoid conflicts of interest and to encourage wider democracy and participation. The restrictions on employees of individual credit unions (as distinct from League employees) from being ILCU directors were relaxed at the 1998 AGM but would still apply if the relevant credit union already had a representative as a League director, supervisor or member of standings order committee. A maximum of two ILCU directors may also be credit union employees. The restrictions are complex and liable to change. Therefore, it would be advisable to consult the relevant rules of the ILCU in specific circumstances.

REGIONAL CHAPTERS

There are 25 local groups of credit unions, geographically related, to facilitate communication and education. Chapters, created by the ILCU, are directly responsible through their elected officers to the League Board. Chapters are a basic and essential part of the ILCU structure and are provided for in League rules. Participation in local chapters helps credit unions in a practical way because ideas and experiences can be exchanged between credit unions. They are also kept in touch with wider issues such as co-operative ideals. Leadership can be fostered through training and discussion. Social events, such as golf outings, promote friendship.

Section 9 of the ILCU's rules deals with Chapters. The League has also published a guide and Chapter Standard Rules which are distinct from model rules for credit unions. Chapter Standard Rules outline the duties of the various officers: chairman, vice-chairman, secretary and treasurer. They, together with the public relations officer, constitute the executive committee. Its function is to give direction and purpose to the chapter's activities throughout the year by planning and co-ordination.

Educational Role of Chapters

Subcommittees may also be formed, such as for education, a vital topic which relates back to basic credit union principles, and for plans for future developments. Topics suggested for lectures and discussions organised by Chapters include: Functions of various officers and committees within credit unions, delinquent loans and bad debts, insurance, procedure for meetings, understanding legislation, ILCU services and functions, and credit union philosophy. Within a chapter area, study groups may be formed and assisted where there is interest in forming new credit unions. Such study groups are an essential part of credit union philosophy and practice. The Liaison Committee's functions include informing credit unions of the chapter's education and training programme and encouraging maximum participation in it.

The motto is "Service in Confidence". Headings recommended for training programmes include credit union philosophy, practice and legislation. The role of the Chapters is being reviewed on the initiative of the ILCU.

ILCU ADMINISTRATIVE STRUCTURE

There is a full-time staff based in the modern offices at 33–41, Lower Mount Street, Dublin 2 under the direction of general secretary, Tony Smyth, and Patrick Fay, head of monitoring services and chief operating officer. The staff includes heads of function and specialists in training, legal, finance, insurance, marketing and public relations, international affairs and also information technology. Following reports from a planning committee and Price Waterhouse, management consultants, changes in the structure were made to improve procedures and meet challenges of the financial services sector. The expertise of specialist outside bodies is also used, for example on insurance and investment.

While the need for change is generally accepted, there are various views about details. The ILCU board will have to concentrate on policy matters rather than on details. In general, the trend is likely to be towards more delegation of functions to full-time executives and heads of function with professional expertise. The voluntary input from activists at League board and other levels will be maintained. A balance is necessary between professional and voluntary efforts. The main focus of the voluntary movement, the AGM/convention, will be restructured to make it more effective. The AGM review committee report of 1998 recommended that each credit union should continue to have two votes at convention. Changes envisaged include postal voting for elections to the board of the ILCU and its formal committees and dividing the AGM into plenary sessions and breakout workshops. There will be more emphasis on planning but reporting will continue the vital role of accountability to the wider membership. A strategic plan has been formulated to provide direction to the movement.

COMPUTER MONITORING

As part of the extensive savings protection system described in chapter 7, each credit union must ensure that a call report, as at 31 March, is sent to the League Office each year. Computer analysis and CAMEL score reports at year ending 30 September are prepared on the basis of Annual Returns — AR 25/AR 28 — which are vital elements in the Savings Protection Monitoring Scheme. Returns must also be sent to the Registrars in Dublin or Belfast. In the ILCU office, information submitted by each credit union is analysed and reports sent to them within six weeks. Asset size is taken into account to facilitate comparison. Boards and supervisory committees are expected to study the reports with particular reference to ratios. On reviewing reports, the League office may write to some credit unions regarding ratios, for example, net loans over thirteen weeks in arrears as a percentage of gross loans. As a follow-up, field officers may visit credit unions and also draw attention to other unacceptable ratios. Field officers may also make other visits. Computer score sheets rate each credit union within specific categories ranging from *excellent* down to *remedial action required*. The suitability of each of the CAMEL ratios is reviewed continuously and necessary adjustments made. Where protracted problems exist, actions such as appointment of liaison directors and joint visits by the Registrar and League officials may be necessary. Annual reports of the ILCU include analyses of ratios, delinquency within credit unions classed according to total assets and also financial trends for credit unions.

CENTRAL INVESTMENT MANAGEMENT SERVICE (CIM)

This flexible scheme replaced the Central Agency Agreement (CAA), a common fund which invested on behalf of participating credit unions. Davy Stockbrokers provide specialist services such as visiting local chapters and advising on investment strategy, including the effects of EMU and interest rates. CIM offers improved rates of return combined with the flexibility to lodge or withdraw money on a daily basis. Funds amounting to around £300 millions are invested in a range of options including marketable securities. The Trustee (Authorised Investments) Order, 1998, permits credit unions to invest in a more diverse manner than previously but caution is advised especially regarding equities or shares in commercial companies.

CENTRAL FINANCIAL SERVICES

Loans and stand-by facilities totalling about £3 millions annually are provided for credit unions, for purposes such as computer purchase, purchase, building and renovation of premises, and also liquidity during peak times for loans. Loans may be drawn down as money is required, thereby avoiding unnecessary interest charges. While interest rates fluctuate, they are below normal commercial rates. This is a good example of mutual savings being used for the wider credit union movement.

INSURANCE SERVICES

Although the ILCU itself is not registered as a company or in any other legal format, ECCU Assurance Co. Ltd was registered to comply with company and insurance law. Its operations were outlined in Chapter 7 on Financial Operations. ECCU, although an independent body, works closely with the ILCU which acts as its agent. ILCU holds the entire issued capital of ECCU and its board meets regularly with directors of the League. ILCU arranges for insurance cover for credit unions such as public and employers' liability, fire and special perils and business interruption. Optional extras cover areas such as motor vehicles. These types of business are effected through the usual commercial insurance sector, rather than the specialised ECCU. The League has also arranged a repayment protection insurance scheme (RPI) to provide extra cover during redundancy and illness. Commission from such schemes help to diversify the funding of the ILCU's activities which had traditionally depended mainly on premiums from the basic insurances on life savings (LS) and loan protection (LP) together with affiliation fees. Insurance products and services endorsed by ILCU carry a distinctive new logo for display. It will signify a high standard of service as recommended by the ILCU's insurance services department.

There are also pension, insurance and disability schemes for League and credit union staff. In accordance with rule 4 of the ILCU rules, its directors must report annually to the AGM on the adequacy of insurance cover.

WIDER COMMUNITY INVOLVEMENT

Workers Co-ops

Grants may be made from the Workers Co-op Fund which, following a resolution passed at the 1998 AGM, will be financed by a transfer of monies from the ILCU general fund to restore the balance in the co-op fund to an amount equal 5p per adult member of affiliated credit unions as at 30th June of the previous year. The fund is to be used at the ILCU's board discretion to grant-aid persons who are members of a credit union as well as being bona fide members of a registered workers' co-op which meets specified criteria regarding worker control. The fund is not widely advertised but credit unions are expected to make its existence known to members.

Funds are also provided for education and training in the workers co-op enterprise sector. Such schemes help co-op development and public awareness. There is scope for future expansion in wider co-op involvement, facilitated for individual co-ops by section 44 of the 1997 Act, but there are limits due to prudential considerations and need to protect members savings.

Promotion and Sponsorship

As well as formal training, the ILCU supplies a large selection of promotional and educational material. Poster and other competitions raise awareness of the credit union ethos. Winning posters have been included in calendars. Sponsorship of sporting events such as the Community Games and Junior Cycle Tour of Ireland help to involve participation at national and local levels.

In accordance with resolution 71 of the convention in 1987, financial support was given to the Society for Co-operative Studies (SCSI) and specifically for its newsletter, *Co-op Contact* and also to other groups such as the Co-operative Development Society and the Co-operative Way for education and promotion. ILCU supports the efforts of the SCSI, a voluntary body comprising members from various co-operative sectors as well as individual academics, public servants and professionals. ILCU was represented by the late Séamus MacEoin and Jack Flahive on the Society's special committee on the wider application of the co-operative system (chaired by Dr Trevor West, TCD) which issued a major report in 1986.

AFFILIATIONS

The ILCU is affiliated to the World Council of Credit Unions (WOCCU). Irish representatives including the late Gus Murray, former ILCU president and later WOCCU president, and Gerry Foley, WOCCU executive secretary in 1996 and subsequently treasurer, have contributed to international developments. WOCCU has almost a hundred affiliated members in 50,000 credit unions world-wide. Another international connection is with the Plunkett Foundation, Oxford, which is engaged in research and consultancy for the world-wide co-operative movement.

ILCU International Development Foundation Ltd

This is a non-governmental organisation (NGO) funded by contributions from members of credit unions. The fund, which has potential for further growth, has spent over £2 million in sponsoring over 85 projects in credit unions and other co-op development in countries including Bangladesh, Nepal, Haiti, South Africa, the Gambia, Montserrat and increasingly in Eastern Europe, especially Russia. The foundation's work helps to promote good relations between Ireland and the developing world. Irish and overseas credit unions are twinned. Visitors are shown Irish credit unions in operation and Irish volunteers work abroad. In Albania, the ILCU's efforts were co-funded with the European Union.

Other International Connections

ILCU board members and executives are involved in WOCCU and EU level initiatives in countries such as Russia. Training materials from Ireland are used in a transfer of knowledge from West to East as explained in the *World of Co-op Enterprise* (Turula, 1998) published by the Plunkett Foundation in an article called *Credit Unions: Sustainable Financial Organisations in Emerging Democracies*. The ILCU has a vital role in the development, consolidation, administration, supervision and servicing of the Irish credit union movement in a technological era of increased competition.

The ILCU maintains good working relations with the official Registrars in Dublin and Belfast and also with relevant government departments. It is clear, from the activities outlined, that the League, in conjunction with its associated bodies, has increasingly widened its key role in community and co-operative development at home and abroad.

Chapter 14

CREDIT UNION ADVISORY COMMITTEE (CUAC)

"Advice is judged by results; not by intentions."

Cicero: *Ad Atticum IX*

Section 180 of the 1997 Act provides for the appointment by the Minister for Enterprise, Trade and Employment of CUAC and for the committee's constitution, functions, membership and expenses.

BACKGROUND

Section 27 of the Credit Union Act, 1966, provided that the Minister (then of Industry and Commerce) should appoint a committee which would be known, and was referred to in the Act as the Credit Union Advisory Committee. Its function was to advise the Minister, and such other persons as he thought fit, in relation to specified matters:

a) The improvement of the management of credit unions;

b) The protection of the interests of members and creditors of credit unions;

c) Other matters relating to credit unions upon which the Minister could, from time to time, seek advice.

The CUAC consisted of not more than seven persons appointed for such period as the Minister thought fit. Persons appointed to membership of the committee are (and were) chosen by the Minister for such appointment because of their knowledge of matters pertaining to credit unions or because they were capable of giving substantial practical assistance in the committee's work. Members of parliament, of either house of the Oireachtas, the Dáil or Seanad, could and may not be members of CUAC. The Minister nominated a member as chairman. Members were paid remuneration and expenses as the Minister, with the consent of the Minister for Finance, would determine.

Section 180 of the Credit Union Act, 1997, provided for the continued existence of the advisory committee with some minor adjustments as explained later in this chapter under current statutory provisions.

EARLY MEMBERS

Pioneers Nora Herlihy and Séamus MacEoin served on the Advisory Committee for many years after its inception in 1967, and contributed their practical expertise to relevant developments. Nora Herlihy chaired the first committee which advised on suitable model rules and ministerial regulations. The committee included other former League directors and some experts who had served on the Committee on Co-operative Societies which had issued an important report in 1963.

Another significant member was James Ivers who gathered information from Wisconsin, USA. He served for many years as Director General of the Incorporated Law Society, the professional body for Irish solicitors. Ivers' MBA thesis (1970) *The Further Development of Credit Unions in Ireland*, UCD, provided insights into the rationale for advisory committees, as summarised below.

WHY AN ADVISORY COMMITTEE?

The advisory committee concept was not original. In the USA there was a specific Federal Credit Union Agency and in Australia an approach similar to the Irish one was adopted. The need for an advisory committee, despite the existence of the Registrar of Friendly Societies, was argued by civil servants in the Department of Industry and Commerce for various reasons. For example, there had been problems with previous credit co-operatives, especially from the Registrar's point of view in relation to annual returns. The advice of interested and suitably qualified people would help to ensure growth and development while keeping problems under review. A senior civil servant in the department, J.A. O'Dwyer, assistant secretary, in a reservation to the *Report of the Committee on Co-operative Societies* (1963) stressed the hazards of voluntary organisations receiving money on deposit from members and lending it to other members. O'Dwyer considered that the proposed safeguards might not be adequate to meet the risks involved. Those reservations may have influenced the government's decision to include an advisory committee as an integral part of credit union legislation.

As explained in the Ivers' thesis, the Minister and Dáil accepted the proposition of an advisory committee. During the parliamentary debate, there were some references to the proposed committee making jobs for members of the Minister's political party. Ivers' thesis added that the nearest equivalents might be the regulatory bodies for the medical and other professions. Such bodies' main function is to protect the public, not, as is commonly thought to protect the professions or vested interests.

THE ILCU AND THE ADVISORY COMMITTEE

The Ivers' thesis also stated that an active League with a high rate of affiliation from registered credit unions might not leave much scope for the CUAC, which had already carried out basic functions such as formulating standard rules and an annual return form. Ivers also stressed the need for a sympathetic approach to ensure that cordial relations existed between the League and CUAC.

In the early years of the CUAC, however, tensions existed between it and the League. Some voluntary workers in the movement resented other credit union activists serving on an officially-appointed body which had an inside track to the Minister and civil servants. Nora Herlihy seems to have been caught in the crossfire between CUAC, an official body under civil service aegis, and the ILCU as a voluntary body.

The above remarks are not intended as a reflection on the dedicated efforts over the years by many CUAC members, including Séamus MacEoin and Nora Herlihy, both now deceased.

There is no statutory prohibition on ILCU directors being CUAC members. Under rules governing the League (as distinct from the standard rules for affiliated credit unions) section 4(7) (f), CUAC members would be ineligible to hold office as a director or supervisor or member of the standing committee or member of the nominating committee of the ILCU. The intention is presumably to avoid conflicts of interest.

In recent years, earlier tensions have been replaced by a mutual effort for the good of the credit union movement. CUAC, the ILCU, the Department of Enterprise, Trade and Employment and also the Registrar have worked together jointly, especially on the new legislation. Amendments suggested by CUAC were included in the final version of the legislation. Michael Woods, former manager of St Mary's Credit Union, Navan, in particular as chairman, has made a significant contribution to the effective role of CUAC.

CURRENT STATUTORY PROVISIONS

Section 180(1) of the Credit Union Act, 1997, provides that there shall continue to be a body known as the Credit Union Advisory Committee (the Advisory Committee) which shall exercise the functions assigned to it by the Act.

Subsection (2) provides that the Committee shall advise the Minister, and such persons as the Minister thinks fit, in relation to

a) the improvement of the management of credit unions;

b) the protection of the interests of members and creditors of credit unions; and

c) other matters relating to credit unions upon which the Minister, *the Registrar, or such persons as may be specified by the Minister*, may from time to time seek the advice of the Committee.

The words italicised above for emphasis, which are additional to earlier provisions in section 27(2) (c) of the 1966 Act, broaden the scope of CUAC to allow it to advise formally the Registrar and other persons as may be specified by the Minister. As indicated in his annual statutory reports, the Registrar already had discussions with CUAC, especially regarding the new legislation.

The residue of section 180 of the 1997 Act re-enacts similar details in section 27 of the 1966 Act providing that the Minister shall appoint not more than seven persons for such period as he thinks fit; and that persons shall be chosen for appointment by reason of their knowledge of matters pertaining to credit unions or because such persons are capable of giving substantial assistance in committees' work. The prohibition on members of the Dáil or Seanad being members of CUAC was continued, as were the provisions about the Minister nominating a chairman, and for payment of expenses and remuneration as the Minister, with the consent of the Minister for Finance, may determine.

The experience of co-operating with other relevant bodies regarding the new legislation in the 1997 Act and providing expertise and experience augurs well for CUAC to contribute effective advice with fruitful results.

Chapter 15

NORTHERN IRELAND

"Whereas success in the North would not necessarily
be followed by success in the South, if they were
successful in the South they would have no difficulty
in succeeding in the North."

Sir Horace Plunkett (1854-1932), Irish co-operative leader

The above statement made in relation to the wider co-op movement at the turn of the 20th century seems apt in reference to the
Irish credit union movement which, from Southern roots, became
well established in the North. On further examination, however,
the position is more complex.

BACKGROUND

There was a co-operative tradition on a limited scale in the North
of Ireland. Following the visit to Dublin in 1823 of Robert Owen,
the British co-op pioneer, the Belfast Co-operative Trading
Association was founded in 1830 with a very ambitious programme ranging from factories to farms. That initiative failed to
maintain a momentum. George Russell (Æ), the Irish co-op leader
during the early twentieth century, was based in Dublin but had
been born in Lurgan, Co. Armagh.

The relationship between the co-op leader, Sir Horace Plunkett
and Ulster has been traced by his biographer Dr Trevor West in
an essay in *The Golden Triangle-the Æ Memorial Lectures* (1989).
The North seemed to provide fertile soil for co-operative ideas.
Friendly societies and small savings banks for mutual self-help
were also established in the North East.

During World War One, a speaker named W.H. West expressed optimistic views at the opening of a branch shop of the Enniskillen Co-operative Society at Ballinmallard. He hoped that the day was near when the people could come together to solve community problems. He hoped that "one day co-operation would achieve wonderful things in Ireland — constructive nation-building — and other lesser accomplishments to make us wonder and grow glad."

After the partition of Ireland, during the 1920's, the Northern co-ops formed the Ulster Agricultural Organisation Society (UAOS) which severed from the Irish mainstream many people who had given splendid service to the all-Ireland co-operative movement.

CREDIT UNIONS IN THE NORTH

The spread of the credit union movement to Northern Ireland was traced by Séamus MacEoin, a credit union pioneer, in his contribution to *The Golden Triangle* (Quinn 1989). The starting point was when Fr Paddy Gallagher, League President, spoke at a Christus Rex Conference in Carrigart, Co. Donegal in 1960. Among the audience was Fr Anthony Mulvey from Derry. Fr Mulvey encouraged John Hume and a few others to form the first Northern credit union in the Bogside, Derry, in October 1960. The movement spread to Armagh and throughout Ulster under the leadership of John Hume. He became the second President of the Irish League, international vice-president, and later leader of the SDLD, MP, MEP and Nobel Peace Laureate.

As outlined in John Hume's book, *Personal Views* (1996), a small group of volunteers, including his wife Pat, and also teachers, clergy and community activists such as Paddy Doherty, founded Derry Credit Union in the Bogside, a working class Roman Catholic enclave. At its inception in 1960, Derry Credit Union had only a handful of members and £4 in savings. By the late 1990's, membership had grown to almost 20,000 members with over £20 million in savings and assets. A smaller and more recent group, the Society Credit Union Ltd based at the Apprentice Boys Memorial Hall, Londonderry, reflects diversity of tradition.

John Hume also contributed to the constructive debate at the Northern Ireland parliament at Stormont resulting in 1969 in the credit union legislation within the industrial and provident societies framework. Success in co-operative savings encouraged positive self-help initiatives in local communities throughout Northern Ireland.

Jack Carney also made a significant contribution to the movement and was elected to the League Board. His daughter, Caroline Carney, continued the family tradition by participating in the Law Library Credit Union Study Group, Dublin, leading in 1998 to the Law Library Credit Union Ltd.

Northern Ireland (NI) credit unions have been traditionally associated with the League (ILCU), the all-Ireland body based in Dublin. The ILCU is still the main umbrella body representing about 58 per cent in 1998 (a declining proportion compared with earlier years) of credit unions in Northern Ireland and over 90 per cent of members.

The credit union movement is non-sectarian and non-political. Roman Catholics, however, have traditionally formed the bulk of Northern credit union membership, and initial efforts, by John Hume and his associates to spread the credit union message in East Belfast fell on stony ground (Hume, 1997).

Following growing interest among the Protestant community, the British-based National Federation of Savings and Co-operative Credit Unions (NFCU) set up a regional office in Northern Ireland in the mid-1980's but a distinct Ulster Federation was subsequently formed. Of the 178 registered credit unions, about 62 had by 1998 affiliated to the Ulster Federation of Credit Unions (UFCU). These credit unions were mainly based in areas with Protestant residents.

For example, Society Credit Union Ltd, founded near the historic walls of Derry in 1990, had 1,300 members and total assets of £750,000 by 1998. The Association of British Credit Unions (ABCUL), based in Britain and affiliated to the World

Council of Credit Unions (WOCCU), is not active now in Northern Ireland.

The credit union movement is much more widespread in Northern Ireland than in Britain. There are over 178 credit unions in Northern Ireland with savings of over £230 million sterling and a total membership of about 250,000, representing a significant segment of the population but leaving scope for expansion. There are 12 independent credit unions in Northern Ireland which are not affiliated to either the ILCU or the UFCU and there are three independent credit unions in Belfast which follow the Antigonish model of Nova Scotia.

Registrar of Credit Unions

The NI Registrar comes within the ambit of the Department of Economic Development, Belfast. The present holder of the office is Raymond McKeag. Unlike the position in Dublin, the Registry of Credit Unions and Registry of Companies in Belfast come under the same direct administration. For credit unions, the Northern Registrar performs similar functions to his counterpart in Dublin but details differ, reflecting different emphasis in the relevant legislation. The NI Registrar maintains a public search facility for records based on annual returns submitted. He also has a registration and prudential role, enforces the law and codes of conduct, and ensures that legislation is harmonised with British and EU standards.

The Registrar's statutory report dated July 1997, covering returns received during 1996, stated that most bodies submit satisfactory returns on time. The Registrar keeps in close contact with the ILCU, the UFCU and also with local credit unions, their officers and auditors.

Legislation — the 1985 Order

The basic legislation is the Credit Unions (Northern Ireland) Order, 1985 (SI 1985/1205, NI 12) — the 1985 Order. It came into operation on 1 June 1986 and consolidated, with amendments and repealed provisions, the Industrial and Provident Societies Act (Northern Ireland) 1969 which regulated credit unions as a special type of society.

The 1985 Order provided a modern legal code for credit unions and varied in detail from the Irish 1966 Act. The main provisions were:

- A minimum membership of 21 plus a secretary, and a maximum of 5,000, were specified for any one credit union;

- Members who no longer have a common bond could retain full borrowing powers for one year, subject to a maximum of 10 per cent of members availing of that facility;

- Under Article 25, deposit-taking was prohibited but section 26 facilitated deposits by persons too young to be members, that is, under 16 years of age. Such deposits are to be held in trust until the attainment of 16 years and then converted to shares, or else withdrawn by depositors;

- The maximum dividend on shares was increased to 8 per cent per annum;

- Article 37 required compulsory insurance against fraud or other dishonesty.

Registration Requirements

The Registrar, in accordance with Article 3 of the 1985 Order, requires credit unions to comply with statutory conditions for registration including:

1) Minimum membership of 21 plus a secretary and a maximum of 5,000;

2) Rules providing for all matters specified in Schedule 1 to the 1985 Order, many of which reflect the usual criteria such as registered office, admission of members, adminis-tration and mode of application of surplus income (the Registrar may also determine that additional matters be included in the rules);

3) Societies formed with the objectives of promoting thrift among members by accumulation of savings, creation of credit at reasonable rates of interest, control and use of members' funds for their mutual benefit, and training and education of members in the wise use of money and in the management of their financial affairs;

4) The place under those rules, to be the society's registered office situated in Northern Ireland;

5) Admission to membership to be restricted to persons each of whom has, in relation to all the other members, not less than one common bond.

The name must not be undesirable in the Registrar's opinion.

The requirements listed above reflect generally acceptable co-operative and credit union principles. Model rules of the ILCU, the UFCU and the Antigonish model facilitate registration at reduced fees.

Deregulation

The Credit Union Deregulation (Northern Ireland) Order, 1997, (SI 1997 No. 2984 (NI 22) came into force in February 1998. According to guidance notes issued by the Registrar, the Order's purpose is to facilitate the growth of credit unions whilst continuing to ensure the safety of members' funds. The Order removes or reduces some of the burdens of the 1985 Order. The term deregulation may give a misleading impression but the new system allows flexibility, especially on shareholding and loans, subject to prudential checks by the Registrar who still retains effective regulatory powers.

The Deregulation Order, subject to specified conditions, provides:

• A statutory declaration, in the appropriate legal format by people specified below, may be used in connection with the common bond.

- Limits on shareholding were increased.

- Shares may be permitted to be used as security.

- Restrictions on non-qualifying members were relaxed.

- Limits on loans to members of credit unions issued with a certificate under section 28 of the 1985 Order may be increased.

The above is explained in more detail below.

Statutory Declaration regarding Common Bond

Article 3 and schedule 1, paragraph 1, of the 1997 Order amended article 3 (5) of the 1985 order to provide that the Registrar, in ascertaining whether a common bond exists between members may, at his discretion, treat a statutory declaration as sufficient evidence that a common bond exists. The statutory declaration may replace supporting evidence and must be signed by three members of a prospective credit union seeking registration, and by the secretary in the presence of a witness (a solicitor, commissioner for oaths, notary public or justice of the peace) who must also sign the declaration. The Registrar may reject the statutory declaration if he considers it proper in the circumstances under the amended article 3(5) of the 1985 Order.

Other requirements such as management structures and necessary expertise must also be in place before registration.

Shareholding

Each member was restricted to a shareholding of £10,000 prior to the 1997 Order. Article 14(3) of the 1985 Order, as amended by article 3 and schedule 1(2) of the 1997 Order, allows individual members to hold more than £10,000 in a credit union provided that the individual's shareholding does not exceed 1.5 per cent of the total shareholdings in the respective credit union. A member may not hold shares exceeding whichever is the greater of £10,000 and 1.5 per cent of the total shareholdings. Therefore, if total shareholdings were £45,000 at the last financial year, a member could hold shares up to £10,000 although that limit exceeds £675 which is 1.5 per cent of £45,000. In a large credit union with total shareholdings of £2 million, a member could hold shares up to £30,000, that is 1.5 per cent of £2 million. According to the Registrar's annual report, in 1996, out of a total 165, there were 32 credit unions with assets over £2 million each.

The use of percentages of total assets as a criterion for individual shareholding and loans was included in the Credit Union Act, 1997 (Republic of Ireland), but on a simpler basis than in Northern Ireland.

Secured Loans

Loans may be granted under article 28 of the 1985 Order on a secured or unsecured basis. Article 28 of the 1985 order, as amended by article 3 and schedule 1(5) of the 1997 Order with the insertion of article 28A, allows a credit union to make a secured loan to a member using that member's shares a security. When the loan is being made, however, the member's paid-up shareholding must exceed or be equal to that member's total liability to the credit union. Other forms of security are not restricted or excluded. The status for unsecured loans is not affected and other forms of security may be used. The use of shares as security for secured loans is now permitted but is not compulsory.

Shares issued as security for a loan may not be withdrawn if that would reduce the member's shareholding below their total liability to the credit union. In other cases, for example where shares were not used as security for a loan, members may withdraw only at the discretion of the board of directors or management committee.

Non-qualifying Members

These are members ceasing to have the common bond with other members and they are restricted to 10 per cent of total membership of a credit union. The inclusion of that class of member in the

Irish Credit Union Act, section 17(4), was controversial. Article 3 and schedule 1(2) (c) and (4) of the Northern Ireland Order, 1997, amends the 1985 Order to remove borrowing and withdrawal restrictions on non-qualifying members. Such members, especially if they move away from the common bond area, may be a greater risk than full members, and stricter controls and monitoring by management committees would be advisable.

Loans

The maximum amount which a credit union could make to a member, under 1985 Order, was £10,000 in excess of the member's shareholding. A new section 28B of the 1985 Order, added by article 3 and schedule 1(5) of the 1997 Order, enables credit unions, which have been issued with a certificate of approval, to grant loans exceeding existing limits on total paid-up shareholding. Section 28B(2) (a) and (b) sets out the factors for determining the total amount which may be loaned to a member in excess of paid-up shareholding. The combination of comparison factors, including the calculation of 20 per cent of general reserves and 1.5 per cent of total paid-up shareholding, is fairly complex and the relevant Orders and guidance notes which provide practical examples should be consulted.

Two examples illustrate the general principles: A small credit union has total paid-up shareholdings of £45,000 and a general reserve of £3,500. 1.5 per cent of shareholding equals £675; 20 per cent of general reserve is £700. Loans may not be made in excess of £10,000 above shareholding. In contrast, a large credit union has total shareholdings of £5 million and general reserves of £400,000. As 1.5 per cent of shareholdings (£75,000) exceeds £10,000 and 20 per cent of general reserves (£80,000) is greater than £10,000, loans may be made up to whichever is the lesser of shareholding calculation and the general reserve calculation. Therefore, the limit on loans is £75,000 in excess of paid-up shareholdings.

The limits are restricted in cases where an additional loan would take the credit union above the limits on the aggregate of large loans permitted in article 28B of the 1985 Order, as explained in the guidance notes issued by the Registrar.

Certificates of approval may be issued only where the Registrar is satisfied that the specific credit union has a general reserve which is not less than 10 per cent of total assets plus adequate management and control systems. In summary, requirements include details of officers and staff including relevant experience, a three-year business plan, and also a letter of comfort from the auditor confirming the adequacy of the relevant arrangements. Before deciding whether to grant a certificate, the Registrar will consider the information supplied together with the annual returns. An official inspection of policy and procedures manuals may also be necessary. Guidance notes on management and systems provide details for officers and staff of credit unions. The Registrar may refuse to grant a certificate or withdraw one following a review. Fair procedures will allow representations to the Registrar. He maintains good relations with the credit union movement through user groups and regular contacts with representative bodies and individual credit unions.

Some Comparisons between Legislation in the Republic of Ireland and Northern Ireland (NI)

There is now free-standing legislation in both jurisdictions, but that in the Republic is more comprehensive and differs in many details from that in Northern Ireland. Registration confers advantages such as corporate status, limitation of members' liability to the amount of their shareholding and the facility to withdraw share capital. These are common to both legislations.

Examples of other common areas are general but not detailed requirements for accounts and audits, annual returns to Registrar and his powers of inspection, hearing of disputes by the Registrar, dissolution of credit union and specified offences. There are also provisions for members to nominate persons to become entitled at members' death to the whole or part of the member's property in the credit union.

The common bond concept based on residence or employment in a particular locality also features in both jurisdictions but finer details differ. The objectives of encouraging thrift and creating sources of credit and controlling savings, as well as encouraging education and training, are also common to both jurisdictions.

Some features already in Northern Ireland legislation were included as new provisions in the Irish Credit Union Act, 1997. For example, under article 31 of the 1985 Order, Northern Ireland credit unions are exempt from the Bills of Sale (Ireland) Acts, 1879–1883. The practical effect of this reform, long advocated in the Irish jurisdiction and implemented in section 34 of the 1997 Act, is to facilitate the creation of floating charges on the assets of the relevant society or credit union.

Because of the exemption from the Bill of Sales Acts, such charges need not be recorded under the cumbersome Bills of Sale registration procedures. The Registrar registers the charges on a system somewhat like that for companies. That reform and the special registration system facilitates borrowing by credit unions.

Loans

The Northern Ireland 1985 Order strictly regulated the operations of credit unions but the criteria were relaxed in the 1997 Order as outlined above. Section 35 (3) of the Irish (Republic) Credit Union Act, 1997, relaxing limits on loans to members exceeding the greater of £30,000 or 1.5 per cent of the total assets of a credit union, provided a simpler solution than did the Northern Ireland Deregulation Order of 1997.

Loans may be made under the Northern Ireland Order upon such security (or without security) and terms as the rules of the credit union may provide.

Under S.R 1993, No. 429, the Credit Unions (Loans and Deposits) Order (Northern Ireland), 1993, maximum periods of unsecured loans are four years or such longer period as may by order be specified, and, in other cases, such period as an order may specify. Section 35(2) of the Irish Act of 1997 specifies the circumstances under which loans may be made for periods exceeding five and ten years.

Interest not exceeding 1 per cent per month on the outstanding balance may be charged in NI but the rate may be varied by order. The same maximum percentage rate was provided for in section 38(1) of the Irish Act, 1997.

Bad Debts

The Registrar's recent annual reports stated that it was gratifying to note that credit unions are continuing to adopt a stringent approach regarding bad debts. He pointed out, however, that whilst prudence and a realistic attitude towards irrecoverable debt must be encouraged, writing off debts must never be regarded as an easy option to be used in preference to rigorous pursuit of delinquent loans.

Reserves

Under article 36 of the Northern Ireland 1985 Order, a credit union must build up and maintain, by means of annual transfers of at least 20 per cent of its surplus for the year, a general reserve amounting to not less than 10 per cent of total assets. Section 45 of the Irish 1997 Act also stipulates a 10 per cent statutory reserve figure. In recent annual reports, the Registrar in Belfast noted that, in general, progress had been made in achieving the statutory reserves of 10 per cent of total assets. In such cases where the total value of assets is increasing, the Registrar recommended that a higher proportion of annual surplus be transferred to reserves, so that the minimum may be reached.

Fraud

The Northern Ireland Registrar has warned repeatedly that directors and committee members must be fully aware of their responsibilities and be especially vigilant in performing their duties. Supervisors and internal auditors must be at all times vigilant and alert to the possibility of fraud. The rules require checks. Supervisors and auditors should also be persistent in questioning directors, committee members, members and employees until they are fully satisfied with the answers provided. Directors should be familiar with bookkeeping methods and computer systems and they should also review insurance cover.

CREDIT UNIONS IN BRITAIN

An analysis of the British credit union movement was included in Donnelly and Haggett (1997). Despite significant growth in recent years, the movement in terms of a few hundred thousand members and about 500 credit unions is not widespread compared with Ireland. Trends indicate that British credit unions are beginning to experience a long-expected development, especially as anti-poverty initiatives in deprived areas and also in employments such as local authority employees and the police. The Registrar of Friendly Societies, as the regulatory authority, insists that employment-based credit unions are given payroll deduction facilities so that members save regularly and in predictable amounts.

The abovementioned study concludes that British credit unions have come a long way since 1985. They are no longer a financial secret but will play an important role in the financial sector, especially as a repository for mutual funds. The Association of British Credit Unions Ltd. (ABCUL), the main central body, is affiliated to the international body WOCCU. The British movement could learn from the total Irish experience.

Under article 82 of the Northern Ireland 1985 Order, regulations may make provision for conferring rights and obligations under that Order on a Great Britain credit union. That is defined as a society registered as a credit union under the law for the time being in force in Great Britain for purposes corresponding to those of the 1985 Order and which carry on or intend to carry on business in Northern Ireland. The provision is interesting in the all-Ireland and EU contexts in the provision of financial services across national frontiers.

CONCLUSION

Credit unions contribute significantly to community development in Northern Ireland. There are many differences in detail and emphasis between the Republic of Ireland and Northern Ireland legislation, as outlined above. In general, the 1985 Order as amended by the 1997 Order modernised the law and provided free-standing legislation drafted specifically to meet the needs and aspirations of the Northern credit union movement, as distinct from other parts of the UK. Experience arising from the 1997 Act in the Republic of Ireland, and the motion passed at the ILCU's AGM in, 1998 seeking similar legislation for Northern Ireland, should encourage further legislative developments north of the border. Noel Treacy, TD, Minister of State at the Department of Enterprise, Trade and Employment at the annual dinner of the ILCU in 1998, suggested that, in the context of the Belfast Agreement of the same year, credit unions could be supervised on an all-Ireland basis. That would have implications for the credit union movement north of the border and the roles of the Registrars in Dublin and Belfast.

Chapter 16

FUTURE TRENDS AND DEVELOPMENTS

"I have seen the future and it works."

Lincoln Steffens (1866–1936).

The above statement, made optimistically about a visit to the former Soviet Union after World War One, would have been more apt as a prediction regarding the credit union movement. What does the future hold for Irish credit unions in the new century and the third millennium? To quote G.K. Chesterton: "Let us look to the future because that is where we are going to be".

MAIN AGENTS OF CHANGE

- New Legislative Framework — especially the Credit Union Act, 1997 in the Republic of Ireland, matched by ILCU's revised standard rules facilitating additional services and stimulating competition with mainstream financial services sectors;

- The supervisory and regulatory framework;

- Involvement with the wider community and the social economy;

- The European Monetary Union and the related Euro currency and lower interest rates;

- Demographic, social and other trends in the Irish economy;

- New technology and its effects on services to members;

- Balancing the traditional voluntary ethos with increased professional management at all levels within the credit union movement.

- Strategic planning by the credit union movement under the ILCU's leadership: *Focus on the Future*.

Changes will also affect Northern Ireland to various degrees but new comprehensive legislation will be required in that jurisdiction.

THE CREDIT UNION ACT, 1997

The effects of the new legislation and the consequent revised standard rules of the ILCU were examined in detail in this book. In summary and subject to the specific statutory provisions, the main practical effects of the changes in respect of financial transactions as explained in detail in Chapter 7 and 8 will be as follows:

- Loans to individual members may be larger in size, up to £30,000 or 1.5 per cent of the total assets (whichever is the greater) of the specific credit union in accordance with section 35 of the 1997 Act and ILCU standard rule 44(3).

- Compared with the previous situation, loans may be for longer periods, for over five years and over ten years subject to overall limits related to total outstanding in the relevant credit union within the formula in section 35(2) (a) and (b) of the 1997 Act and ILCU standard rule 44(4). Further increases in the limits by Ministerial order are possible but unlikely in the short term.

- It is difficult to predict the pattern of future lending but many loans are likely to be for relatively modest amounts as credit unions facilitate the needs of a wide range of members. While a few credit unions with very large assets could legally grant individual loans approaching £1 million, many credit unions will be restricted by their asset base, cash flows and practical operations from granting large loans. Members should check the position within their own credit union and the varying policies on lending.

Additional Services

Subject to the statutory constraints in sections 48 to 52 of the 1997 Act, reflected in rules 59 to 63, a credit union may provide, as principal or agent, additional services of a description that appears to the Registrar to be of mutual benefit to its members. Such services would be other than those already provided for, such as loans, shares and acceptance of deposits. When this book was being written, a commencement order had not yet been made by the Minister to bring the sections on additional services into operation.

Pending details in Ministerial orders and regulations, it is difficult to predict precisely what additional services would be allowed. They could include commercial-type loans at higher rates of interest, special savings products, savings related to life insurance and pensions, mortgages, laser cards, and also the issue of cheque books. There could be a much wider range of financial and insurance products than those already provided.

Advertising by individual credit unions, and by groups and associations of credit unions (including the ILCU), is likely to increase to draw attention to existing and new services in the competitive financial services environment. Such advertising would be subject to the constraints and conditions in section 86 of the 1997 Act.

The Supervisory and Regulatory Framework

Despite criticism of some aspects and the credit union movement's fears of over-intrusiveness, the supervisory and regulatory regime in the 1997 Act provides a balanced approach to meet the public interest and allow credit unions to operate effectively. The functions of the Registrar of Friendly Societies have been examined throughout this book, and specifically in Chapter 9. The full implications will take time and experience in the actual operation of the Act. Continued excellent relations between the Registrar, who understands the special nature and ethos of credit unions, and the ILCU are essential to ensure efficiency to the ultimate interest of members.

The Oireachtas Joint Committee on Finance and the Public Service examined allegations about the commercial banking sector and, following a comparative study in some other European states, concluded that current regulation and supervision were inadequate. In its report — *Review of Banking Policy and the Regulation and Supervision of Financial Institutions* (1988) — the joint committee recommended that an independent financial services authority be established to regulate and supervise the financial services sector, including banks, building societies, friendly societies and, significantly, credit unions. The joint committee may have taken too broad an approach by including voluntary bodies with the commercial sector, without evidence of malfunctioning within credit unions or inadequacies in the existing framework. As credit union operations expand, however, there will be further pressure for the supervisory functions to be subsumed in a wider framework. Government policy favours an independent overall financial services authority. Details will be decided when the implementation group, appointed in October 1998, with Michael McDowell, SC, as chairman, makes its advisory recommendations. A super regulator on the UK model would have implications for the Registrar's role and could lead to the separation of registration and regulatory functions for credit unions. The ILCU would prefer that the Registrar retain the regulatory role.

In Northern Ireland, despite a policy of statutory deregulation allowing greater discretion and flexibility, the Registrar of Credit Unions will have a vital role in considering, and then implementing, new comprehensive legislation which will be influenced by the 1997 Act in the Republic of Ireland.

INVOLVEMENT WITH THE WIDER COMMUNITY
AND THE SOCIAL ECONOMY

Operating Principles, detailed in appendix 2 to this book and in appendix 1 to the ILCU's standard rules, restate the high ideals of co-operation and social responsibility including a vision of social justice and regard for the broader community. The ILCU's standard rule 6 requires each credit union to conduct its affairs in accordance with those principles, but increased awareness at all levels is essential to combat criticism by mainstream financial institutions and media commentators who often misunderstand the co-operative ethos.

Arguments against wider community involvement by credit unions have focused on fears that members' savings could be lost in risky enterprises. As examined in Chapter 8 of this book on Financial Operations, a structured and balanced approach is, however, facilitated by the 1997 Act in section 44. It enables the general meeting of a credit union to approve the establishment (and subsequent winding-up) of a special fund for specified social, cultural, charitable or community purposes. Safeguards require adequate provision for current and contingent liabilities, maintaining proper reserves, limits on the amounts of the special funds relative to the accumulated reserves, and the directors, being satisfied that the payment will not affect financial stability.

The social economy covers a spectrum outside the market economy, between the activities of the private commercial sector and of the public sector. There are differences of opinion as to whether credit unions, as voluntary co-operatives with a self-help ethos should be considered as part of the social economy, or whether credit unions should financially assist social economic initiatives, including combating unemployment and social exclusion. Paddy Candon, an experienced credit union activist in New Ross Credit Union Limited and the Co-operative Way education group, considers that co-operation has the potential to reverse the negative effects of the market economy. He is critical of outside funding and control inherent in the social economy concept. Paddy Candon echoed the views of many activists when he argued that the Irish credit union movement utilising its co-operative basis is ideally placed, financially and geographically, to stimulate secondary development and alternatives to the market economy (Candon, 1998).

If there is a renewed awareness, by education and training, of the basic co-op ethos underlying the credit union movement, and a more imaginative approach, there will be greater involvement in wider community development.

Surplus funds in credit unions have again stimulated the concept of an Irish co-operative bank to provide a third force in banking but it will be increasingly difficult to realise that aim in the current era of large-scale financial institutions.

EMU, THE EURO AND LOWER INTEREST RATES

The ILCU's documents on the Euro, including detailed timetables and a glossary of technical terms, will be supplemented by regular checklists highlighting important points. Credit unions and members must familiarise themselves with the necessary details.

As emphasised in the editorial in *Credit Union Review*, Vol.16, issue 110 (1998), EMU may seriously affect the way in which credit unions do business and the interest rates charged on loans and given on savings. Falling interest rates will intensify the need to give value for money. Fine-tuning will be required periodically to balance minimum returns on savings with minimum costs of borrowing. The balance must be assessed against the market rates of interest and the value of the credit union must be obvious to the members. The co-operative ethos should not penalise vulnerable sections in order to maximise the dividend or reward to other sections.

EMU and the wider investment choices allowable under the Trustee (Authorised Investments) Order, 1998, have implications for investments by credit unions having regard for their varying needs of security, liquidity, yield and flexibility. Credit unions, in planning future strategy, need specialised information which is available from Davy Stockbrokers, professional advisors to the ILCU Central Investment Management.

As many Irish holiday destinations will be in the Euro zone, demand for foreign exchange facilities, a service provided by some Irish credit unions, will be affected.

Although the UK remains outside EMU, at least in the medium term, credit unions in Northern Ireland, especially in border counties should not ignore the implications, especially on currency transactions.

DEMOGRAPHIC, SOCIAL AND OTHER TRENDS IN THE IRISH ECONOMY

"Bringing young people to the credit union movement is important — it is important to teach young people that saving is the key to spending — because to have grasped that concept at an early age creates a life long discipline that can be handed down from generation to generation", President Mary McAleese, at the opening of ILCU new offices in Dublin, 21 February 1998.

Youth — defined as under 30 years of age, and especially under 25 years — is under-represented in the credit union movement. *The Youth Policy Task Force's (YPTF) Interim Report*, based on a very well researched nationwide study, and adopted by the ILCU's AGM in April, 1998, referred to a lost generation of young people with no credit union involvement. Most credit unions lack specific initiatives to cater for third-level students. There are no campus credit unions and Belfield Credit Union Limited caters only for university staff. In contrast, banks actively encourage young people by providing user-friendly services, including easy access to cash. Increased use of ATMs by credit unions will facilitate students living away from home, provided that they are already credit union members.

On the broader front, there will be more imaginative approaches to attract a higher proportion of youth including: an ILCU nationwide youth policy, supported by a practical measures such as a designated youth development officer, web sites, partnerships with schools, colleges and youth bodies, a strategic alliance with at least one national youth organisation and greater involvement by young people at all levels of the credit union movement.

At the other end of the scale, it will be necessary to retain the loyalty of the traditional core membership base which is becoming older in accordance with general trends in Irish society. Special savings products, possibly linked to insurance and pensions, will have to be devised and marketed by credit unions as principals or agents.

Women have been active leaders since the era of Nora Herlihy and Muriel Gahan but a study of the special needs of female members should be undertaken to encourage more involvement at all levels. The gender perspective in the broader context was examined in "Women in Co-operatives: the Policy of the International Co-op Alliance" (Urquijo, 1998).

Social Class

Although all social classes are represented within the Irish credit union movement, the trends identified in a survey by Landsdowne Market Research and quoted in an article by Jim Aughney (1996) in the *Irish Independent* are likely to intensify:

> A declining farmer base and a rising membership by the middle classes and professional people. They are becoming increasingly alert to the advantages of co-operative credit and are exercising their democratic right to form or join credit unions.
>
> A slowing-down of, or possible recession in, the Irish economy would probably affect the rate of growth of credit unions. They would remain, however, a safe option for savings.

New Technology

As ATM networks for cash withdrawals and electronic funds transfer systems for direct payment of wages (such as Paypath) and for crediting accounts with State welfare benefits become the norm in the wider financial services sector, members will expect similar facilities from their credit unions. Some already share in the IQ Cash network. ILCUTech, a specialised company owned by ILCU, aims at providing long-term, affordable systems making new services available to all members while not placing smaller credit unions at a disadvantage. Standard software systems and harmonised computer networks are essential to attract all credit unions as appropriate to their circumstances and to ensure that credit unions remain competitive. ILCU propose the ISIS system which was specially adapted from an international system.

State-of-the-art technology is expensive and cost effectiveness will be vital. There will be the inevitable conflicts of interest and differing priorities. Some credit unions may not require elaborate new systems or may be unwilling to pay for them. Large and small credit unions could have different priorities. Debates between various interest groups will continue as technology develops through the ILCUtech credit union system project.

BALANCE BETWEEN THE VOLUNTARY ETHOS AND PROFESSIONAL MANAGEMENT

The voluntary nature of co-operation, as manifest in the operation of credit unions at local and national level, is both a weakness and a strength. A balance is necessary between the energy and enthusiasm of voluntary officers and members, and management by full-time professionals. Frank Lynch, ILCU president, was quoted in *The Irish Times*, 9 October 1998, (article by Jane O'Sullivan on credit union savings) as estimating the voluntary efforts to be worth £35 to £40 millions annually. That voluntary effort helps to reduce costs and keeps down the interest rates on loans. The management and specialist staff of the ILCU will play an increasingly important role in future. Credit unions, especially the larger ones, will have full-time professional managers with experience and specialist qualifications, especially the Diploma in Credit Union Studies from the (UCC)–NUI, Cork. Training by the ILCU and the Institute of Credit Co-operative Administration will be vital for managers and other staff. Volunteers will need more specialised professional training in management, finance, legal frameworks and the human dimension, which the ILCU provides.

STRATEGIC PLANNING BY THE CREDIT UNION MOVEMENT UNDER THE ILCU'S LEADERSHIP

Focus on the Future, Irish Credit Unions in the New Millennium, issued by the ILCU in 1998 states the vision:

> Our vision is that credit unions will satisfy the economic and social needs of their members, with dignity and integrity, by offering, in the co-operative manner and on a not-for-profit basis full financial services for everyone who wishes to join.

To that end, a strategic plan maps out a detailed strategic plan to achieve that vision of unifying the movement in a common purpose to satisfy the needs of all its members. Detailed goals, specific objectives and practical strategies cover: sustainability, mutuality, inclusiveness, governance, impact and funding.

Internal systems, including the ILCU AGM, are being reviewed and streamlined to meet the practical needs of the Irish credit union movement. It has grown in recent years at 20 per cent annually, a rate which exceeded the record growth rate in the Irish economy. According to an analysis by Madden (1998) in 1998 savings represented by shares (about £3 billion) exceed loans (about £2.3 billion). The gap is projected to continue and to increase to over £900 million unless there is a new policy on lowering interest rates. As indicated by Jill Kerby, in her article on the challenge of low interest rates in the Family Money column, *The Irish Times*, 23 October 1998, an excess of accumulated savings would have serious implications for credit unions. They could effectively become savings unions by attracting an increasing number of short-term investors lacking in understanding of, or loyalty to, the co-operative ethos. Short-term savings could also distort the cash flow and cause liquidity problems.

Improved premises throughout Ireland, although criticised by some co-operative activists, are a physical manifestation of the success of the Irish credit union movement. It will be increasingly difficult for small-scale credit unions to operate outside the ILCU and its ancillary services. The common bonds in some areas of cities and suburbs seem artificial and restrictive, having regard to shopping and other social patterns. Mergers and alliances are likely. Large credit unions will be able to negotiate directly with commercial companies, for example to provide insurance cover. Telecom Éireann Staff Credit Union Ltd., one of the largest in Ireland, was recently expelled from the ILCU in a dispute about insurance payments, part of which comprises commission to the ILCU to fund its general activities and the savings protection scheme. A two-tier structure could damage the cohesiveness of the credit union movement.

The ILCU will provide enhanced services, underpinning the official statutory framework and protection for members' savings. A reasonably favourable taxation policy, including exemption from corporation tax and concessions on reporting to the Revenue Commissioners and on DIRT for small savers is important.

Because of their ethos and legislative restrictions on holding and transfer of shares and the one-member-one-vote system, credit unions cannot revoke their mutual status and follow some building societies down the plc route. It is likely, however, that smaller credit unions, especially in urban areas, will combine or merge to achieve economies of scale and to provide additional services.

As indicated by Norman Murphy, in his presidential address to the ILCU 1998 AGM, referring to the many imaginative but realistic initiatives by the credit union movement: "The best way to predict the future is to invent it".

Appendix 1

PROFILES OF CREDIT UNIONS

BALLYPHEHANE CREDIT UNION LTD, CORK

This was the first credit union to be formed south of the Dublin area. It was appropriate that Cork should be in the vanguard as Nora Herlihy, a pioneer of the Irish credit union movement, was a native of County Cork.

A prime mover in this southern initiative was the Roman Catholic Bishop of Cork, Dr Cornelius Lucey. As outlined in chapter 2 on the origins and development of the Irish Credit Union Movement, Dr Lucey had previously lectured on the UCD social studies course which played a vital role in stimulating interest in co-operative development. As Bishop of Cork, Dr Lucey put social theory and the principles of Papal Encyclicals into practice. He envisaged this credit union as a pilot scheme to meet local personal banking needs. He had staunch support from dynamic clergy especially Archdeacon Duggan, Fr Robert Ormond and Fr Ned Fitzgerald assisted by lay people including Bryan Lougheed, Dave McAuliffe and Dermot (Der) Cogan. Mr Cogan was president of the ILCU, 1971–1973. During the frugal fifties, Ballyphehane was a new parish based in a housing area for workers and their families. Their economic situation was characterised by unemployment and lack of credit facilities. Moneylending, pawnbroking and hire purchase aggravated the plight of families caught in a cycle of debt and deprivation.

At the study group meetings in the sacristy rooms of the Roman Catholic Church in Ballyphehane, Fr Fitzgerald explained the basic concepts of co-operative credit. He emphasised that it involved the exchange of savings and loans between members and also dealing with other people's money. The initiative was parochial in the best sense of that word. The pioneering group obtained information and literature from the USA where Bishop Lucey had observed the credit union system operating effectively. The careful preliminary work bore fruit when Ballyphehane Credit Union opened to the public on 1 July 1960. There were 38 members who contributed £62 in shares. The first loan of £5, to be repaid over twenty weeks, was to cover medical bills for a member's child.

This pioneering credit union was well organised and alert to wider developments. It affiliated to the Credit Union National Association (CUNA) in the USA. It was mentioned, as a good example of local co-operation, in correspondence between Nora Herlihy and President Eisenhower. Local members played their part in establishing the ILCU.

Success was cumulative. The credit union system became popular and helped to break cycles of debt. Women and young people became active and availed of access to credit. Members were involved in the wider credit union movement at chapter, league and international level. On its 30th anniversary in December 1990, Ballyphehane Credit Union was honoured with a civic reception by the Lord Mayor of Cork, Councillor Frank Nash. Local efforts and hospitality were recognised in a resolution which the WOCCU passed at the international forum in Cork, July 1994.

Fitting its innovative role, Ballyphehane prides itself as the first Irish credit union to have its own fully-owned permanent premises. At the formal opening of the premises, Mr James J. Ivers, representing the ILCU, acknowledged Ballyphehane's efforts in spreading the credit union message.

In modern offices, efficient systems, including computers, were installed. By 1995, in addition to the volunteers, there were fifteen staff employed including the manager, George Cantwell. Account enquiries can now be dealt with immediately. Services include money management systems, payment of household bills, home insurance and foreign exchange.

Approximate current statistics for 1997 illustrate the extent of financial success: current membership of 12,000, total loans of £19 million, total savings of £25 million, 17 people on the payroll between full and part-time, and a core group of 30 volunteers.

The remarkable story of this Cork credit union, however, relates also to its pioneering initiatives which contributed to social solidarity in the local community and set an inspiring example to the wider co-operative credit movement. The achievements were crowned when the credit union won the Credit Union Cup in 1997 for representing the best in service to members.

References

McCarthy, O., *History and Development of Ballyphehane Credit Union, 1960–1994*, Centre for Co-operative Studies, NUI, Cork and in *Credit Union Review*, ILCU, June/July 1997, p. 11.

Thanks to Anthony Drummond, honorary secretary of the credit union, for his help.

DONORE CREDIT UNION LTD

Based in the Donore Avenue neighbourhood of South Circular Road, Dublin, the origins and development of this credit union are inextricably linked with the evolution of the Irish credit union movement. The common bond embraces the area from Leonard's Corner to the Stadium, through Cork Street, Ardee Street, into Blackpitts and back by Raymond Street to Leonard's Corner.

The credit union was registered initially in 1958 as Cumann Muintir Dún Óir (Donore Parishioners Union) with the Registrar under the Friendly Societies Act, 1896 as amended. The main object was to provide by members' contributions for life assurance. In addition to the mortality fund, there was a loan fund. There were originally 94 members, with £240 shares and loans of £283. The friendly society status was unsatisfactory but it was a useful legal device pending specific credit union legislation.

Donore rivals Dún Laoghaire in claiming to have formed Ireland's first credit union. In Nora Herlihy's view, however, both Donore and Dún Laoghaire were twins. Two of Donore's pioneers, Eileen and Angela (Aingil) Byrne (Ní Bhroin) had participated in earlier co-operative initiatives at Red Island Holiday Camp, Skerries, Co. Dublin. From its early years, Donore has played an active role in the wider credit union movement. Donore was a founder member of the League in 1960 and Angela Byrne was elected to the first League Board.

The original office of Donore Credit Union was in the Byrne home, a red-bricked house at 35 Hamilton Street, where co-operative credit ideas had been discussed at fireside chats. Nora Herlihy, eminent credit union leader, cut the tape at the opening of new premises in Ebenezer Terrace in 1969.

In 1986, Bertie Ahern, TD, then Lord Mayor and later Taoiseach, formally switched on a computer system in the offices. In 1991, modern purpose-built offices at 22 Rutledge Terrace, South Circular Road, were opened with an ecumenical blessing. The cost of £0.5 million was met without any borrowing, a measure of the credit union's growth to over 3,000 members and shareholding of over £3 million.

Councillor Brendan Lynch, Lord Mayor of Dublin, 1996/97, has been an active member of Donore Credit Union for over thirty years. As a community councillor on Dublin Corporation, Mr Lynch was especially aware of the neighbourhood aspects of the credit union. Practical results include financing of extensions to houses. The Donore Credit Union in the best co-operative tradition, includes people of all religions, professions and occupations.

Donore, celebrating its fortieth year in 1998, had over 3,000 members and loans of about £3 million. It is parochial effort in the best sense of that phrase. The co-operative seeds sown by the pioneers have yielded a ripe harvest in Donore Credit Union. It can be justly proud of its record of practical community service.

References

Donore Credit Union Limited, 1958–1993, 35 Years of Serving the People of Donore, souvenir book (1993).

Culloty, A.T., (1990) "Nora Herlihy, Irish Credit Union Pioneer", *Review*, ILCU, pp. 59–62.

Review, (1997) "Dublin's Lord Mayor is a Long-Time Credit Union Man" ILCU, June/July p. 13.

Review, (1998/99) "First Credit Union Reaches 40", ILCU, Vol. 16, No. 112, December/January.

BALLYJAMESDUFF CREDIT UNION LTD

Having shared in the economic boom during the 1960s, the County Cavan town of Ballyjamesduff, provided fertile soil for a credit union. Through the initiative of Rev J. Duffy, CC, and Bill Ryan a study group worked during the Winter of 1969/70 in conjunction with personnel from the ILCU. By the first AGM in March 1971, there were 80 members, with savings of £1,860 and loans of £1,354.

Office accommodation was a problem. From club-rooms at St Joseph's Hall, the base moved to a store room in a corner of Mackey's shop. A mobile home beside St Joseph's Hall provided privacy but depended on members' car batteries for lighting. Run-down batteries caused further problems. The common bond's extension from three to six miles radius from the town led to rapid increases in membership. New premises in Main Street were opened in 1977 by Michael O'Doherty, ILCU secretary.

During the 25th anniversary celebrations in 1996, Mrs. Mary Robinson, President of Ireland, visited the premises on a sunny June morning. By then, membership had grown to almost 2,500, with shares and deposits of over £3 million and loans exceeding £2 million. The offices are being extended again to cater for growth.

This credit union is also active in wider community activities and initiatives including the Credit Union Junior cycle tour of Ireland, the poster competition and primary school quiz. Bally-jamesduff members are also involved in local chapter 6 which covers Cavan, Louth and Meath.

Paddy McInerney, a long-time officer, was appointed part-time manager in 1995. Membership by 1997 had reached 2,800, with savings of £3.7 million and £2.5 in loans. Growth is combined with continuity in this progressive credit union which has an urban-rural mix, serving the town of Ballyjamesduff and the adjoining agricultural area.

If Paddy Reilly, renowned in Percy French's song, came back to Ballyjamesduff, he would surely join its thriving credit union.

References and Sources

Ballyjamesduff Credit Union, 25 Years, Jubilee Souvenir booklet, 1996, foreword by Norman Murphy, president, ILCU and background articles by Séamus Ó Dubthaigh and Paddy McInerney, whose assistance is acknowledged.

Review, "Mrs. Mary Robinson, then President of Ireland, helps Ballyjamesduff celebrate its Jubilee". ILCU, April/May 1997, p. 20.

TALLOW AREA CREDIT UNION LTD

Based in County Waterford, this credit union has grown substantially in thirty years: from sixteen members and share capital of £14 in 1968 to a membership of almost 4,000 in 1998 with assets of over £5 million and loans of about £3 million. Interest rates are being reduced in line with current trends.

The town of Tallow has a population of less than 1,000 but the common bond area covers about 6,000 people. Described as the "Heart of the Community", the credit union became involved in the wider economic life of the area. The credit union members include over seventy local clubs and associations. Many of these received loans to develop their facilities. Initiatives included fostering small industries and projects.

The Tallow Enterprise Group Ltd, was established following a survey which identified the area as having a very high rate of unemployment. Initial aims were modest but many people were trained to form their own businesses. The credit union provided support services including office space, meeting room, and facilities such as telephone, fax, photocopying and typing. Viable business ideas required premises. A group of budding entrepreneurs approached the credit union for financial assistance and help in acquiring workspace.

In 1989, as a practical measure, the credit union bought an old grain warehouse and converted it into an enterprise centre, named Nora Herlihy House after the co-founder of the Irish credit union movement. This development was funded by loans from the credit union and also grant aid. Over two hundred people were assisted to set up their own businesses, while others were employed by local companies. The consequent enterprise culture enhanced Tallow as a suitable location for outside investors.

A garage premises, which was subsequently acquired and refurbished through a loan and grant, is the base for a food company and a local photographer.

Séamus MacEoin, co-founder of the Irish credit union movement, in a silver jubilee tribute in 1993, wrote: "Not content with being extremely well-managed and run, it (Tallow Credit Union) has provided all possible ancillary services for the benefit of its members. Even more significantly it has had the concern, courage and initiative to involve itself directly with the community and government agencies in the very challenging task of job creation. It should be remembered that the Irish credit union movement originated in the intensive and unrewarding efforts of its founders at co-operative job creation. The focal point of your great work is therefore the Enterprise Centre, very appropriately named 'Nora Herlihy House'".

The Tallow experience is widely recognised as a model of community development. It has inspired other Irish credit unions to support co-operative initiatives to ease social and economic problems on a mutual basis. The international dimension includes visitors from all over the world who come to learn from this success story. Sheila Ryan, manager of Tallow Credit Union and honorary secretary of the enterprise group, has spoken at a rural development conference in Cornwall. Tallow provides practical inspiration at home and abroad.

References

Annual reports of Tallow Credit Union Ltd. Tallow Credit Union Ltd. Silver Jubilee, 1968-1993, 25 Years of Caring and Sharing.

Coffey, Áine, "Community Service", *Business and Finance*, April 1998.

Dungarvan Leader, "Tallow Celebrates 21st Birthday in Style", May 26, 1989.

Thanks to Sheila Ryan for her enthusiastic help.

Comment

A cautionary note of general application, without any reflection on individuals: as credit unions become identified with their associated enterprises in the same locality, it is possible that business failure could damage the credit union despite its separate legal existence. Credit union officers must be especially careful in such circumstances.

The Credit Union Act, 1997, facilitates wider community involvement by credit unions, especially in section 44 on special funds for social, cultural or charitable purposes, including community development, within a stricter regime of supervision by the Registrar of Friendly Societies.

St Raphael's Garda Credit Union Ltd

This has the largest asset base, in terms of loans, of all Irish credit unions. Membership is about 19,000, with loans of almost £70 million and savings of about the same amount. There is a policy of interest rebates rather than lowering current interest rates.

Background

It all began in the Special Branch in 1964. Dan Norrison, from St Joseph's Aviation Credit Union (mainly Aer Lingus employees), addressed a meeting in the Detective Branch on 22 April 1964. Participants decided to form a credit union within the Garda Síochána. Officers elected were: president, James F. Walsh; vice-president, James Hayes; treasurer, Patrick K. Kearney; secretary, Brian A. Sheehan. Other founder members were: William J. Smaul, William N. Hynes, John Hamill, Sean P O'Connell, Daniel P. Boyle, Joseph Higgins, Christopher P. Godkin, Michael Mescall and James Healy.

The Garda Commissioner was informed of the decision. His permission was sought to organise the credit union and for pay sergeants to deduct monies from members' pay. The standard by-laws of the ILCU were adopted and affiliation applied for. A room in Dublin Castle was obtained as an office. Fr Clarence Daly, CP, Mount Argus, was appointed as spiritual director, following a traditional Dublin police connection with the Passionist Order.

On the recommendation of Nora Herlihy, ILCU, it was later agreed to change the name from St. Michael's to St. Raphael's. The inaugural meeting and first AGM were held on 19 August 1964. Publicity was obtained through the Garda Representative Body magazine. It was decided to hold an open meeting in the Garda Club, Harrington Street, Dublin and to invite Deputy Commissioner, William P. Quinn, and also credit union activists — Nora Herlihy, Michael O'Doherty, Dan Norrison and Kathleen Matthews.

By Christmas 1964, there were 119 members with shares of £638 and five loans totalling £222 had been granted.

Success

It is a long way from that modest start in 1964 to 1998 and a membership of 19,000, and loans of almost £70 million and savings in shares and deposits of about the same amount. The original small office in Dublin Castle contrasts with the excellent bright premises at St Raphael's House, 81/84 Upper Dorset Street, Dublin 1. The old redbrick school was converted to provide state-of-the-art office facilities to serve the members throughout Dublin and the country. (There is another large Garda credit union, St Paul's, based in Cork).

The common bond of St Raphael's covers: enlisted and serving members of all ranks (including student gardaí) of the Garda Síochána in the Republic of Ireland, and retired personnel of the force who were members of either Garda credit union before their retirement. Members' families are also eligible for membership. The Registrar classified St Raphael's under the "Other" miscellaneous common bond category to cover pensioners under the pre-1997 legislation.

Major advantages are the stable member base in single State employment and direct deductions from payroll.

Services

The geographic dispersal of members throughout the country does not cause any major problems. Payroll deductions facilitate members and management. Using a confidential pin number, members can have direct access to account information, including requests for loans, share or budget withdrawals, plus information on personal accounts and foreign currency rates.

Competitive rates of interest are paid on shares and deposits. The low interest rate climate is reflected in interest rebates, currently at 25% of interest paid during the year. The rebate is paid into the members' share accounts.

Insurance on shares and loans is provided in accordance with the general practice, and wider services are envisaged. Without any charge to members, a budget account scheme is operated to cover mortgage payments and other basic household outgoings. Annual bureau de change transactions total about £9 million but that figure may decline when the Euro becomes fully operational.

Loans

The main purposes for loans are: car purchase, house improvements and purchase, with a smaller proportion for education, health costs and holidays. Demand for loans is almost completely met. Unlike some credit unions, loans and savings totals are almost identical. Loans for shorter rather than long periods are currently favoured to meet members' needs.

Youth

New generation members are fostered through imaginative initiatives: classes are provided in the credit union offices to prepare family members for Garda entrance tests; the credit union ethos is explained to students at the Garda College in Templemore, Co Tipperary; the undergraduate computer bureau is available free at the Dorset Street offices to assist trainees in preparing and presenting projects; annual youth golf classics and art competitions are sponsored.

Other Social Projects

Financial support is provided for charities, sports and other relevant projects such as the *Garda Gazette*, the journal of the Garda Síochána Historical Society. Further initiatives being considered include a plan to assist deprived communities in the north inner city of Dublin, adjacent to the Dorset Street offices. The credit union is an active member of chapter 21.

The Future

There is awareness of current trends including the Euro and technological developments. Information technology is utilised and modern computer systems have been installed. When official restrictions are overcome, Paypath will facilitate payment of salaries into credit union accounts. Access to laser cards and ATMs through a common system would be helpful, provided that costs are not excessive.

Officers

The officers elected for 1998 were: chairman/president, Oliver Harrington; vice-chairman, Martin Walsh; secretary, Patrick Fox; treasurer, Aidan Ó Murchú. Supervisory Committee: chairman, John O'Driscoll; Con McCarthy and Kevin Dolan.

Michael O'Brien, an experienced credit union activist, succeeded Michael Murphy as general manager during 1997/8. Eugene Lynch is assistant manager, bringing the total management and staff to 11 persons. With its dedicated members, officers, management and staff, St. Raphael's continued success is assured.

References and Sources

Author's interview with James O'Brien, general manager, whose courtesy and assistance were appreciated

Garda Review, Phibsboro Tower, Dublin 7, Andy Needham (ed).

Minutes of early meetings and also annual reports.

LAW LIBRARY CREDIT UNION LTD

After a relatively long gestation period of a few years at the study group stage, history was made as this was the first credit union to be registered under the 1997 Act, on International Credit Union Day, 15 October 1998. Delay in registration was due to the interval between the commencement of the main provisions of the 1997 Act and the adoption and finalisation of new standard rules of the ILCU, following negotiation with the Registrar and other authorities.

The name derives from the Law Library as the traditional place in the Four Courts, Inns Quay, Dublin 7 where barristers practise law and share common facilities. The communal ethos of the Bar of Ireland provided a starting point.

Although many of the founder members already had relevant experience and expertise, the study group procedure was followed in accordance with the practice and requirements of the ILCU. The motto of pioneer Nora Herlihy was applicable: No education, no credit union. ILCU representatives, especially director Mary Griffin and field officer Brian Douglas, were particularly helpful and supportive at study group meetings. The local chapter 21, comprising many large industrial credit unions covering service and professional employments, was also helpful.

Rosemary McLaughlin edited an informative newsletter. Practical enthusiasm was generated by the formation of a savings fund. As that was an unincorporated body, trustees were appointed. Loans could not be issued prior to registration because of legal restrictions under moneylenders' and consumer credit legislation. The representative body for practising barristers, the Bar Council, supported the initiatives but the study group and the credit union operate independently and distinct from that Council. The common bond was drafted to include practising barristers in Dublin, Cork and on circuit, and employees within the Law Library, and also family members in accordance with section 2 of the 1997 Act.

The first board of directors elected at the organisation meeting on 13 November 1998 was: Ercus Stewart, SC (chairman); Dan

Feehan (vice-chair); Teddy O'Neill (secretary); Sinéad Ní Chúlacháin (treasurer); Mary Phelan, Tessa Feaheny, Vivian McDonnell, Denis Daly, Caroline Carney.

The first Supervisory Board elected at the organisation meeting was: Anthony P. Quinn, chairman; Francis Gallogly and Cormac Corrigan, secretary.

Comment

Some misinformed media commentators, especially columnists, confuse credit unions with charities and begrudgingly refer to credit unions in specific occupations and professions such as the Bar, commerce and the public service as somehow reflecting on the co-operative ethos. In reality, however, individuals sharing a common bond in such occupations have varying income levels and needs at various stages throughout their careers. Such people have a democratic right to form or join credit unions to cater for their financial needs on a mutual co-operative basis.

Further contribution to the co-operative ethos can be made individually or through the wider credit union movement. Co-operation is a valid concept at all levels of society, including the legal profession.

Appendix 2

(A) CREDIT UNION OPERATING PRINCIPLES

The genesis of these principles can be traced back to the English Rochdale Pioneers who founded an equitable co-operative society and store at Toad Lane, Rochdale, Lancashire, in 1844. The modernised version of the Rochdale principles, as adopted by the International Co-op Alliance at Manchester in 1995, are listed at (B) below.

The operating principles were adopted at the AGM in 1984 of the Irish League of Credit Unions (ILCU) and approved at the International Credit Union Forum in August of that year by representatives of membership council, the World Council of Credit Unions (WOCCU). The principles were issued by ILCU following the AGM of 1992 and are included as Appendix 1 to the standard rules as revised in 1998 and adopted by the ILCU's annual convention.

Copies of the principles are displayed in the offices of some credit unions but members' awareness of the philosophy and its practical implication needs to be improved.

The principles are also included as an appendix to the rules of ILCU, that is the rules governing the relationship between credit unions and the League, as distinct from the standard rules for individual credit unions. In the rules of the ILCU, the objects, at section 1(3), include encouraging its members to operate in accordance with the Credit Union Operating Principles, as set out below.

Introduction

These Credit Union Principles are founded in the philosophy of co-operation and its central values of equality, equity and self-help. At the heart of these principles is the concept of human development and the brotherhood of man expressed through people working together to achieve a better life for themselves and their children.

1) **Open and Voluntary Membership** — Membership in a credit union is voluntary and open to all, within the accepted common bond of association, who can make use of its services and are willing to accept the corresponding responsibilities.

2) **Democratic Control** — Credit union members enjoy equal rights to vote (one-member-one-vote) and participate in decisions affecting the credit union, without regard to the amount of savings or deposits or the volume of business. The credit union is autonomous, within the framework of law and regulation, recognising the credit union as a co-operative enterprise serving and controlled by its members. Credit union elected officers are voluntary in nature and incumbents should not receive a salary for fulfilling the duties for which they were elected. However, credit unions may reimburse legitimate expenses incurred by elected officials.

3) **Limited Dividends on Equity Capital** — Permanent equity capital where it exists in the credit union receives limited dividends.

4) **Return on Savings and Deposits** — To encourage thrift through savings and thus to provide loans and other member services, a fair rate of interest is paid on savings and deposits, within the capability of the credit union.

5) **Return of Surplus to Members** — The surplus arising out of the operations of the credit, union after ensuring appropriate reserve levels and after payment of dividends, belongs to and benefits all members with no member or group of members benefiting to the detriment of others. This surplus

may be distributed among members in proportion to their transactions with the credit union (interest or patronage refunds) or directed to improved or additional services required by the members. Expenditure in credit unions should be for the benefit of all members with no member or group of members benefiting to the detriment of others.

6) **Non-discrimination in Race, Religion and Politics** — Credit unions are non-discriminatory in relation to race, nationality, sex, religion and politics within the limits of their legal common bond. Operating decisions and the conduct of business are based on member needs, economic factors and sound management principles. While credit unions are apolitical and will not become aligned with partisan political interests, this does not prevent them from making such political representations as are necessary to defend and promote the collective interests of credit unions and their members.

7) **Service to Members** — Credit union services are directed towards improving the economic well-being of all members, whose needs shall be a permanent and paramount consideration, rather than towards the maximising of surpluses.

8) **On-going Education** — Credit unions actively promote the education of their members, officers and employees, along with the public in general, in the economic, social, democratic and mutual self-help principles of credit unions. The promotion of thrift and the wise use of credit, as well as education on the rights and responsibilities of members, are essential to the dual social and economic character of credit unions in serving member needs.

9) **Co-operation Among Co-operatives** — In keeping with their philosophy and the pooling practices of co-operatives, credit unions, within their capability, actively co-operate with other credit unions, co-operatives and their associations at

local, national and international levels in order to best serve the interests of their members and their community. This inter-co-operation fosters the development of the co-operative sector in society.

10) **Social Responsibility** — Continuing the ideals and beliefs of co-operative pioneers, credit unions seek to bring about human and social development. Their vision of social justice extends both to the individual members and to the larger community in which they work and reside. The credit union ideal is to extend service to all who need and can use it. Every person is either a member or a potential member and, appropriately, part of the credit union sphere of interest and concern. Decisions should be taken with full regard for the interests of the broader community within which the credit union and its members reside.

(B) STATEMENT OF THE CO-OPERATIVE IDENTITY

The operating principles, listed above, reflect the philosophy of the modernised co-operative principles which were adopted by the International Co-operative Alliance at Manchester, UK, in 1995:

Definition

A co-operative is an autonomous association of persons united voluntarily to meet their common economic, social and cultural needs and aspirations through a jointly-owned and democratically-controlled enterprise.

Values

Co-operatives are based on the values of self-help, self-responsibility, democracy, equality, equity and solidarity. In the tradition of their founders, co-operative members believe in the ethical value of honesty, openness, social responsibility and caring for others.

Principles

The co-operative principles are guidelines by which co-operatives put their values into practice.

1st Principle: Voluntary and Open Membership

Co-operatives are voluntary organisations, open to all persons able to use their services and willing to accept the responsibilities of membership, without gender, social, racial, political or religious discrimination.

2nd Principle: Democratic Member Control

Co-operatives are democratic organisations controlled by their members, who actively participate in setting their policies and making decisions. Men and women serving as elected representatives are accountable to the membership. In primary co-operatives members have equal rights (one-member-one-vote) and co-operatives at other levels are organised in a democratic manner.

3rd Principle: Member Economic Participation

Members contribute equitably to, and democratically control, the capital of their co-operative. At least part of that capital is usually the common property of the co-operative. They usually receive limited compensation, if any, on capital subscribed as a condition of membership. Members allocate surpluses for all or any of the following purposes: developing the co-operative, possibly by setting up reserves, part of which would be indivisible; benefiting members in proportion to their transactions with the co-operative; and supporting other activities approved by the membership.

4th Principle: Autonomy and Independence

Co-operatives are autonomous, self-help organisations controlled by their members. If they enter into agreements with other organisations, including governments, or raise capital from external sources, they do so on terms that ensure democratic control by their members and maintain their co-operative autonomy.

5th Principle: Education, Training and Information

Co-operatives provide education and training for their members, elected representatives, managers and employees so that they can contribute effectively to the development of their co-operatives. They inform the general public — particularly young people and opinion leaders — about the nature and benefits of co-operation.

6th Principle: Co-operation among Co-operatives

Co-operatives serve their members most effectively and strengthen the co-operative movement by working together through local, national, regional and international structures.

7th Principle: Concern for Community

While focusing on member needs, co-operatives work for the sustainable development of their communities through policies accepted by their members.

Appendix 3

CREDIT UNION INVOCATION

LORD, make me an instrument of Thy peace.

Where there is hatred, let me sow love;

Where there is injury, pardon;

Where there is doubt, faith;

Where there is despair, hope;

Where there is darkness, light;

And where there is sadness, joy.

DIVINE MASTER, Grant that I may

Not so much seek to be consoled as to console;

To be understood as to understand;

To be loved as to love;

For it is in giving that we receive,

It is in pardoning that we are pardoned,

And it is in dying that we are born

To eternal life.

St Francis of Assisi

ACHAINÍ AN CHOMHAIR CHREIDMHEASA

A THÍARNA, déan díom uirlís de Do shíocháin

Áit a bhuil fuath, lig dom grá a chur;

Áit a bhuil dochar déanta, pardúin;

Áit a bhuil amhras, creideamh;

Áit a bhuil éadóchas, dóchas;

Áit a bhuil dorchadas, solas;

Agus áit a bhuil brón, áthas.

A MHÁISTIR DHIAGA, deonaigh nach niarriam

Comh mór sólás a fháil le sólás a thabhairt;

A bheith tuigthe chomh mór le tuiscint a bheith agam;

Grá a fháil le grá a thabairt;

Óir is ó bheith ag tabhairt a fhaighimíd;

Is ó phardún a thabhairt a fhaighimid pardún;

Agus is trí bhás a fháil a saolaítear sinn

Don bheatha shíorraí.

Naomh Proinsías Assisi

In Memoriam: Séamus P. MacEoin

Pioneer of the Irish Credit Union Movement a d'éag 14 Deireadh Fómhair 1993.

On a cold October morning, at the funeral Mass in St Therese's Church, Mount Merrion, Dublin, Fr Dermot McKenna, SJ, spoke about Séamus MacEoin's contribution to the community and Ireland. It was apt that a Jesuit, and fellow co-operative activist, should give the homily because that order had been active in the UCD extra-mural course which lit a spark for Séamus. His life's work was devoted to Irish credit unions. Séamus was not content to rest on the laurels of the very successful credit union movement. In more recent years the wider co-operative movement, specifically the Co-operative Development Society Ltd, was the subject of Séamus's idealism, as a practical response to the lack of jobs. He was a true patriot whose work received little public or media acclaim. He had admonished a well-known historian who had failed to acknowledge the credit union success story. Fr. McKenna spoke about how Séamus had touched so many people's lives.

My first encounter with Séamus was during the 1950's in the Technical Students Literary and Debating Society which met in 18, Parnell Square, Dublin (now the Writers' Museum). We were both junior civil servants who thought that we could change the world.

Séamus expressed a fervent interest in Irish economic and social topics. His concerned outlook came into focus for me only years later when he recounted his extra-mural studies at UCD which had sharpened his social conscience. Early efforts, expressed in the Folk School movement and the Credit Union Extension Service led to practical results: the League in 1960 and new legislation in 1966.

I lost touch with him during those glorious years of achievement when credit unions were formed and the movement took root. During that time, Séamus did change the world for the better.

As a civil servant dealing with credit unions in the Department of Industry and Commerce during the late 1970s and early 1980s, my path again crossed that of Séamus. He had served for many years on the Advisory Committee under the 1966 Act and was a League director. He was a credit union representative on the Special Committee of the Society for Co-operative Studies (SCSI) which studied the wider application of the co-operative movement. I represented the Registry of Friendly Societies on the committee which issued a comprehensive report in 1986. During the committee meetings Séamus argued strongly for co-operative principles. Typically of Séamus, he was not content to allow the report to accumulate dust in pigeon-holes, either in the official or voluntary sectors. Despite his illness, he framed a motion at the Society for Co-operative Studies' AGM in 1992 to try and achieve some action on the report's recommendations. Séamus was a practical idealist.

As a civil servant, he managed Dún Laoghaire Employment Exchange towards the end of his official career. In this cynical, consumerist and materialistic age, it may be difficult to understand the motivation of activists like Séamus MacEoin. During his last illness at St Michael's, Dun Laoghaire, he made contact with many of the people whose lives he had touched. In response to my question about his motivation, he spoke of his late mother. As a teacher in Co. Kilkenny, she had been involved in community work all her life. His mother passed the torch of public service to Séamus. His wife, Eilis, and family encouraged his labour of love. Let's keep that flame of co-operative idealism burning brightly in his memory.

Ar dheis Dé go raibh a anam dílis

Anthony P. Quinn, 1994

GLOSSARY OF LEGAL AND OTHER TERMS

TERMS EXPLAINED SIMPLY

For more detailed definitions, consult: statutory definitions in acts, especially the Credit Union Act, 1997, section 2(1) on interpretation; legal dictionaries, particularly *A Dictionary of Irish Law*, Murdoch, H., revised second edition, Dublin, 1993. References to rules, unless otherwise stated, are to the standard rules for credit unions registered in the Republic of Ireland and affiliated to the ILCU. The Act, unless otherwise stated, means the Credit Union Act, 1997 (No. 15 of 1997). "Chapter", unless otherwise stated, refers to the relevant chapter of this book where the specific topic is dealt with in more detail. Local and regional groups of credit unions are also called "chapters".

- **Administrator**: Person nominated by the **Registrar** and appointed by the Court, in specified circumstances under section 137 of the Act, to administer the affairs of a credit union which is experiencing difficulties. The administration system, based on the Insurance (Number 2) Act, 1983, allows a credit union to continue as a going concern but the eventual outcome may be winding-up. Part XI of the Act, sections 137 to 141, and Chapter 11 on administrators and examiners provide more detail.

- **Advisory Committee**: The Credit Union Advisory Committee, CUAC, explained in Chapter 14. Section 180 of the 1997 Act continued the existence of CUAC, originally established under section 27 of the 1966 Act. Appointed by the Minister,

CUAC provides expert advice to the Minister and other relevant persons, including the **Registrar**.

- **Annual General Meeting, AGM**: Meeting of members must be held in the State during October to January, after the end of the each financial year, at a time and place provided for under the rules of a **credit union**. Detailed provisions are in section 78 of the 1997 Act, rule 128, as explained in Chapter 5 on meetings and voting. The AGM is the policy-making body where members elect the **Board of Directors** and the **Supervisory Committee** (except in new credit unions where it is elected at the **Organisation Meeting**.)

- **Annual Accounts**: Accounts, including an income and expenditure account and balance sheet, required under section 111 of the Act, rule 147, in respect of a credit union's financial year, together with the notes to them. Accounts must give a true and fair view. Accounts and **audits/auditors** are dealt with in Chapter 10.

- **Annual Return**: The annual return which each credit union is required to prepare under section 124 of the Act, rule 157, and to send the Registrar (and to the ILCU for affiliated credit unions) not later than 31st March each year.

- **Audit**: Detailed inspection of accounts by an independent qualified person called an auditor which each credit union must elect under section 113 of the Act, rule 149. The first auditor is appointed by the directors before the AGM but subsequently the auditor is appointed at the AGM. In default, the Registrar may appoint an auditor under section 113(5).

- **Automated Teller Machines, ATM**: Electro-mechanical terminals allowing individuals with an ATM or cash card and Personal Identification Number (PIN), to obtain cash from their accounts and, increasingly, to access other services. These "hole-in-the-wall" systems, commonly available to consumers in banks and building societies are becoming increasingly accessible to credit union members through the integrated IQ Card being developed by the ILCU through the ILCUtech system.

- **Board of Directors**: The committee of management or other directing body of a credit union, responsible for its general control, direction and management. Sections 53 to 57 in part IV of the Act, and rules 64 to 77 and also Chapter 6 on governance refer. Board members, also called directors, serve in a voluntary capacity and are not paid, but may be allowed expenses

- **Budget Account Schemes**: Many credit unions provide this ancillary service to members who wish to regularise their household expenditure patterns over a specified period within the credit union's framework. Members should carefully plan and estimate their expenditure over a twelve-month period to ensure that at the end of that time the total payroll deductions credited to their credit union account correlates to outgoings. Credit unions must also be careful in administering budget schemes and avoid subsidising them from mainstream activities.

- **Chapter**: A regional grouping of credit unions which acts as a forum for exchanging information and training programmes. Each of the 25 chapters meets regularly and provides an important part of the movement's structure.

- **Credit Institution**: Recognised bank within the meaning of the Central Banks, 1942 to 1997; a trustee savings bank; the Post Office Savings Bank; or a building society within the meaning of the Building Societies Act, 1989. The main relevance is for investments by credit unions under section 43 of the Act, rule 52. Credit unions are not defined as credit institutions and are exempt from relevant banking, building societies and consumer credit legislation.

- **Common Bond**: A basic concept peculiar to credit unions, membership of which is based on a common bond between members. For example, members must be in the same occupation, residing or being employed in a particular locality, be employed by a particular employer or have retired from employment with a particular employer, or be members of the same association (other than one formed for the purpose of forming a society to be registered as a credit union). The Registrar may approve other common bonds. Section 6(3) of the Act, rules 1, 14, 20 and 44 (6) refer. An individual could have more than one common bond and thus be entitled to membership of more than one credit union. Family members, as defined, of the same household are also qualified for membership.

- **Co-operative (Co-op)**: Broad term covering a wide and diverse range of bodies and associations, run for the mutual benefit of the members as users of their services, rather than for profit. Co-ops can be identified by their purpose and objectives rather than by their legal form. They generally follow the International Co-operative Principles including open and voluntary membership, democratic control, limited or equitable return on capital, mutual co-operation and education, as outlined in chapter 1. The principles are being adapted to modern needs, and co-operatives are sometimes referred to as people-centred businesses, as distinct from the normal commercial enterprise.

  The related Operating Principles adopted by the AGM of the ILCU in 1984 and subsequently by affiliated credit unions are in appendix 2 to this book and appendix 1 to the ILCU standard rules.

  Co-operative societies were traditionally registered under the Industrial and Provident Societies Acts, 1893–1978. Due to the inadequacies of that legislation, however, in recent years the Companies Acts are being used to register some forms of co-operatives including worker co-ops.

- **The Companies Acts**: The Companies Acts, 1963–1990, together with any enactment which is stated under such Act to be construed with those Acts.

- **The Court**: Where that term is used in the 1997 Act, it means the High Court in the Irish jurisdiction. Where other courts have the relevant jurisdiction, they are specifically referred to in the Act, mainly the Circuit and District Courts.

- **Credit Union**: In a simple and general explanation, a financial co-operative in which members save money to provide loans to other members. The current specific definition in the Irish jurisdiction is: a society registered as such, that is as a credit union under the 1997 Act and also existing societies deemed to be registered as credit unions under section 5(3). That transitional provision applies to societies registered before the commencement of the Credit Union Act, 1997, as credit unions under the Industrial and Provident Societies Acts, 1893 to 1978. Each credit union is a separate legal and corporate entity distinct from other credit unions.

- **Credit Committee**: In accordance with section 67(1) (a) of the Act and its third schedule, reflected in rules 94 to 97, each credit union must have a credit committee consisting of at least three members including one director/board member. Members of the **Credit Control Committee**, the **Credit Control Officer**, **Credit Officer**, **Treasurers** or their assistants are ineligible for membership of the credit committee. Its basic function is to consider and decide on members' applications for credit. Effective credit committee members must know how to interpret loan applications and analyse applicants' creditworthiness.

- **Credit Control Committee**: In accordance with section 67(1) (b) of the Act and its third schedule, reflected in rules 104 to 107, each credit union must have a credit control committee consisting of at least three members including one director/board member. Members of the **Credit Committee**, the **Credit Control Officer**, the **Credit Officer**, **Treasurers** or their assistants are ineligible for membership of the credit control committee. Its basic function is to seek to ensure that members repay loans in accordance with their loan agreements.

Common statutory requirements for the two committees outlined above include submitting written reports to the board at each meeting of the board and complying with its instructions. Committee members serve in a voluntary unpaid capacity. The Act requires meetings to be held as often as necessary but the rules specify meetings to be held not less frequently than once a month.

- **Credit Officer**: A person appointed by the board of directors to work under the credit committee's supervision. Delegated powers include approval of credit (a) that is fully secured by the borrowing members' shareholding or an amount specified in writing in excess of such shareholding or (b) that qualifies as emergency credit within terms approved by the board. Under section 65 of the Act, this is an optional position but rule 99 makes is compulsory for credit unions affiliated to the ILCU.

- **Credit Control Officer**: A person appointed by the board of directors to work under the credit committee's supervision and to assist it. Under section 65(4) of the Act, this is an optional position but rule 108 makes is compulsory.

  Treasurers and their assistants and other persons with a potential conflict of interest due to membership of credit or credit control committees are excluded from holding the above positions.

  The above officers and committees concerned with credit are dealt with in more detail in Chapter 6 on Governance.

- **Debentures**: Defined in section 2 of the 1997 Act and rule 1 as debentures, debenture stock or bonds of a credit union, whether constituting a charge on the assets or not. Debentures are relevant to borrowing by a credit union under sections 33 and 34 and rule 42, as outlined in Chapters 7 and 8 on Financial Transactions. A broader general definition of a debenture is: an instrument, often but not necessarily under seal, issued by a borrowing body as evidence of a debt or as security for a loan of a fixed sum of money on which interest is paid. A debenture is often given a charge over the borrower's assets. The Credit Union Act, 1997, facilitates such borrowing by providing exemption in section 34, rule 41, from the Bills of Sale (Ireland) Act, 1879 and 1883, if the charge is registered by the Registrar.

- **Deposits**: In financial institutions, money placed in an account whereby it will be returned to the depositor with or without interest. The term was not defined in Irish law according to the High Court in *Irish Commercial Society Group Ltd*, in receivership and liquidation, 1987, a case concerning industrial and provident societies.
  The Credit Union Act, 1997, sections 27, 28, 31 and 32 and rules 33, 37, 38 and 39 provide detailed provisions and restrictions on deposits which provide a method of saving in a credit union as an alternative, or addition, to shares.

- **Examinership**: A legal mechanism for rescuing and reconstructing ailing but potentially viable companies under the Companies (Amendment) Act, 1990. Adapted with some changes for use in comparable credit union situations by part XII of the Credit Union Act, 1997, sections 142 to 170 and by rule 165. The examiner, usually a specialist accountant, determines whether the credit union would be likely to continue operating viably and satisfy its creditors. The relevant credit union would be placed temporarily under the protection of the Court. Chapter 11 of this book refers.

- **General Meeting**: Meeting of members at an AGM or SGM in accordance with the rules and wider law, as explained in more detail in chapter 5 on Meetings and Voting. A credit union is required to hold an annual general meeting in the State in respect of each financial year in accordance with the rules.

- **ILCUtech** is an company set up originally to develop automated, computer-based, ATMs and payment services for credit unions. Supporting services including paypath to credit salaries direct to credit union accounts, direct debits, debit card services and social welfare payments, require a standard network and harmonisation of computer systems in the various credit unions.

- **Industrial and Provident Society, I & P Society**: A society formed to carry on any industry, business or trade specified in its rules under the I & P Societies Acts, 1893 to 1978. Registration confers corporate status and limited liability. Most, but not all, the societies registered under those Acts are co-ops. Credit unions were previously registered under the I & P legislation as amended by the Credit Union Act, 1966. Now the stand-alone Credit Union Act, 1997 provides a registration and wider statutory framework.

- **Invocation**: Prayer, following that of St. Francis and regarded and generally accepted as non-denominational. The invocation, in Appendix 3, is usually said by members when commencing meetings.

- **Irish League of Credit Unions, ILCU**: The unincorporated service body which acts as an umbrella and representative organisation for about 540 credit unions throughout Ireland, both in the Republic and Northern Ireland. The ILCU formulates model rules for affiliated credit unions in each jurisdiction and issues directions and guidance to them. It also provides training and other support services. Most, but not all, Irish credit unions are affiliated to the ILCU. It was statutorily recognised in the 1997 Act, section 181 of which includes the ILCU as an expert or knowledgeable body may be consulted by the **Minister** or **Registrar**, for example before making regulations under section 182.

- **Member**: A person who has complied with the formalities and other requirements and is admitted to membership of a credit union. Only members are entitled to the privileges of membership including savings by shares and deposits, and borrowing money by loans. Chapter 3 refers.

- **Membership Committee**: A statutory requirement under section 67(1) (c) of the Act, rule 109. This committee, appointed by the board of directors, considers and decides on applications for membership of a credit union. A least one director must be a member and the treasurer and assistant treasurer are ineligible for membership of this committee.

- **The Minister**: The Minister for Enterprise, Trade and Employment, (ETE), who is the successor in title to the Minister for Industry and Commerce. Credit union functions are normally delegated to a Minister of State at the Department of ETE. The Minister appoints the Registrar.

- **Mutual**: Used to describe a society or body which is owned and controlled by persons, usually the members, who use the service or product provided by the society. Ownership and ultimate control is vested in the members on the basis of equality rather than in proportion to financial interest as would be the position in the usual commercial enterprises. Building societies were traditionally mutual bodies but recently some have become public limited banking companies on commercial lines. Credit unions are mutual societies because of their nature especially the one member one vote provision, as underpinned by the legislative framework, up-dated in the 1997 Act.

- **Nomination**: This has the general meaning of nominating an individual for a specific committee or position as officer. There is also a more specific meaning, under sections 21 and 22 of the 1997 Act, rules 27 and 28, of nomination of a member's specified property in a credit union so that such property will pass, on the member's death, to the nominee.

- **Non-qualifying Member**: According to section 17(4) of the 1997 Act, a member who ceases to have the common bond required of members of the relevant credit union. Such people may retain their voting rights and membership and also may continue saving but shall be left out of account in determining for any purpose whether a common bond exists between members. Restrictions apply to loans to non-qualifying members under section 36 (3) of the 1997 Act. The related rule 44(6) does not use the term, non-qualifying member, which is not favoured by the credit union movement.

- **Officer**: Under section 2 of the Act, rule 1 includes the following: chairman (or president); vice-chairman (vice-president); treasurer; secretary; member of board of directors or of principal committee or supervisory committee; employee; credit officer or credit control officer. Auditors are excluded. It is important to note the inclusion of employee. Officers are dealt with in more detail in Chapter 6 on Governance.

- **Organisation Meeting**: A once-off meeting in new credit unions only held in accordance with section 77 of the Act and rule 127. This meeting is called by the signatories to the registration application (the founder members) to be held not later than one month after a credit union is registered. Attendance includes the founder members and others, usually study group participants, admitted to membership. The main function is to elect, by secret ballot, the first board of directors and supervisory committee. The first auditor was appointed by the organisation meeting under the previous legislation but now the board of directors makes that appointment under the 1997 Act. Chapter 5 on Meetings and Voting refers.

- **Passbook**: The traditional book serving as a current statement recording a member's transactions including savings as shares or deposits, and also other financial transactions. To reflect the changes arising from new technology, passbook is now defined in section 2 of the Act, rule 1, as including any type of written statement of account.

- **Principal Committee**: Any committee — credit committee, credit control committee, membership committee, as outlined above. Each must include at least one board member and have the usual positions of chair and secretary. Chapter 6 on Governance refers.

- **The Register**: The register which the Registrar maintains in accordance with section 8(5) for the purposes of the Act. The Registrar is required to enter the name of every credit union in the register which is a continuation of the register kept for the purposes of the Credit Union Act, 1966.

- **Registered**: Means for the time being entered in the register and registration under the Act shall be construed accordingly.

- **Registrar**: The Registrar of Friendly Societies is appointed by the Minister but is independent in the exercise of his statutory duties. The Registrar, who is distinct from the Registrar of Companies, is required to make an annual report to the Minister under section 106 of the Act, with respect to his statutory functions under the Act. The reports are laid before the Dáil and Seanad and published to provide useful information. Chapter 9 deals with the Registrar's supervisory and control functions. As explained in Chapter 15, in Northern Ireland the Registrar known as the Registrar of Credit Unions also issues statutory reports.

- **Regulations**: Regulations made by the Minister under an Act, in the form of statutory instruments which are cited by their number, year and title. After consulting the Registrar, the Advisory Committee and other expert bodies, the Minister may make regulations on a wide range of areas specified in section 182, including altering financial limits, and under section 183, for the purposes of removing difficulties experienced in operating the Act.

- **Regulatory Directions**: In contrast to the formal ministerial regulations outlined above, regulatory directions are written directions given by the Registrar to a credit union which do one or more of the actions specified under section 87(3) of the Act. Examples are: prohibiting, on certain conditions, credit unions from raising funds, making payments or acquiring or disposing of assets or liabilities, and also requiring investments to be realised or prohibited.

- **Rules**: The registered rules for the time being of a credit union, including any amendments to the rules registered with the Registrar. Societies and credit unions traditionally have rules as their constitutions, as distinct from the memorandums and articles of association which govern the operations of registered companies. Chapter 4 deals with rules in general and there are many other references to them in the book. Standard or model rules are made available by various co-operative groups to facilitate registration. The ILCU has revised standard rules for its affiliated credit unions under the 1997 Act and a separate set of model rules in respect of Northern Ireland.

- **Resolution**: A formal expression of intention or opinion by a meeting of members in accordance with rules, law and procedures.
  Resolutions are either ordinary, that one which needs a simple majority of votes cast to be passed, or special, passed by not less than three-quarters of votes cast, and as defined below.

- **Savings**: Monies saved by members and lodged with a credit union as shares, deposits or other funds held by a credit union on behalf of its members. Savings are a vital element and provide the life-blood of a credit union. A more general description of savings is monies, surplus to an individual's immediate requirements, which are placed aside or invested for future use.

- **Savings Protection Scheme**: Under section 46(2) of the Act, a scheme to protect, in whole or in part, members' savings in a credit union, in the event of insolvency or other financial default on the part of the credit union. ILCU standard rule 1 (interpretation) for affiliated credit unions is more specific by stating that the scheme is that established by the ICLU.

- **Share**: Each sum of one pound standing to a member's credit in a credit union in the register of members required by the Act to be kept by that credit union. As explained in Chapter 7 on Financial Transactions, shares in credit unions are different from shares in the usual commercial companies. Credit union shares confer ownership rights on a member but cannot be traded on the stock exchange. Multiple shareholding does not confer extra voting rights as each member has only one share irrespective of shareholding.

- **Special General Meeting, SGM**: A meeting of members convened by the Board of Directors in special circumstances in accordance with section 79 of the Act and rule 129. In accordance with procedures under section 79(3), a qualifying group of members may request that a SGM be called. Chapter 5 on Meetings and Voting refers.

- **Special Resolution**: A resolution which:

  ◊ Is passed by a majority of not less than three-quarters of such members of a credit union for the time being entitled under the rules to vote as may have voted in person at any General Meeting of which notice, specifying the intention to propose the resolution, has been duly given according to the rules; and

  ◊ Is confirmed by a majority of such members for the time being entitled under the rules to vote as may have voted in person at any subsequent General Meeting of which notice has been duly given. This subsequent meeting must be duly held not less than 14 days and not more than 28 days from the date of the meeting at which the resolution was first passed. Chapter 5 on Meetings and Voting refers.

- **Statutory**: Used to describe a requirement under statute, that is under the body of law enacted by the parliamentary process and, in this book, usually the Credit Union Act, 1997, and relevant regulations.

- **Supervisory Committee**: Each credit union must have such a committee, consisting of three or five members including a chairman and secretary. Its general and vital duty is to oversee the directors' performance of their functions in accordance with the Act. Sections 58 to 62, rules 78 to 88, and Chapter 6 on Governance provide specific details. The maximum period of service of a Supervisory Committee member is three years but retiring members are eligible for re-election unless the rules provide otherwise. There is also a supervisory committee for ILCU itself.

- **Surplus Funds**: Funds in respect of a financial year ascertained after providing for all operating expenses of the credit union in that year, together with any necessary provision for depreciation but without providing for amounts to be paid as dividends. In accordance with section 45(1) and rule 54(1), not less than 10% of the surplus funds of each credit union must be allocated to a statutory reserve.

- **Statutory Reserve**: As a prudential measure, each credit union must establish a reserve fund to which is allocated in each financial year not less than 10% of the surplus funds.

- **Voluntary Assistant**: A member who, although not an officer, is engaged in any way (but without remuneration) in the operation of a credit union. The voluntary input into the credit union movement is substantial and basic to the co-operative ethos.

- **Winding-up**: The process, also known as liquidation, whereby the existence of a credit union is formally terminated. Assets are collected and realised, proceeds are applied to discharge debts and liabilities and any balance is distributed in accordance with specific procedures. Details of the various modes of winding-up are given in Chapter 12 on Termination which deals with part X, sections 133 to 136 of the Act and rule 164.

- **World Council of Credit Unions (WOCCU)**: An influential international body which regulates and organises the credit union movement in many diverse countries. ILCU is affiliated to WOCCU and international conventions are held in different places including Ireland.

Useful Addresses

Centre for Co-operative Studies, National University of Ireland, Cork. Tel: (021) 902719; Fax: (021) 903358; email: CCS@ucc.ie

Co-operative Development Society Ltd., (CDS), 5 Fitzwilliam Square, Dublin 2. Tel: 01 6789660

Consumers' Association of Ireland, (CAI), 45 Upper Mount St., Dublin 2, Tel: (01) 6612466; Fax: 6612464 — publishers of *Consumer Choice* magazine, Tel: (01) 6686836.

Department of Enterprise, Trade and Employment, Frederick Building, Setanta Centre, South Frederick Street, Dublin 2. Tel: (01) 6614444, LoCall, from outside Dublin area, 1890 220222; email: [name of relevant officer] @entemp.irlgov.ie

Irish Banks Information Service, (IBIS), Nassau House, Nassau Street, Dublin 2, Tel: (01) 6715299; Fax: (01) 6796680; email: ibf@ibf.ie

Irish Co-operative Organisation Society, (ICOS), Plunkett House, 84 Merrion Square, Dublin 2, Tel: (01) 6764783 or 6624816; Fax: (01) 6624502; email icos@iol.ie

Irish League of Credit Unions, (ILCU), 33 Lower Mount Street, Dublin 2, publishers of *Credit Union Review*, Tel: (01) 6146700; Fax: (01) 6146701; email: info.ilcu@creditunion.ie; www.creditunion.ie

Irish Mortgage & Savings Association, (IMSA), 23 St Stephen's Green, Dublin 2 Tel: 01 6766333; Fax: 01 6618622; email mortgage@indigo.ie

Government Publications Sales Office, Sun Alliance House, Molesworth Street, Dublin 2. Tel: (01) 6613111 or 679 3515; LoCall 1890 213434.

Irish Trade Union Trust, (ITUT), Liberty Hall, Eden Quay, Dublin 1, Tel: 01 8787272.

Oireachtas, Houses of, Dáil Éireann and Seanad Éireann, Leinster House, Dublin 2. Tel: (01) 618 3000; LoCall 1890 337889 (Dáil); 1890 732623 (Seanad). Website: www.irlgov.ie/oireachtas. There are also individual email addresses.

Plunkett Foundation, 23 Hanborough Business Park, Long Hanborough, Oxford OXB 8LH, England, Tel: +44 (0) 1993 883636; Fax: + 44 (0) 1993 883576; email: plunkett@gn.apc.org

Registrar of Friendly Societies, Parnell House, 14 Parnell Square, Dublin 1, Tel: 01 8045499; LoCall 1890 213434.

Registrar of Credit Unions — Northern Ireland, Department of Economic Development, IDB House, 64 Chichester Street, Belfast BT1 4JX, Tel: (080) 1232 234488.

The Society for Co-operative Societies in Ireland Ltd., (SCSI), publishers of *Co-op Contact*, Tel: 01 6764783, c/o Plunkett House, 84 Merrion Square, Dublin 2. Or c/o CDS, 5 Fitzwilliam Square, Dublin 2, Tel: (01) 678 9660.

Money Advice and Budgeting Services, (MABS), (funded by the Department of Social, Community and Family Affairs). Check telephone directory for local addresses and numbers.

It is advisable to consult telephone directories for current addresses and numbers as they may change from time to time. Information about credit unions in neighbourhoods or places of employment is usually available locally. The ILCU will also provide relevant data. Web sites and e-mail, which are increasingly becoming available, are also useful for information and communications. Acts of the Oireachtas are also available on CD-ROM from Government Publications Sales Office.

SELECT BIBLIOGRAPHY

1. CREDIT UNIONS

Aughney, J. (1996) "Credit Unions Lay it on the Line — They're Cheaper", *Irish Independent*, 22 July.

Berry, J. and Roberts, M. (1984) *Co-op Management and Employment*, Industrial Common Ownership (ICOM): London.

Bird, T.C. (1998) "Credit Union Act 1997", annotation in *Irish Current Law Statutes Annotated*, (ICLSA), R.62, August, Round Hall Sweet and Maxwell: Dublin.

Bolger, P. (1993/94) "Irish Credit Union Movement", in *Donegal Annual Historical Society Journal*,

Bussy, P, (1994) "Credit Unions — The Next Ten Years" in *World of Co-operative Enterprise*, Year Book, Plunkett Foundation: Oxford

Candon, P. (1995) "Whither Credit Unions?", in *Credit Union Review* Irish League of Credit Unions (ILCU), August/September: Dublin.

Candon, P. (1997) "Cash as Cash Can", in *Co-op Contact*, Issue 6, Vol. 2, Summer, SCSI: Dublin.

Candon, P. Credit Union Management, The Co-operative Dimension, forthcoming.

Coffey, A. (1998) "Credit Unions, Banking's Biggest Threat; Community Service", in *Business and Finance*, 16 April: Dublin.

Coffey, A. (1998) "Lending Rate Cut to Materialise", Personal Finance, *The Sunday Tribune*, 15 November: Dublin.

Credit Union Act, 1997, Explanatory Guide, (1997) Department of Enterprise, Trade and Employment: Dublin.

Crowley, D. (1997) "Concern about Credit Unions", article in *The Sunday Tribune*, 13 April: Dublin.

Culloty, A.T. (1990) *Nora Herlihy, Irish Credit Union Pioneer*, foreword by John Hume, MP, MEP, ILCU: Dublin.

Donnelly, R. and Haggett A.R. (1997) "The End of the Beginning — Growth in British Credit Unions between 1985 and 1994", in *World of Co-operative Enterprise*, Year Book, p. 207, Plunkett Foundation: Oxford

Dublin, J., and S. (1966) *Credit Unions Theory and Practice*, Wayne State University Press, MI: USA.

Dublin, J. and S. (1983) *Credit Unions in a Changing World*, Wayne State University Press, MI: USA.

Forde, S. *Memories are Made of This*, and *As it was in the Beginning*, origins of Irish credit unions, dates and sources, not clear.

Guidance Notes series (1998 et seq). and other training and advisory material, ILCU: Dublin.

Herlihy, N., unpublised correspondence, 30 September 1961 and 25 November 1985 to Muriel Gahan.

Herlihy, N. (1969) *Before the Dawn*, ICLU archives, Dublin, originally published in magazine of Chapter 3 credit unions, Belfast.

Ivers, J.J. *The Further Development of Credit Unions in Ireland*, (1970) unpublished MBA thesis, Department of Business Administration, Faculty of Commerce, University College Dublin: Dublin.

Kerby, J. (1998) "Credit Unions Challenged by Low-interest Loans", Family Money, Business This Week, *The Irish Times* 23 October.

Killeen, J. (1993) Credit Unions: Unique Financial Institutions — A Bright Future? unpublished BBS degree dissertation.

Lloyd, Rev. Canon, C. (1974) letter to Nora Herlihy from 23 November.

McCarthy, O. (1996) *History and Development of Ballyphehane Credit Union,* 1960–94, Centre for Co-op Studies, University College Cork (now National University of Ireland, Cork)

McCluskey, D. (1998) "Smoother Path for Clients and Managers", article about Sandymount Credit Union, Computers in Business section in *The Sunday Business Post*: Dublin, 5 April.

MacEoin, S. (1987) "The Development of the Credit Union Movement", in O'Sullivan, J. and Cannon, S. (eds.) *The Book of Dun Laoghaire*, Blackrock Teachers' Centre: Dublin.

MacEoin, S. (1964) "The Credit Union and the Farmer", in *Biatas*, Irish Sugar, Vol. XVII, No.11, February: Co. Dublin.

Madden, N. (1998) "One Per Cent Per Month is not a Philosophy", article in *Credit Union Review*, Vol. 16, Issue 111, October/November, ILCU:Dublin.

Ó Cearbhaill, D. (1985) "Comhair Chreidmheasa: Prionsabail agus Feidhmiú", *Central Bank Review*, Spring: Dublin.

Ó Céirín, Kit, (1993) "Foundress of the Credit Union", article on Nora Herlihy, *Ireland's Eye, Cú Chulainn Annual*: Mullingar, Co. Westmeath.

O'Dwyer, J. (1994) "The Changing Face of Irish Credit Unions", unpublished thesis: Dublin.

O'Leary, D.M. (1988) *Credit Unions in Ireland, Past Present and Future*, dissertation for National Diploma in Business Studies (Banking) NIHE, Limerick (now University of Limerick).

Oliver, E. (1998) "Registrar's Report Highlights Failings in Management of Credit Unions" *The Irish Times*, 17 December.

Price Waterhouse (1992) Summary Report on Review of Organisational and Financing Requirements (of Irish League of Credit Unions): Dublin.

Report of AGM Review Committee (1998), ILCU: Dublin.

O'Reilly, P. (1994) *Credit Unions — The Quiet Revolution*, unpublished thesis.

O'Sullivan, J. (1998) "League Welcomes Moves on Status of Credit Unions"; "Report Backs Tax Breaks for Savers", articles in *The Irish Times, Business This Week*, 9 October: Dublin.

O'Sullivan, R. (1999) "Debt Managers Help Over-spenders Walk Tall Again", *The Irish Times, Business this Week*, 8 January: Dublin.

Quinn, A.P. (1995) "Irish Credit Unions: A Success Story", *History Ireland*, Graham T. (ed.) Vol. 3, No. 1, Spring: Dublin.

Quinn, A.P. (1995) "Credit Union Law, from Hybrid to Thoroughbred?" lecture to Summer School, Diploma in Credit Union Studies, July, NUI, Cork.

Quinn, A.P. (1997) "New Laws for Co-ops but What About Other Co-ops", in *Co-op Contact*, Vol. 2, Issue 5, Spring, SCSI: Dublin.

Quinn, A.P. (1997) "The Credit Union Bill, 1996" *Bar Review*, Bar Council, Vol. 5, Issue 2, March: Dublin.

Quinn, A.P. (1998) "Tea Scones, Homespuns and a Fiver for Postage Stamps", article about Muriel Gahan and origins of Irish credit union movement, *Credit Union Review*, Vol. 16, Issue 111, October/November, ILCU: Dublin.

Seekamp, G. (1998) "Team Spirit Key to Setting up a Credit Union", article in *The Sunday Business Post*, 4 January: Dublin.

Scott, F. (1995) "Credit Union: Quo Vadis", dissertation for Masters in Rural Development degree, University College Galway.

Sisk, N.M. 1995 "The New Credit Union Act — Implications for Credit Union*s*" Registrar of Friendly Societies, address given to summer school, University College Cork, (now NUI Cork), 11 July

Smyth, S. (1998) "New Row as Credit Unions Face Tax", *Irish Independent,* 22 October.

Smyth, Sam, Credit Unions' pleading for special status is a bit rich, *The Sunday Tribune*, 25 October 1998.

Standard Rules for Credit Unions, (Republic of Ireland), (1998) registered under the Credit Union Act, 1997, ILCU: Dublin.

Theodora, T. (1998) "Credit Unions: Sustainable Co-operative Financial Organisations in Emerging Democracies", *World of Co-operative Enterprise*, Year Book, p. 113, Plunkett Foundation: Oxford

World of Co-operative Enterprise, Year Book, Plunkett Foundation, Oxford, various articles.

Youth Policy Task Force (YPTF) Interim Report (1998) ILCU: Dublin

2. CO-OPERATIVE BACKGROUND AND HISTORY

Anderson, R.A. (1935) "With Plunkett in Ireland: The Co-op Organisers Story", London. New edition (1983) with foreword by Ross, W., Irish Academic Press and Society for Co-operative Studies, (SCSI): Dublin.

Bolger, P. (1977) "The Irish Co-operative Movement, its History and Development", Institute of Public Administration": Dublin.

Bolger, P. (ed.) (1986) "And See Her Beauty Shining There, The Story of the Irish Countrywomen", Irish Academic Press and SCSI: Dublin.

Cahill, Prof. E. (1998) "Co-ops Lack Investment Power", address to ICOS AGM, NUI Cork, (news item in *The Irish Times*, 3 November).

Candon, P. (1998) "The Social Economy — A Critical Response" *Co-op Contact*, Vol. 2, Issue 2, SCSI: Dublin

"Co-operative Education, Challenge for the Future" (1998) *The Co-operative Way: The Co-op Education and Promotion Group*, The Co-op Education and Promotion Group: Dublin.

Craig, E.T. (c.1920) introduction by Æ, *An Irish Commune, The Experiment at Ralahine, Co. Clare, 1831–1833*: Dublin. New edition (1983) with material by James Connolly, Terence O'Brien and Cormac Ó Gráda, (ed.) Irish Academic Press and SCSI: Dublin.

Dodaro, S. and Pluta, L. (1995) *The Antigonish Movement, Past Success, Current Circumstances, Future Options*, Co-ops Branch, Nova Scotia Economic Renewal Agency, Truro, Nova Scotia: Canada.

Fingall, Elizabeth Countess of, (1937) *Memories — Seventy Years Young*, Collins: London. Reprinted (1991) Lilliput Press: Dublin.

Gallagher, P. (1939) *My Story, Paddy the Cope*, first edition with Peadar O'Donnell's foreword, Jonathan Cape: London. Revised edition (c.1945) with foreword by E.P. McDermott, Templecrone Co-op Society Ltd: Dungloe, Co. Donegal.

Henry, M. (ed.), (1994) Fruits of a Century, an Illustrated Centenary History, 1984-1994, ICOS: Dublin.

King, C. and Kennedy, L. (1994) "Irish Co-operatives from Creameries at the Crossroads to Multinationals", in *History Ireland*, Graham, T. (ed.) Vol. 2, No. 4, Winter: Dublin.

Laidlaw, A.F. (1961) The Campus and the Community, the Global Impact of the Antigonish Movement, Harvest House: Montreal, Canada.

Laidlaw, A.F. (ed.) (1971) with commentary, *The Man from Margaree, Writings and Speeches of M.M. Coady, Educator, Reformer, Priest*, McClelland and Stewart: Toronto, Canada.

MacLellan, M. (1985) *Coady Remembered*, St Francis Xavier University Press: Antigonish, Novia Scotia, Canada.

Mitchell, G. (1997) *Deeds Not Words, The Life and Work of Muriel Gahan, Champion of Rural Women and Craftworkers*, Town House: Dublin. (Reviewed (1998) by Quinn, A.P. in *Co-op Contact*, SCSI, Vol. 2, No. 8., Spring.)

Plunkett, H. (1904) *Ireland in the New Century*, First edition, John Murray: London. New edition (1983) with foreword by West,
Dr T., Irish Academic Press and Society for Co-op Studies: Dublin.

Quinn, A.P. (1989) *The Golden Triangle — The Æ Commemorative Lectures*, ed. with additional material, Society for Co-operative Studies, sponsored by ILCU.

RTE Television, (1998) "The Money Box", item on credit unions, presenter George Lee, 29 November.

Smith, R. (1998) The Centenary Co-operative Creamery Society Ltd., A Centenary of Co-operative Endeavour, 1898–1998, Mount Cross: Dublin.

Thompson, D.J. (1994) *Weavers of Dreams, Founders of the Modern Co-operative Movement*, 150th Anniversary edition, Centre for Co-operation, University of California, CA: USA.

West, Dr. T. (1986) *Horace Plunkett, Co-operation and Politics, An Irish Biography*, Colin Smythe, Gerrards Cross, Bucks, and Catholic University of America, Washington, DC.

3. CO-OPERATIVE REPORTS, LAWS AND PRINCIPLES

Bolger, P. Working Together — the Co-operative Concept, O'Brien Press, Dublin, 1985.

Briscoe B. et al. (1982) *The Co-operative Idea*, Centre for Co-operative Studies, (CCS), University College Cork, (UCC).

Co-op Guides, practical booklets and videos, CCS, Cork

Fuller, F.B, (1910) The Law Relating to Friendly Societies and Industrial and Provident Societies, third edition, Stevens: London.

Keating, C. (1983) (ed.) Plunkett & Co-operatives — Past, Present and Future, CCS, Cork.

Linehan, M. (ed.) (1982) "Co-operatives and the Law", papers presented at Institute of Public Administration seminar, CCS, Cork.

Parnell, E. (1995) Reinventing the Co-operative, Enterprises for the 21st Century, Plunkett Foundation: Oxford.

Quinn, A.P. (1994) Co-ops and Their Hazy Legal Environment, in *Commercial Law Practitioner*, Vol. 1, No.6 June, pp. 149–176: Dublin.

Quinn, A.P. (1998) "New Legislation for Industrial and Provident Societies?", article in *Irish Law Times*, No. 12 (177–192), Vol. 16, new series, July, Round Hall Sweet and Maxwell: Dublin.

Phelan, M. (1998) "The Relationship between paid staff and voluntary staff, with case study on credit unions", MA thesis, National College of Ireland, (NCI), formerly National College of Industrial Relations, (NCIR): Dublin.

Report of the Departmental Committee on Agricultural Credit in Ireland (1914) presented to both Houses of Parliament at the command of HM George V, CD 7375/6, HMSO: London.

Report of Committee on Co-operative Societies, (1963) Pr. 7411, committee established by Seán Lemass, Minister for Industry and Commerce, later Taoiseach.

Snaith, I. (1984) *The Law on Co-operatives*, Waterlow: London.

Snaith, I. (1993) *Handbook of Industrial and Provident Society Law*, Holyoake Books: Manchester, England.

Small Business Co-ops, (1986) Joint (Parliamentary) Committee of Oireachtas on Small Businesses, Government Publications Sales Office, Dublin 2.

Sisk H. (ed.) (1992/4), Society for Co-operative Studies, SCSI, Papers and Proceedings of Annual Conferences and also Newsletters.

Wider Application of the Co-op System in Ireland, (1986) SCSI, The Plunkett House, 84 Merrion Square, Dublin 2.

Watkins, W.P. (1986) *Co-operative Principles, To-Day and Tomorrow*, Holyoake Books: Manchester, England.

4. SPECIALIST PERIODICALS

Co-op Ireland, old series up to 1992, (ed.) Henry, M., Tara Publications, Poolbeg St., Dublin for ICOS. New series 1993, Irish Farming Publications, Deansgrange Rd, Blackrock, Co. Dublin.

Co-op Contact, editor Ann-Marie Kennedy, 1995–1998 series, Anthony M. Quinn (ed.) 1998 to date, SCSI (with funding from ILCU): Dublin.

Review of International Co-operation, International Co-op Alliance: Geneva, Switzerland.

Credit Union Review, Irish League of Credit Unions, 33–41, Lower Mount Street, Dublin 2.

Consumer Choice, editor Kieran Doherty, Consumers Association of Ireland, 45 Upper Mount Street, Dublin 2

5. ANNUAL REPORTS

Registrar of Friendly Societies, Government Publications Sales Office: Dublin. (Some years are combined in one report).

Registrar of Credit Unions Northern Ireland HM Stationery Office, Belfast.

Irish League of Credit Unions: Dublin.

Irish Co-operative Organisation Society (ICOS): Dublin. Details and addresses in separate list

6. CO-OP AND CREDIT UNION REPORTS FROM ABROAD:

Desjardins Group, Quebec, Canada

World Council of Credit Unions (WOCCU)

Plunkett Foundation, Oxford

7. MISCELLANEOUS INCLUDING GENERAL LEGAL TEXTS

Ahern, D., Minister for Social, Community and Family Affairs, (1998) "Consumer Credit and Debt Management Initiatives relevant to Money Advice and Budgeting Service" (MABS) address, to 3rd European Conference on Consumer Debt, Malahide, Co. Dublin, 23 September.

Bennion, F.A.R, (1992) *Statutory Interpretation, a Code*, second edition, Butterworth: London

Bird, Timothy C. (1998) *Consumer Credit Law*, Round Hall Sweet and Maxwell: Dublin.

Carrigan, M.W. (1998) *Handbook on Arbitration Law in Ireland*, Law Society: Dublin.

Company Law Review Group, (1994) First report, Department of Enterprise, Trade and Employment: Dublin.

Clark, R. (1998) *Contract Law in Ireland*, fourth edition, Round Hall, Sweet and Maxwell: Dublin.

Consumer Credit, (1997) Office of the Director of Consumer Affairs: Dublin.

Forde, M. (1984) *Arbitration Law and Procedure*, Round Hall: Dublin.

Forde, M. (1991) *Reorganising Failing Businesses* Mercier: Dublin.

Gaughan, J.A., (1992) Alfred O'Rahilly, 111: Controversialist, Part 1: Social Reformer, Kingdom Books: Dublin.

Hogan, D., O'Neill, B., Bowen-Walsh, J. (1991) *Combined Companies Acts, 1963–1990*, Bastow Charleton Publications: Dublin.

Hogan G., and Morgan, D.G. (1998) *Administrative Law in Ireland*, Third edition: Dublin.

Hume, J. (1996) Personal Views, Politics, Peace and Reconciliation in Ireland, Town House: Dublin.

Kelly, J.M. (1997) *The Irish Constitution.* Third edition, Hogan, G. and Whyte, G., Butterworth: Dublin.

King, C.A, (1996) Obituary of Fr Paddy Gallagher, in *Donegal Annual, Journal of the Co. Donegal Historical Society*, Golden Jubilee Issue, No. 48.

McRedmond, L. (1991) To the Greater Glory, A History of the Irish Jesuits Gill and Macmillan: Dublin.

Maloney, M. and Spellman, J. (1999) *The Law of Meetings* Round Hall, Sweet and Maxwell: Dublin

Maxwell, P.B. *The Interpretation of Statutes*, various editions, Sweet and Maxwell: London

Miller, R.J. (1947) *Forty Years After: Pius XI and the Social Order, a Commentary*, Radio Replies Press, St Paul, Minn: USA.

McCann, L. (1993) *Companies Acts*, Butterworths: Dublin.

Mulholland, J. (1996) "The Writers of Donegal" (with references to Paddy 'The Cope' Gallagher) in *Donegal Annual, Journal of the Co. Donegal Historical Society*, Golden Jubilee Issue, No. 48: Donegal.

Murdoch, H. (1993) *A Dictionary of Irish Law*, second edition, Topaz: Dublin.

Handbook on Debt Management, Coolock Community Law Centre, Barrycourt Mall, Northside Shopping Centre, Coolock, Dublin 17.

Marry, E. (1998) "The Company Examinership — Looking for a Life Line After in re Springline" (in Liquidation), in *Bar Review*, Vol. 3, Issue 4, January/February, Bar Council: Dublin.

O'Connor, E. (1992) *A Labour History of Ireland 1824–1960*, Gill and Macmillan: Dublin.

O'Donnell, J.L. (1997) "Appointing an Examiner, Learning to Live with the Culture of Corporate Rescue" *Bar Review*, April, Bar Council: Dublin.

O'Donnell, J.L, (1994) Examinership, The Companies (Amendment) Act, 1990, Oak Tree Press: Dublin.

Rapple, C. *Family Finance*, issued annually, Squirrel Press: Dublin

Routledge, P. (1987) *John Hume, A Biography*, Harper Collins: London.

Securing Retirement Income, (1998) National Pensions Policy Initiative, (NPPI), Irish Pensions Board, reference to credit unions providing Personal Retirement Savings Accounts, (PRSA): Dublin.

Tallon, F. (1993) Getting Down to Work — Creating Jobs in Your Community, Brandon: Co. Kerry.

Twining, W. and Miers, D. (1982) *How to Do Things with Rules*, second edition, Weidenfeld and Nicolson: London.

Urquijo, L.G. (1998) "Women in Co-operatives: the Policy of the International Co-op Alliance" *Journal of Co-operative Studies*, Vol. 31, No 2 (No. 93) September: UK Society for Co-operative Studies.

8. PARLIAMENTARY DEBATES ON CREDIT UNION LEGISLATION, 1996–97

475 Dáil Debates: col. 523 (Order for second stage), cols. 523–527 (second stage), 552–566, 682–696, 720–746, 895–922, 954–985, 1673–1692, (second stage resumed); 476, cols 38–51, 78–87, 1041–1065, (second stage resumed); 477, col. 16 (Credit Union Bill, 1996, motion), col. 1308-1325 (Report and final stages); 150, cols. 38–72 (second stage); 151, cols 260–2262 (committee final stages).

Seanad Debates, (1997) Vol. 151, No. 1, cols. 38–71, 17 April.

Seanad Éireann, (1997) Committee and final stages, Vol. 151, No. 3, 23 April, cols 278; 260–262

INDEX

achainí an chomhar
chreidmheasa, 264
accounting
expertise, lack of, 159
guidelines, 154–5
internal control procedures,
159
records, 147–8
requirements, basic, 146
true and fair view, 146–7
accounts, auditors and
watchdogs, 145–59
accounts,
monitoring of, 157
by the ILCU, 158
additional services to members,
103–6
and the Credit Union Act,
1997, 231
Registrar's approval of, 104–5
right to appeal against
Registrar's decision, 106
supplementary provisions for,
105
administration
order by High Court, 171–2
administration,
effects of, 172–3
termination and outcome of,
173
administrative functions of the
Registrar, 141–2
administrators
and examiners, 162–74

administratorship and the
Registrar, 171, 173
advertising, 125–6
agricultural banks, 12
Agricultural Credit Corporation
(ACC), 14
agricultural credit societies,
12–13
lessons from failure of, 14
Ahern, B., 244
Albania, 206
Alfred O'Rahilly:
Controversialist, Part 1: Social
Reformer, 15
amalgamation, 184
confirmation of, 185–6
distribution of funds to
members on, 186
statement to members about
proposed, 185
amalgamations and transfers of
engagements, 184–6
Ancient Order of Hibernians
(AOH), 15
annual
percentage rate (APR), 95
return to Registrar, 156
annual general meeting (AGM),
49–53
and the Registrar, 133
business at, 51–2
elections at, 52–3
voting procedures at, 51
Antigonish, 5, 20–1, 218
appeal against refusal of loan, 94

Apprentice Boys, 216
approval of loans, 94
Arbitration Acts, 1954-98, 140–1
Armagh, 216
assets, charges on, 113–14
Association of British Credit
  Unions (ABCUL), 217, 227
Auditing in a Computer
  Environment, 155
auditors
  and auditing, 149–50
  , watchdogs and accounts,
    145–60
auditors,
  appointment and removal of,
    152–3
  duties of credit union and of,
    distinction between, 153–4
  exclusions from appointment
    of, 151–2
  resignations of, 155–6
  responsibilities of, 158–9
  statutory requirements for,
    150–1
Aughney, J., 236
Australian parish credit unions,
  21
automated teller machines
  (ATMs), *xxx*, 116, 235–6
autonomy and independence,
  261–2

Bacon, F., 175
bad debts, 226
Ballyjamesduff Credit Union
  Ltd, 246–7
Ballyphehane Credit Union Ltd,
  241–3
Bangladesh, 206
bankruptcy, 199
banks
  compared with credit unions,
    xxviii–ix
banks,

co-operation and competition
  with, *xxix–xxxi*
Barrington, J., 43, 122–3
Barron, J, 137
Belfast Agreement, the, 228
Belfast Co-operative Trading
  Association, 215
Belfield Credit Union Ltd, 235
Bell, M., *xxxiii*
Berry, J., 59
bills of exchange, 96–7
Bills of Exchange Act, 1882, 96
Bills of Sale (Ireland) Acts
  1879-83, 113, 225
Bird, T.C., 103, 105–6, 139, 166,
  168
Blayney, J., 123
board of directors, 60–4,
  disqualification from the,
    76–8
  functions of the, 62–3
  lack of succession planning by
    the, 132
  meetings of the,
    agenda for, 63–4
    minutes of, 66
  non-participation in the credit
    union running by members
    of the, 132
  personality differences on the,
    132
  removal of director from the,
    64
  special provisions for the,
    61–2
borrowing by credit unions,
  112–14
  charges on assets for, 113
  limitations on, 113
Boyle, D.P., 251
Brady, Fr J., 193
Brennan, C., 41
British credit unions, 35, 227
building societies,
  comparisons with, *xxx-xxxi*

Building Societies Acts, 1928 and
1989, *xxix–xxx*, 28, 84, 109,
125–7, 146, 152, 156
BUPA, 99
Byrne (Ní Bhroin), A., 244
Byrne, D., 17
Byrne (Ní Bhroin), E., 191, 244

caisses d'économie, 5
Cahill, Prof. E., 60
Caisse Populaire de Levis, 4
caisses populaires, 4–5, 17, 21
CAMEL score report system,
158, 202–3
cancellation of registry, 186–8
restriction on, 183
Candon, P., 17, 233–4
capital,
dividends on equity, 258
returns on share, 8
Cantwell, G., 242
Carey, E., 117
Carney, C., 217, 256
Carney, J., 217
Central Agency Agreement
(CAA), 192, 203
Central Bank, *xxi*, 126
Central Bank Acts, 1942-97,
xxix, 28, 39, 84, 109, 127
Central Financial Services
(CFS), 192, 203–4
Central Investment
Management, 109, 203, 234
chapters, 36, 56–7, 192
standard rules for, 200
change, main agents of, 229–30
charges on assets, 113–14
Chartered Association of
Certified Accountants, 150, 154
Chesterton, G.K., 229
Christus Rex, 216
Cicero, 209
Clark, R., 92
Clones Credit Union, 191
Coady, Mgr M., 5, 18, 20

Cogan, D., 241
Committee on Co-operative
Societies, Irish Government,
22–3, 210
report of, 211
committee members,
payments to, 74–5
committees,
ILCU, 199
mandatory, 71
credit, 71–2, 94
credit control, 71–2,
membership, 71–3
nomination, 52
optional, 71
supervisory, 53, 68–70
common bond, 24
enshrined in law, 32–3
in Northern Ireland,
statutory declaration re, 221
Community Development
Movement, 22, 119
Community Games, 205
community involvement, 12, 262
of credit unions, 233–4
of the ILCU, 204–5
Companies Acts, 1963 and 1990,
37, 44, 76–7, 114, 136, 149–50,
161, 166–70, 176–81
Company Law Review Group,
162
complaints and disputes, 140–1
computer monitoring by the,
202–3
computers, 116
confidentiality, 73
Congress of Irish Unions, 16
Consultative Committee of
Accounting Bodies in Ireland
(CCAB-I), 150, 154
Consumer Credit Act, 1995, *xxix*,
xxxi, 28, 84, 105, 126, 168
Consumers' Association of
Ireland, *xxxi*
contracts, 107

control and supervision by the
  Registrar, 124
    of assets and liabilities, ratios
    and structures, 125
co-operation,
  social and economic studies
    in, 15–16
  translating ideas about into
    action on, 17–18
co-operation among
  co-operatives, 259–60
co-operative
  background, the, 1–10
  context, the, 2
    in Ireland, 11–12
  identity, statement of the,
    260–2
  movement, historical outline
    of the, 2–7
  principles, 7
    international, the, 7–10,
      27, 196, 260–2
      and credit unions, 10
Co-op Contact, 205
Co-operative Development
  Society Ltd (CDS), 22, 205
Co-operative Education and
  Promotion Group, 17
Co-operative Way education
  group, 205, 233
co-operatives,
  autonomy and independence
    of, 261–2
  concern for community by,
    262
  co-operation among, 259–60,
    262
  democratic member control of,
    7–8, 258, 261
  economic participation by
    members of, 261
  education, training and
    information in, 8, 17, 201,
    205, 233, 259, 262
  values of, 260

voluntary and open
  membership of, 7, 258, 261
Corrigan, C., 256
Country Workers Ltd, 19
Coyne, Fr E., 15, 193
Craig, E.T., 11
credit union
  cancellation, 183
  dissolution, 183
  governance, 59–81
  invocation, 263
  a legal entity, 25
  legislation, Irish, 23–5
  management, 60
  membership, basics, 27–36
  movement self-regulatory, 143
  officers, 60, 64–7
  operating principles, 9–10, 59,
    193, 196, 233, 257–260
  rules, 34, 37–45
    legal effects of, 43–5
    specific requirements for,
      37–40
    standard, 40–3
  termination, 175–88
credit union,
  forming a, 27–30
  joining a, 30–2
  transfer of engagements of a,
    175
  winding-up a, 176
Credit Union Act
  1966, *xxiv*, 23–4, 66, 85, 118,
    123, 145, 213, 219
  1997, *xxvi, xxviii, xxx, xxxii,
    xxxiv*, 1, 9, 24–5, 28–35,
    38–44, 47–51, 53–6, 60–2,
    64–78, 84–9, 91–5, 97–110,
    112–5, 117–31, 133–42,
    146–57, 159, 161–74, 176–8,
    181, 183–8, 194, 200, 205,
    209–10, 212–3, 222–3,
    225–6, 228–33
  and additional services, 231

and the supervisory and
    regulatory framework,
    231–2
Credit Union Advisory
  Committee (CUAC), 40, 66, 91,
  102, 105, 124, 209–13, 151, 155,
  200
    and the ILCU, 211–2
    background to the, 209–10
    early members of, 210
    reasons for a, 210–1
    statutory provisions for,
        current, 212–3
Credit Union
    of Canada, 5
    Cup, 243
    Extension Service, 18–9,
        22–3, 191
    League of Ireland, 22, 25, 192
    National Association (CUNA),
        6, 18, 20, 191
    Mutual Insurance Society
        (CUMIS), 98, 115, 192, 242
    Review, 234
    Studies, Diploma in, 80, 194,
        237
credit unions and the
  international co-operative
  principles, 10, 193, 196
credit unions,
    acquisition, holding and
        disposal of land by, 107–8
    amalgamation of, 184–6
    borrowing by, 112–14
        charges on assets for, 113
        limitations on, 113
    campus, 235
    cannot convert into a
        company, 188
    compared with
        banks, *xxviii-ix*
        building societies, *xix-xxxi*
        finance houses, *xxi*
        insurance industry, *xxi*
        moneylenders, *xxi*

the Post Office Savings
    Bank, *xxxi*
control of, democratic, 7–8,
    258, 261
in context, *xxvi–vii*
insurance cover for, 114–15
investments by, 108–12
judgments against, 114–15
profiles of, 241–256
wider operations by, 107–116
Credit Unions Deregulation
    Order (Northern Ireland),
    1997, 220–5
Credit Unions (Loans and
    Deposits) Order (Northern
    Ireland), 1993, 225
Credit Unions (Northern
    Ireland) Order, 1985, 101, 113,
    218–9, 221–3, 225, 227
*Credit Unions: Sustainable
    Financial Organisations in
    Emerging Democracies*, 206
Creidmheas, 192
Criminal Justice Act, 1994, 91,
    139–40
Culloty, A.T., 16
CUMIS bond, 115
Cumann Muintir Dún Óir, 19,
    191, 244–5
CUTECH Society, 116

Dáil Éireann, *xxxiii*, 12, 137, 210
    Select Committee on
        Enterprise and Economic
        Strategy, *xxxiii*, 89, 91, 95,
        108, 112, 113–4, 121, 127–8,
        151, 155, 170, 190
Daly, Fr C., 251
Daly, D., 256
daonscoileanna, 19
Davies, N., 20
Davy Stockbrokers, 109, 203, 234
debts from members, remedy for,
    97
decision making, 79

de Valera, E., 20
democratic control, 7–8, 258, 261
demographic, social and other
    trends in the Irish economy,
    235–7
Department of Economic
    Development (Northern
    Ireland), 218
Department of Enterprise, Trade
    and Employment, *xxxiv*, 24,
    118, 212, 228
Department of Industry and
    Commerce, 22, 24, 210
Department of Social,
    Community and Family
    Affairs, *xxvii*
deposit interest withholding tax,
    (DIRT), 106, 239
deposits, 87–91
    in joint accounts, 89–90
    money-laundering and, 90–1
    receipting for money in, 90
    records of, 89
    restriction on holding of, 87–8
    restrictions on withdrawal of,
        88–9
    return on, 258
deregulation in Northern
    Ireland, 220–1
Derry Credit Union, 216
Desjardins, A., 4, 17–18
Dictionary of Irish Law, A, 267
Diploma in Credit Union Studies
    (NUI-Cork), 80, 194, 237
Diploma in Social and Economic
    Science (UCD), 15–7, 21, 191
Director of Consumer Affairs,
    xxix, xxxii, 125
Director of Public Prosecutions
    (DPP), 137
directors,
    payments to, 74–5
disputes and complaints, 140–1

disqualification from board or
    other functions, 76–8
dissolution, 180–3
    restriction on, 183
dividends, 86–7
Doherty, P., 216
Dolan, K., 254
Doneraile credit society, 13
Donnelly, R., 227
Donore Credit Union Ltd, 19,
    191, 244–5
Douglas, B., 255
Dublin Central Co-op Society
    (DCCS), 17–18, 22–3, 191
Duffy, Fr J., 246
Duggan, Archdeacon, 241
Dún Laoghaire Credit Union, 19,
    191
Dún Laoghaire Grocery Co-op,
    19, 191
duties, fiduciary, 77–8
duty to account and security, 76

ECCU Assurance Company Ltd,
    26, 34, 98, 192, 199, 204
education, 8, 17, 201, 205, 233,
    259
Eisenhower, D., 242
elections to board and
    supervisory committee, 52–3
Electricity Supply Board (ESB)
    Credit Union, 30, 32
electronic funds transfer (EFT),
    116
Enniskillen Co-operative Society,
    216
equity capital, limited dividends
    on, 258
European Commission, 106
European Community, 150
European Monetary Union
    (EMU), *xxvii–viii*, 95, 229
    , the euro and lower interest
        rates, 229, 234–5

European Union, 206
examiner,
consideration of members'
and creditors' proposals by,
169
detailed procedures of,
168–70
effect of petition to appoint,
on creditors and others,
165–6
on powers of receiver or
provisional liquidator,
167
production of documents and
evidence to an, 168
proposals of an, court's
consideration of, 170
examiners
and administrators, 161–74
examinership,
Circuit Court's powers re, 164
court rules re, 170
ending and outcome of, 170–1
High Court's power to
appoint, 163
independent accountants
report re, 165
petition for court's protection
re, 163–4
interim, pending report,
165
publicity for, 169
Registrar, and the, 163–4,
169–70
expulsion of a member, 54–5

family members, 33
Fay, P., 201
Federal Credit Union Agency,
210
Feaheny, T., 256
Feehan, D., 256
fiduciary duties, 77–8
Filene, E.A., 6, 18
Finance Bill 1998, 106

financial
legislation, general, 84–5
transactions, 83–106
Finlay, C.J., 136
Finlay, Fr T.A., 12, 15, 21, 189,
193
Fitzgerald, Fr E., 21, 241
Fitzgibbon, L.J., 158
Flahive, J., 205
Flanagan, S., 23
Flood, J., 70
*Focus on the Future, Irish Credit
Unions in the New Millennium,*
230, 238
Foley, G., 194, 206
folk high schools, 19–20, 22, 191
Forde, S., 18–19, 27, 191–2
*Forty Years After: Pious XI and
the Social Order,* 5
Fowler, H., 21
Fox, P., 254
fraud, 197, 226–7
friendly societies, 14–15
Friendly Societies (Amendment)
Act, 1977, 117,
*Further Development of Credit
Unions in Ireland, The,* 13,
210–1
future trends and developments,
229–39

Gaffney, M., 16
Gahan, M., 19–22, 236
Gallagher, Fr P., 21, 192, 194,
216
Gallogly, F., 256
Gambia, 206
Garda Gazette, 252
Garda Síochána credit unions,
30, 32, 251
Gateaux Employees' Credit
Union, 188
Gaughan, A., 15
Germany, co-operation in, 2–4
Godkin, C.P., 251

Golden Triangle, The: the Æ Commemorative Lectures, 19, 216–7

Greater Glory, To The: A History of the Irish Jesuits, 193

governance, 59–81

Government Committee on Co-operative Societies, 22

Griffin, M., 255

Grundvig, 20

Haggett, A.R., 227

Haiti, 206

Hamill, J., 251

Harney, M., 194

Harrington, O., 254

Hayes, J., 251

Healy, S., 191

Herlihy, N., 15–8, 20–3, 27, 191–3, 210–2, 236, 241–2, 244, 251, 255

Herlihy House, Nora, 248–9

Hibernian Philanthropic Society, 11

Higgins, J., 251

Higgins, M.D., 194

Hillery, Dr P., 23, 193

Hogan, G., 33, 70, 136

Home Union scheme, 35

Horace Plunkett, Co-operation and Politics, an Irish Biography, 12

Hume, J., 25, 192, 194, 216–7

Hume, P., 216

Hynes, W.N., 251

ILCUtech, 116, 237

Incorporated Law Society, 210

Industrial and Provident Societies Acts, 1893 and 1978, *xxxii*, 22–4, 37–8, 44, 70, 97, 100, 107, 118–9, 122–3, 129, 134, 136, 145, 150, 176, 180–1, 184

Industrial and Provident Societies (NI) Act, 1969, 192, 218–9

ineligibility for office with the ILCU, 199–200

Insolvency Act, 1986 (UK), 162

inspection by the Registrar, 129–31

   of accounts and other records, 131

   weaknesses revealed by, 132–3

Institute of Certified Public Accountants in Ireland, 150

Institute of Chartered Accountants, 150, 154

Institute of Credit Co-operative Administration, 79, 237

Institute of Incorporated Public Accountants, 150

insurance

   cover for credit unions, 114–15

      cumis bond for, 115

   services of the ILCU, 204

insurance, 34–5, 97–9

   life savings, 99

   loan protection, 98–9

Insurance Acts, 172–3, 267

interest

   on loans, 94–5

      criticism of rate of, 96

   rates, EMU, the euro and lower, 234–5

internal control procedures, 159

international connections of the ILCU, 206–7

International Co-operative Alliance, 7, 9, 20, 236, 257, 260

International Co-operative Principles, 193, 196, 257-60

International Credit Union Day, *xxiv*, 193, 255

International Credit Union Forum, 194, 257

International Development
Foundation Ltd, 2, 199
investigations by the Registrar,
133
  costs of, 137
  examination on oath by court
    during, 135–6
  follow-up on reports of,
    137–138
  procedures for, 134
    company law comparisons
      of the, 136–7
  supplemental provisions for,
    135
    sanctions for non-
      compliance, 135
investments by credit unions,
  108–12
  in land and buildings, 139
  and money-laundering,
    139–40
  and the Registrar, 138–40
  in special funds for social,
    cultural or charitable
    purposes, 110–2
    rationale for provisions for,
      112
IQ Cash service, *xxix*, 116, 237
Iris Oifigiúil, 105, 122, 127,
  1397, 164, 169, 179, 182
Irish Agricultural Organisation
  Society (IAOS), 12, 15, 22
Irish Banking Commission, 14
Irish Banks' Information Service
  (IBIS), *xxvii–viii*
Irish Constitution, The, 33
*Irish Co-operative Movement, its
  History and Development, The*,
  12
Irish Co-operative Organisation
  Society (ICOS), 12, 22, 60
Irish Co-operatives, from
  Creameries at the Crossroads
  to Multinationals, 11

Irish Countrywomen's
  Association, (ICA), 18, 20, 22
Irish credit union
  legislation, 23–5
  movement,
    future trends and
      developments in the,
      229–40
    German and American
      influences on the, 18
    growth in the, *xxv*
    origins and development of
      the, 11–26
    pioneers and inspirational
      leaders of the, 19-22
Irish Credit Unions, a Success
  Story, 12
Irish Current Law Statutes
  Annotated (ICLSA), *xxxv*, 33,
  103, 106, 122, 139, 166, 168
Irish Farmers' Association (IFA),
  18, 191
Irish Independent, 236
Irish League of Credit Unions
  (ILCU), *xxv, xxx, xxxii, xxxiv*,
  9–10, 22, 25–9, 32–6, 40–3, 45,
  47, 50–1, 53, 56–7, 60, 62–3, 67,
  69, 71, 73, 78–80, 84, 87, 91,
  95–6, 98–102, 105, 109–10, 112,
  115–6, 119, 125–6, 128–30, 132,
  139, 141, 143, 176, 180–1,
  188–207, 216, 229–35, 237–9
  administrative structure of
    the, 201–202
  affiliations of the, 206
  annual convention/AGM and
    elections to Board of the,
    198
  Central Financial
    Services(CFS) of the, 203–4
  Central Investment
    Management Service of the,
    203
  committees of the, 199

Irish League of Credit Unions
  (ILCU), (cont'd.)
  computer monitoring by the,
    202–3
  and the Credit Union
    Advisory Committee
    (CUAC), 211–2
  format and history of the,
    190–5
  ineligibility for office with the,
    199–200
  insurance services of the, 204,
    239
  international connections of
    the, 206–7
    International Development
      Foundation Ltd, 206
    other, 206–7
  membership of the, 189–90
  monitoring systems of the,
    162
  in Northern Ireland, 190, 218,
    220, 228
  objects of the, 196–7
  recognition of status of the,
    195
  regional chapters of the,
    200–1
    educational role of, 201
  rules of the, 195, 163, 189–90
  savings protection scheme of
    the, 35, 99–100, 158, 162
  supervisory committee of the,
    199
  vision and mission statement
    of, 197
  wider community
    involvement of the, 204–5
    in promotion and
      sponsorship, 205
    in workers' co-ops, 204–5
Irish Mortgage and Savings
  Association, *xix*
Irish National Foresters, 15
Irish Press Credit Union, 188

Irish Times, The, 128, 237
Irish Trade Union Congress, 16
ISIS system, 237
Italy, co-operative credit in, 14
Ivers, J.J., 13, 210–1, 242

Jay, P., 6
Jesuits, Irish, 193
joint accounts, 89–90
Junior Cycle Tour of Ireland, 205

Kearney, P.K., 251
Kelly, J.M., 33, 136
Kennedy, L., 11
Kent, Fr E., 193
Keogh, H., *xxv*
Kerby, J., 238
King, C., 11
King's X, 20, 191

Labour History of Ireland, A, 15
land,
  acquisition, holding and
    disposal of, 107–8
Lansdowne Market Research,
  236
Law Library Credit Union Ltd,
  xxxii, 30, 217, 255–6
legislation in Northern Ireland,
  218–9
  on bad debts, 226
  compared with Republic of
    Ireland, 224–5
  on fraud, 226–7
  on loans, 225–6
  on reserves, 226
Lemass, S., 22–3
liaison committee, 201
life savings insurance, 99
Llewellyn, K., 37
Lloyd, Canon C., 21
loan protection insurance, 96,
  98–9
loans and savings in summary,
  35

loans, 91–7
  appeal against refusal of, 94
  approval of, 94
  detailed provisions on, 92–3
  interest on, 94–5
    criticism of rate of, 96
  in Northern Ireland, 222–6
  promissory notes, bills of
    exchange and, 96–7
  restrictions on, 91–2
Lougheed, B., 241
Lucey, Dr C., 16, 21, 241
Luzzatti, L., 4
Lynch, B., 245
Lynch, E., 254
Lynch, F., 195, 237
Lynch, J., 23

McAleese, M., 194, 235
McAughtry, S., *xxv*
McAuliffe, D., 241
McAuliffe, P., 22
McCarthy, C., 254
McCarthy, T., 193
McDonnell, V., 256
McDowell, M., 232
MacEoin, E., 266
MacEoin, S.P., 16–9, 21–3, 27,
  191–2, 194, 205, 212, 216, 248,
  265–6
McInerney, P., 246
McKeag, R., 218
McKenna, Fr. D., 193, 265
McKevitt, Canon P., 21
McLaughlin, R., 255
McQuaid, Dr J.C., 16
McRedmond, L., 193
Madden N., 238
management, 60
managers,
  specific duties of, 80–1
  professional, 79–80
Mangan, K., 22
Manorhamilton Credit Union, 30
Masters of Their Own Destiny, 5

Matthews, K., 23, 251
meetings,
  and voting, 47–57
  active participation at, 57
  annual general, (AGM), 49–53
  board, 61–4,
  chapter, 56–7
  decision making at, 79
  organisation, 48–9
  quorum at, 78–9
  resolutions at, 55–7
  special general, (SGM), 53–5
  supervisory committee, 68, 70
meitheal, 2
members,
  democratic control by, 7–8,
    258, 261
  economic participation by,
    261
  service to, 259
membership committee, 72–3
membership, 84–5
  basics of credit union, 27–36
  main benefits of, 35–6
  open and voluntary, 7, 258, 261
mentally handicapped persons,
  payments in respect of, 103
  validity of, 103
Mescall, M., 251
Mitchell, G., 19
money,
  receipting for, 90
money-laundering, 90–1, 139–40
Money, Advice and Budgeting
  Service (MABS) *xxvii*
Montserrat, 206
Morgan, D., 70
Muintir na Tíre, 18
Mulvey, Fr. A., 216
Murdoch, H., 267
Murphy, C., 20
Murphy, J., 190, 194
Murphy, M., 254
Murphy, N., 194
Murray, G., 194, 206

Nash, F., 242
National College of Industrial
   Relations (NCIR), 80
National College of Ireland
   (NCI), 80
National Co-operative Council
   (NCC), 17–9, 21–2, 191
National Diploma in Business
   Studies, 142
National Farmers' Association,
   18, 191
National Federation of Savings
   and Co-operative Credit Unions
   (NFCU), 26, 217
National Institute for Higher
   Education, Limerick, 142
National Land Bank, 12
National University of Ireland -
   Cork, 15, 79, 237
Nepal, 206
New Harmony, 6
New Lanark, 6
New Ross Credit Union Ltd, 233
Ní Chúlacháin, S., 256
nominations for transfer of
   financial interest upon death,
   101–2
non-discrimination, 259
non-qualifying members in
   Northern Ireland, 222–3
*Nora Herlihy: Irish Credit Union
   Pioneer*, 16
Norrison, D., 251
North America, co-operative
   credit in, 4–6
North William Street Credit
   Union, 194
Northern Ireland, 25–6, 215–28
   background to credit union
      movement in, 215
   common bond in, statutory
      declaration re, 221
   credit unions in, 216–24
      deregulation of, 220–1
      loans from, 223–4

   non-qualifying members
      of, 222–3
   registration requirements
      for, 219–10
   secured loans from, 222
   shareholding in, 221–2
legislation in, 218–9
   on bad debts, 226
   compared with Republic of
      Ireland, 224–5
   on fraud, 226–7
   on loans, 225–6
   on reserves, 226
Parliament, 217
Registrar of Credit Unions in,
   xxix, 218

O'Brien, Fr, 21
O'Brien, M., 254
Ó Cearbhaill, B., 19–20
O'Connell, S.P., 251
O'Connor, Dr E., 15
O'Doherty, M., 192, 246, 251
O'Donnell, J.L., 161
O'Driscoll, J., 254
O'Dwyer, J.A., 41, 211
Office of Consumer Affairs, *xxxi*
officers, 60, 64–7
   liability and indemnity of, 74
   required signatures of, 75
   terms of office of, 67
Ó Floinn, an t-Athair D., 21
O'Halloran, J., 19
Oireachtas Joint Committee on
   Finance and the Public Service,
   xxix, 232
   report of, 232
O'Kane, F., 194
O'Keeffe, N., *xxxii*
O'Leary, D.M., 142, 190
ombudsman, 141
Ó Murchú, A., 254
O'Neill, E., 256
operating principles, 9–10, 233,
   257–60

O'Rahilly, Prof. A., 15–6
organisation meeting, 48–9
Ormond, Fr R., 242
O'Sullivan, J., 237
Owen, R., 6, 11, 216

Parnell, E., 79
passbooks, 85, 90
Paypath, 236
Personal Views, 216
Phelan, M., 80, 256
Philbin, Dr W., 21
Plunkett Foundation, 12, 206
Plunkett, Sir H., 12, 17, 21–2,
    27, 215
Pope Pius XI, 5
Post, An, *xxiii*
Post Office Savings Bank, 109
Powers of Attorney Act, 1996,
    103
Premier Navan Road Credit
    Union, 23
Price Waterhouse, 201
principles,
    co-operative, 7
        international, the, 7–10,
            27, 196, 260–2
        operating, 9–10, 59, 193, 196,
            233, 257–260
professional managers, 79–80
professional management and
    the voluntary ethos, balance
    between, 237
profiles of credit unions, 241–256
promissory notes and bills of
    exchange, 89, 96–7
promotion and sponsorship by
    the ILCU, 205
provident purposes, 92
proxy voting, 51

Quadragesimo Anno, 5, 16
Quill, M., *xxiv*
Quinn, A.P., 117
Quinn, E., 19

Quinn, F., 19
Quinn, R., 19
Quinn, W.P., 251
quorum, 78–9

Rabbitte, P., *xxxii*, 91, 112, 121,
    151, 190
Raiffeisen, F., 3
Raiffeisen Societies, 3–4, 12–13,
    18–21
Ralahine co-op, 11
receipting for money, 90
receivership, 127
records of shares and deposits,
    89
regional chapters of the ILCU,
    200–1
    educational role of, 201
Registrar of Companies, 181
    in Northern Ireland, 218
Registrar of Credit Unions in
    Northern Ireland, *xxi*, 202, 207,
    218–22, 224–8, 232
Registrar of Friendly Societies,
    xix, *xxxii*, 12, 22, 24, 27, 29, 32–
    6, 38–43, 45, 50, 61, 67–9, 72,
    84, 88, 90, 93, 97, 100, 102,
    104–8, 111, 113–5, 117–43,
    162–7, 176–7, 195, 197, 202–3,
    207, 228, 231–2
    administrative functions of
        the, 141–2
    administratorship and the,
        171, 173
    annual accounts and the, 148,
        156
    attendance at ILCU chapter
        and annual general
        meetings, 143
    auditors and the, 150, 152,
        155–6
    cancellation of registration by
        the, 122
    complaints and disputes and
        the, 140

Registrar of Friendly Societies,
  (cont'd.)
  control and supervision by
    the, 124
    of advertising, 125–6
    of assets and liabilities,
      ratios and structures,
      125
  disputes and complaints and
    the, 140–1
  examinership and the, 163–4,
    169–70
  follow-up action of the, 133
  fulfilling functions of
    Registrar of Companies, 181
  inspection by the, 129–31
    of accounts and other
      records, 131
    weaknesses revealed by,
      132–3
  investigations by the, 133
    costs of, 137
    examination on oath by
      court during, 135–6
    follow-up on reports of,
      137–138
    procedures for, 134
      company law
        comparisons of the,
        136–7
      supplemental provisions
        for, 135
        sanctions for non-
          compliance, 135
    and investments, 138–40
      in land and building,
      139
      and money-laundering,
      139–40
  limits to the functions of the,
    122–3
  mission statement of the, 118
  monitoring of accounts by the,
    157
  prudential role of the, 123–4

  registration by the, 119–21,
    175
  regulatory directions of the,
    126–9
    procedural requirements
      for, 127–9
  role of the, 40
  statutory report of the, 131–3
  time limits on the, 121–2
registration, 119–21
  requirements in Northern
    Ireland, 219–20
regulatory directions of the
  Registrar, 126–9
  procedural requirements for,
    127–9
repayment protection insurance
  scheme (RPI), 204
*Report of the Committee on Co-
  operative Societies*, 211
Rerum Novarum, 5, 16
reserves, 226
resolutions, 55–7
  special, 55–6
*Review of Banking Policy and the
  Regulation and Supervision of
  Financial Institutions*, 232
Reynolds, A., 100
Roberts, M., 59
Robinson, M., 194, 246
Rochdale Equitable Pioneer
  Society, 7, 257
Rochdale Rules, the, 7
rules, 34, 37–45
  appendices to the, 42–3
  legal effects of the, 43–5
  of the ILCU, 195, 200
  re members and the credit
    union, legal effects of the,
    43–4
  members and the, 44–5
  specific requirements for the,
    37–40
  standard, 40–3, 195
  variations in the, 29–30

Russell, G., (Æ), 12, 21, 36, 215
Russia, 206
Ryan, P., 192
Ryan, S., 249
Ryan, T., 193
Ryan, W., 246

St Joseph's Aviation Credit
  Union, 251
St Louis co-operative banking
  system, 6
St Mary's Navan Credit Union
  Ltd, 15, 116, 212
St Mary's parish credit union,
  Manchester, NH, 6
St Paul's Garda Credit Union,
  30, 252
St Raphael's Garda Credit Union
  Ltd, 30, 251–4
savings protection scheme, 35,
  99–100, 120, 158, 162, 202, 239
savings, return on, 258
Schultze-Delitzsch, H, 2
Schultze-Delitzsch Societies, 2–3
Seanad Éireann, *xxv*, 137, 210
secretary, 66–7
security and duty to account, 76
shareholding in Northern
  Ireland, 221–2
shares, 75–7
  dividends on, 76–7
  in joint accounts, 89–90
  money-laundering and, 90–1
  receipting for money in, 90
  records of, 89
  restriction on holding of, 87–8
  restrictions on withdrawal of,
    88–9
  return on, 8
  transfer of, 74
Sheehan, B.A., 251
Sisk, N.M., 117
small payments upon death,
  provisions for, 102
  validity of, 103

Smaul, W.J., 251
Smyth, T., 194, 201
social class and the credit union
  movement, 236–7, *xxv*, *xxvii*
Social and Economic Science
  (UCD), Diploma in, 15–7, 21,
  191
social
  economy, credit union
    involvement with the, 233–4
  responsibility, 260
Society for Co-operative Studies
  in Ireland Ltd (SCSI), *xxxii*,
  205
Society Credit Union Ltd, 216–7
Society of St Vincent de Paul, 21
Solicitors Acts, 1954–94, 102
South Africa, 206
Spetland, O., 191
special funds for social, cultural
  or charitable purposes, 110–2
  rationale for provisions for,
    112
special general meeting (SGM),
  53–5
sponsorship and promotion by
  the ILCU, 205
Stafford, J., 194
*Statement of Credit Union
  Operating Principles*, 193, 196,
  233
Statutory Instruments Act, 1947,
  108, 139
Steffens, L., 229
Stewart, E., 255
strategic planning by the credit
  union movement, 238–9
study groups, pre-formation,
  27–8
Succession Act, 1966, 102
supervisory and regulatory
  framework, 231–2
supervisory committee,
  board, and the, 64, 67
  elections to the, 52–3

supervisory committee, (cont'd.)
functions of the, 68–9, 77
of the ILCU, 199
and loans, 94
procedural provisions for the,
68
removal of a member of the,
55
statutory duties by the,
inadequate performance of
their, 132
suspension or removal of an
officer by the, 70
term of office of the, 69
surplus funds, 109
disposal of, 8
return to members of, 258

Tallow Area Credit Union Ltd,
248–50
Tallow Enterprise Group Ltd,
248
tax, 106
deposit interest withholding,
(DIRT), 106
technology and the credit union
movement, new, 229, 236–7
Telecom Éireann Credit Union,
30, 32, 239
termination, 175–88
Thompson, W., 6
time limits on the Registrar,
121–2
Tompkins, Dr J.H., 5, 83
transfer
of engagements, 184–5
and amalgamations, 184–6
confirmation of, 185–6
distribution of funds to
members on, 186
statement to members
about proposed, 185
of financial interest upon
death, 100–3
nominations for, 101–2

provisions for small
payments, 102
of shares, 86
Treacy, N., 142, 195, 228
treasurer, 65–6
functions of the, 148–9
statutory duties by the,
inadequate performance of
their, 132
Trustee (Authorised
Investments) Order 1998, 109,
125, 138, 203, 234
Trustee Savings Bank (TSB),
109
Turula, 206

Ulster Agricultural Organisation
Society (UAOS), 216
Ulster Federation of Credit
Unions (UFCU), 26, 217–8, 220
Unfair Dismissals Act, 1977, 70
United Irishwomen, 22
University College Cork (UCC),
237
University College Dublin
(UCD), 15–7, 21, 191
Belfield Credit Union Ltd, 235
University of Limerick, 142
Urquijo, L.G., 236

Vandeleur, J.S., 11
village banks, 12
voluntary ethos and professional
management, balance between
the, 237
Voluntary Health Insurance
Board (VHI), 99
voting
at meetings, 48, 51
by proxy, 51
Walsh, J.F., 251
Walsh, M., 254
watchdogs, auditors and
accounts, 145–60
Watkins, W.P., 1, 20, 47

West, Dr T., 215
West, W.H., 216
Whyte, G., 33, 136
wills, preparing, 102
winding-up, 176–83, 127
  under the Companies Acts,
    176–7
  effect of administrators and
    examiners on, 183
  general procedures for,
    179–80
  by the High Court, 177–8
  by instrument of dissolution,
    180–3
  by liquidators and
    liquidations, 180
  voluntary, 178
    creditors', 179
    members', 178–9

withdrawals, 88–9
  restriction of, 87–8
Wollenborg, Dr L., 4
Women in Co-operatives: the
  Policy of the International
  Co-operative Alliance, 236
Woods, M.F., 116, 212
workers' co-ops, ILCU, 204–5
World of Co-operative Enterprise,
  206
World Council of Credit Unions
  (WOCCU), 21, 194, 206, 217,
  227, 242, 257

youth policy task force (YPTF),
  195, 199, 235
Youth Policy Task Force's
  Interim report, 235